MODERN SEXISM

Blatant, Subtle, and Covert Discrimination

SECOND EDITION

NIJOLE V. BENOKRAITIS
University of Baltimore

JOE R. FEAGIN
University of Florida

PRENTICE HALL, Englewood Cliffs, New Jersey 07632

Library of Congress Cataloging-in-Publication Data

Benokraitis, Nijole V. (Nijole Vaicaitis)
    Modern sexism : blatant, subtle, and covert discrimination /
Nijole V. Benokraitis, Joe R. Feagin. — 2nd ed.
        p.   cm.
    Includes bibliographical references and index.
    ISBN 0–13–588617–1
    1. Sex discrimination against women—United States.   2. Sexism—
United States.   I. Feagin, Joe R.   II. Title.
HQ1426.B428   1994
305.42—dc20
                                                        94–22624
                                                        CIP

Editorial/production supervision
        and interior design: Mary Kathryn Bsales
Acquisitions editor: Nancy E. Roberts
Associate editor: Sharon Chambliss
Editorial assistant: Pat Naturale
Buyer: Mary Ann Gloriande
Cover illustration: Jennifer Phillips
Cover design: Jennifer Phillips, Carl Cox
        The Institute for Language, Technology, and Publications Design
        University of Baltimore

Printed in the United States of America

10 9 8 7 6 5 4 3 2 1

ISBN 0-13-588617-1

Prentice-Hall International (UK) Limited, *London*
Prentice-Hall of Australia Pty. Limited, *Sydney*
Prentice-Hall Canada Inc., *Toronto*
Prentice-Hall Hispanoamericana, S.A., *Mexico*
Prentice-Hall of India Private Limited, *New Delhi*
Prentice-Hall of Japan, Inc., *Tokyo*
Simon & Schuster Asia Pte. Ltd., *Singapore*
Editora Prentice-Hall do Brasil, Ltda., *Rio de Janeiro*

This book is dedicated

To Vitalius, my best friend, to my mother, Ona Vaicaitis, a remarkable woman, and to the memory of my father, Pijus Vaicaitis

N.V.B.

and

To all those women who still suffer from the actions of my gender, with the hope that they will continue to organize for change

J.R.F.

CONTENTS

PREFACE

Last year, a young scientist and his colleagues, including a newly-hired female engineer, attended a Christmas lunch at a well-known company:

> Much to our shock, the luncheon was full of jokes and sexual references by the "Santa" of a very degrading and explicit nature. He threw condoms to the crowd and put walking wind-up penises on the table, making comments about the women employees and secretaries. I would have been offended in any case, but considering [the female engineer] we had persuaded to join us, I was furious. We found out later that the company had the same program the previous years and the division leaders had done nothing to stop it.

This is not an isolated example of sexist behavior. As we did the research and conducted more interviews for this edition, we were overwhelmed by how little some things had changed during the last decade. In fact, a more representative title for this book could have been *Modern Sexism:* Even More *Blatant, Subtle, and Covert Discrimination.*

There has been some progress, however. For example, the Anita Hill/Clarence Thomas hearings and the O.J. Simpson trial have heightened national awareness of widespread sexual harassment and domestic violence, the Civil Rights Act of 1991 enabled victims of gender and race discrimination to claim compensatory and punitive damages, the Family and Medical Leave Act provides unpaid leave for the birth or adoption of a child or illness of family members, and Congress is considering a Gender Equity in Education Act.

Compared to a decade ago, more women are challenging discrimination. As this book goes to press, a federal judge ruled that Vassar College illegally denied tenure to a female biologist partly because she was married and a mother. The judge ordered Vassar to reinstate the biologist with tenure if she still wanted the job and to pay her double damages and legal fees. A New York medical school and hospital have agreed to pay a female researcher nearly $1 million to settle a long-running sex discrimination lawsuit. Women are increasingly reporting and seeking legal redress for sexual harassment and other types of discrimination—at television and radio stations, in such federal agencies as the Drug Enforcement Administration, and in educational institutions.

The occasional successes should not eclipse our understanding of the stagnation and backsliding in regard to sexism in this and other countries. A United Nations Human Development Report recently noted that no country treats its women as well as its men; women still constitute "the neglected majority." In the United States, of all the top institutional leaders at the largest industries and corporations, banks, utilities and communication companies, universities, leading law firms, and investment houses, and of all the top elected and appointed government officials, *less than five percent are women.*

Since the early 1980s there has been a strong male-dominated backlash against the advances made by women in the 1960s and 1970s. This backlash has taken many forms, some verbal and some physically violent. In this book we cite extensive empirical data from many sources to challenge the backlash and its denial of the continuing significance of sexism in the United States. Entrenched, pervasive, institutionalized sex discrimination remains one of the most serious problems facing U.S. society today.

Women are responsible for some of the backsliding. A hot selling item is a push-up bra that purportedly gives even the most flat-chested women cleavage. The People for the Ethical Treatment of Animals (PETA), an organization that has harassed and physically attacked women who wear fur coats, raises funds by featuring famous nude women in its "I'd rather go naked than wear fur" ads. "Hooters"—a slang term for breasts—is one of the fastest growing restaurant chains in the United States, Puerto Rico, and Mexico. Waitresses wear revealing uniforms of cropped T-shirts and mini-shorts and hula hoop on command so (male) customers can watch their breasts bounce. (Male employees—bartenders and bouncers—wear long pants and polo shirts.) When it opened in Baltimore, the local television stations interviewed women customers who described Hooters as "a great family restaurant" and a "fun place."

We are born into, grow up in, and grow old in societies where most women are still second-class citizens: Many endure being demeaned, trivialized, and brutalized both verbally and physically. As the earlier examples suggest, sex discrimination encourages and reinforces sex inequality. Whether intentional or unintentional, the values, attitudes, and behaviors due to sex discrimination are harmful not only to women and men as individuals, but also to such basic institutions as the family, the economy, education, health, housing, religion, and the legal and political systems.

This book is about blatant, subtle, and covert sex discrimination. We describe and illustrate several types of sex discrimination, show how discriminatory practices have increased during the past decade, suggest why women are sometimes complicit in the discriminatory behavior, and examine the consequences of all forms of contemporary sex inequality. The last chapter proposes remedies for diminishing and eradicating sex discrimination now and in the future.

We have found that some students become impatient with our analyses of sex discrimination. Halfway through the book we often hear such questions as "Well, what do we *do*?" "How can *I* change what's going on?" *To eliminate sexism, the first step is to expose it.* This continues to be one of our primary objectives. Chapter 9, however, offers both individual and collective suggestions to abolish (or at least decrease) gender inequality.

Modern Sexism has been written for a large audience. The book is relevant for students in the social sciences, the humanities, women's studies, public and business administration, social work, communications, and human relations. Much of the interview data, which come from people in a variety of occupations, should be interesting to the general public, affirmative action officers, policy makers, community planners, corporate executives and mangers, counselors and human resource staff, defense contractors, administrators, criminal justice staff, and educators at all levels.

CHANGES TO THE SECOND EDITION

The second edition is very different from the first edition in several ways. We have honed our theoretical approach, drawing on the recommendations and insights of our students, fellow researchers, and the Prentice Hall reviewers. Some of the chapters are almost entirely new because they incorporate much recent research and data. Besides the heavily-revised chapter on women of color, we have incorporated discussions of race, age, social class, and sexual orientation throughout the book. We have also emphasized policy changes and present new material on women in other societies. The boxed materials draw the reader's attention to some of the most recent sex inequality issues. We have incorporated even more examples from movies, television, political activities, and the popular press to supplement the most recent references from legal cases and scholarly research.

Also new to this edition is a test item file, prepared by Clairece Booher Feagin. For each chapter, the instructor will find multiple-choice items and several essay questions.

ACKNOWLEDGMENTS

We are indebted to many people who helped us write and produce this book. The most important contributors were the 310 men and women who agreed to be interviewed or who sent in written comments about their experiences for the first edition, and the 98 women and men who did the same for the second edition. Although sometimes painful, the responses were always thoughtful and insightful. They provided important illustrative material for most chapters of this book.

At the University of Baltimore, Randall Beirne, Sue Briggs, Richard Caston, Richard Swaim and Robert Poole offered numerous ideas about current discriminatory practices. Garrett Van Meter responded quickly and generously with technical assistance. Graduate students Layne Baumann, Lynda Blute, Alice Delaney, Elizabeth Dibbell, Deborah Dougherty, Alexandra DeGuzman, Paul Ludolph, Betty Maina, Cynthia Wonderly, and Atlisa Young conducted excellent interviews which have been incorporated into the second edition. Also, Deborah Dougherty, Lauren O'Conner, Renita Richardson, Rohit Sachdeva, Judy Shaw, and Jianhong Zhao provided technical assistance and data entry that were critical in handling the enormous amount of research for this book.

At the University of Texas and the University of Florida, Gideon Sjoberg, Christine Williams, Suzanne Harper, Terry Sullivan, Debra Van Ausdale, Julie Netzer, Tiffany Hogan, Herna Vera, and Michael Hodge provided a sympathetic ear for our problems and insight into the workings of modern sexism.

Nijole Benokraitis is grateful to the Yale Gordon College of Liberal Arts at the University of Baltimore for providing a faculty summer grant during the early stages of the research. Despite shrinking budgets, Provost Ronald Legon and Deans Wayne Markert and Irvin Brown managed to find resources for student assistance during several summers. As always, the Langsdale Library staff was invaluable in locating and accessing materials. Colleagues on two electronic mail lists were especially magnanimous in supplying information on published and unpublished research and legal cases: Many thanks to SASH-L, Sociologists Against Sexual Harassment (Phoebe Morgan Stambaugh, moderator/listowner), and to WMST-L, Women's Studies List (Joan Korenman, moderator/listowner).

At Prentice Hall, Nancy Roberts, editor-in-chief of social sciences, has encouraged us to prepare a second edition for many years. Nancy has always been available to answer questions, has inspired us, and has spent much time coordinating the production of *Modern Sexism*. Throughout the years, she has been a valued editor, colleague, and friend. We are grateful to Katy Bsales, our production editor, for her conscientious, unflappable, and intelligent handling of the myriad tasks involved in producing this book.

The constructive criticisms of the Prentice Hall reviewers helped us clarify our perspective and arguments. For both the first and second editions, we thank the following reviewers for their challenging questions, useful comments, and helpful suggestions:

Louise Comfort, California State University at Hayward
Sue Parry, Siena College
Verta Taylor, Ohio State University
Susan Tiano, University of New Mexico

Charlene A. Urwin, Texas Christian University
Jeffery Prager, University of California at Los Angeles
Melissa K. Gilbert, Boston College

Andrius Benokraitis has been a computer godsend. Throughout the years, he has installed hardware and software, and has been an invaluable consultant in solving innumerable word-processing glitches. Gema Benokraitis has been a constant source of encouragement when energy and enthusiasm flagged: The hikes, especially, revived both body and soul. Vitalius Benokraitis is a very rare man. He was practicing sex equality long before it was fashionable to even talk about it and chuckled at the resulting criticisms. He continues to be supportive, encouraging, thoughtful, understanding, and patient. Most importantly, he never loses his temper or his sense of humor.

Michelle Feagin has been supportive in this enterprise and has taught by her life that one can survive and thrive even in the midst of abusive sexism. Trevor Feagin has also been supportive and provided useful suggestions for reshaping the text to make it more accessible for college students. Clairece Booher Feagin has not only been supportive and encouraging, but also has contributed substantial material and insight to this book, making it better than it otherwise would have been. By her example she has shown that one can be both an outstanding mother and a creative intellectual force in her own writings on racism and sexism.

****

We are planning to pursue our research on subtle and covert sex discrimination in the future and encourage reactions from readers. As this book shows, all responses are presented anonymously.

Nijole V. Benokraitis
University of Baltimore
Sociology Department
1420 N. Charles Street
Baltimore, MD 21201
410-837-5294
Fax: 410-592-6006
E-mail: nbenokraitis@ubmail.ubalt.edu

Joe R. Feagin
University of Florida
Sociology Department
3219 Turlington Hall
Gainesville, FL 32611
904-392-0265
Fax: 904-392-6568
feagin2@nervm.nerdc.ufl.edu

ABOUT THE AUTHORS

Nijole V. Benokraitis received her bachelor's degree from Emmanuel College, her master's degree from the University of Illinois at Urbana, and her doctorate in sociology from the University of Texas at Austin. Currently a professor of sociology at the University of Baltimore, Nijole Benokraitis has served as chair and graduate program director of the Sociology Department. She has published *Marriages and Families: Changes, Choices, and Constraints* (1993) and coedited *Seeing Ourselves: Classical, Contemporary, and Cross-Cultural Readings in Sociology* Third Edition (1995). She has also published numerous articles and book chapters on institutional racism, discrimination against women in the federal government, subtle sex discrimination, and family policy. The recipient of grants and fellowships from several institutions, including the National Institutes of Mental Health and the Administration on Aging and the National Endowment for the Humanities, Nijole Benokraitis also serves as a consultant in sex discrimination to women's commissions, business groups, and colleges and universities.

Joe R. Feagin received his bachelor's degree from Baylor University, his doctorate in sociology from Harvard University, and is currently the Graduate Research Professor in sociology at the University of Florida at Gainesville. He taught previously at the University of Texas (1970-1990) and the University of California at Riverside (1966-1970). He does research on gender and racial discrimination and on affirmative action. His racial relations analysis has appeared in the fourth edition of *Racial and Ethnic Relations* (1993). He has recently completed a major research project on the discrimination faced by successful black Americans, a major portion of which was published as

Living with Racism: The Black Middle Class Experience (1994). Working with Hernan Vera, he has completed a new book, *White Racism: The Basics*, to be published in 1995. Joe Feagin has served as Scholar-in-Residence at the U.S. Commission on Civil Rights, Vice-President of the Society for Study of Social Problems, and as chair of the American Sociological Association's Section on Racial and Ethnic Minorities.

CHAPTER ONE
SEX DISCRIMINATION IN THE 1990s: PROGRESS AND ILLUSIONS OF PROGRESS

How far have American women come since *Modern Sexism* was first published almost a decade ago? Consider a few recent situations:

> A veteran female judge was invited to a ceremony at a federal courthouse. When she arrived, the U.S. District judges, all men, were seated at the front of the room. She was escorted to her own "reserved seat" across the way—with the judges' wives.[1]
>
> A faculty member includes ads of naked women or women in subservient roles in an advertising class. Many of the ads are tattered and dated, but he uses the examples anyway. In one class he commented that women gave up being homemakers to take all the men's jobs in advertising. In another class, he became frustrated that no one knew the answer to a question he asked about a particular statistical percentage. He turned to a female student and said, "C'mon, dispel this myth about women not being able to do math." His tone was patronizing and condescending. In one class he also referred to a secretary with a "bimbo" voice.[2]
>
> A young woman in her early twenties fixes and assembles bikes at a local bicycle store. After she tells the customers what's wrong and gives an estimate of the charges, many ask for the manager to confirm the problems and costs. Her male counterpart, who has less expertise and experience, is treated with respect and never challenged. (Authors' files)

These are not isolated examples of paranoid or hypersensitive women. There are numerous gender gaps, gender traps, and much backsliding as we move toward the twenty-first century. Despite blatant, subtle, and covert sex discrimination, many Americans feel that sex discrimination is practically nonexistent and they are optimistic about the future.

WHY MANY AMERICANS ARE OPTIMISTIC

Many Americans feel that women have enjoyed unprecedented break-throughs in the last decade, and especially during the last few years:

- after almost eight years of stonewalling, Congress finally passed the Family and Medical Leave Act, allowing up to 12 weeks of unpaid leave for men and women to care for newborn babies, adopted children, or disabled family members;
- President Bill Clinton appointed an unprecedented number of women to Cabinet and other high-ranking positions (Janet Reno, attorney general; Donna Shalala, secretary of Health and Human Services; Hazel O'Leary, secretary of the Department of Energy; Madeleine Albright, ambassador to the United Nations; Carol Browner, director of the Environmental Protection Agency; Dr. Joycelyn Elders, surgeon general of the United States; Judge Ruth Bader Ginsburg, U.S. Supreme Court; and Florence Joyner, who replaced Arnold Schwarzenegger as head of the President's Commission on Fitness);
- in sexual harassment legislation, the Civil Rights Act of 1991 allowed victims to claim compensatory and punitive damages; in 1992 the Supreme Court affirmed that students can recover damages from schools; and in 1993 (*Harris v. Forklift Systems, Inc.*), the Supreme Court ruled that victims do not have to prove severe psychological damage in sexual harassment cases. All of these decisions supported victims rather than offenders;
- although modest, the budget for breast cancer research and education was doubled in 1993;
- some of the biggest movie hits were directed by women (e.g., Penny Marshall's *Awakenings* and *Big*, Amy Heckerling's *Look Who's Talking*, Barbra Streisand's *The Prince of Tides*, and Penelope Spheeris's *Wayne's World*). Walt Disney studios have featured women in nonstereotypical roles: the "computer hacker" in *Jurassic Park* is a girl; in *Aladdin*, Princess Jasmine is a spunky heroine who sneaks out of the palace in search of adventure, stands up to the wizard, and tries to rescue Aladdin;
- in 1993, Toni Morrison was the first African American, male or female, to win the Nobel Prize for Literature. She was the eighth woman and only the second American woman to receive the prestigious award since its inception in 1901;
- in 1992, the Church of England departed from 450 years of tradition by allowing women to become priests even though leading opponents predicted that the decision would pit "diocese against diocese, parish against parish, even parishioners against parishioners."[3] In the same year, although a panel of U.S. Roman Catholic bishops affirmed the church's ban on ordaining women, their statement on women's issues called sexism "a moral and social evil," criticized businesses that promote men over equally qualified women, and suggested that biblical texts and church liturgy should be rewritten so that "people" be used, for example, instead of "men" or "brothers;"[4]
- in 1992, Edith Cresson became France's first woman prime minister; a year later, Kim Campbell was elected as the first prime minister of Canada; Gro Harlem Brundtland was elected prime minister in Norway for the third time; and Vigdis Finnbogadottir (described as "the only single mother to lead a nation"), president of Iceland since 1980, won the last election with 95 percent of the votes.

Women have made other inroads as well. Since the United States switched to an all-volunteer military force in 1973, the percentage of women serving on active duty in the military has increased from 2 percent to 11 percent. During the Persian Gulf war in 1991, 15 American women died even though they were not officially in combat positions. As a result, and after many months of congressional deliberations and public pressure, some of the bans on women in combat jobs (the typical route to higher ranks in the military services) may be lifted.

Lesbians have also seen some progress. Several cities have passed "domestic partners" legislation, which entitles gay men and lesbians to health benefits for their partners, Increasing numbers of lesbians are becoming mothers through sperm banks, adopting children, and developing support-group networks.

Although some of this progress is real, much is illusory. Many women—regardless of educational levels and occupations—are still hitting glass ceilings and brick walls.

PERSISTENT GENDER GAPS: HITTING GLASS CEILINGS AND BRICK WALLS

Many people are convinced that sex discrimination is no longer a problem. This conviction is based, first and foremost, on a lack of information. The average American rarely sees data on sex discrimination. Everyday sex discrimination is often ignored while the few instances when women win sex-bias lawsuits get headlines. Even when statistics on sex discrimination are occasionally provided by the media, the initial reaction is usually denial or skepticism: "That was last year. What about statistics for this year?" "Even national data aren't accurate." Or, people point to exceptions: "My neighbor just got a job in construction, and she says she's getting the same salary as the men." "But the music industry is different. Look at all the money Madonna makes." "Isn't Oprah Winfrey one of the wealthiest people in America?" Since most women's advancements have been slow, many Americans often ignore even blatant sexism in search of other explanations. Perhaps, many wonder, there really aren't many qualified women. Perhaps women don't want to be in powerful jobs.

Sex discrimination is as robust today as it was ten years ago. In fact, the most recent research shows that, in many areas, sex inequality may be increasing. Although there has been progress, there are persistent gender gaps in employment, politics, education, and other areas.

Employment

There are still numerous gender gaps in employment. Only 7.5 percent of the 1,315 board members at America's 100 biggest companies are women. Of the highest-paid officers and directors of the 799 public companies, virtually none (*less than 0.5 percent*) are women! Only 27 women, or 11.5 percent, hold leadership positions in the country's 25 biggest unions.[5] Less than 5 percent of the executive jobs are held by women or minorities—a number that has barely budged in a decade.[6]

An estimated 7 million women now run their own businesses, generating $500 billion in annual revenues, up from $98 billion 10 years ago. About 30 percent of the small businesses are owned by women. Although women-owned firms employ more workers than all the Fortune 500 companies combined, they are awarded only 1 percent of all federal government contracts. Many women hit their first brick wall when they apply for money to start a business:

> The president of a management and development company in Minnesota was repeatedly forced to send her brother to the bank to secure financing. "They wanted to use his financial statement and not mine, yet I ran the business," she says. When the president of a $7 million-per-year construction corporation first approached bankers about start-up funding for her construction firm, they suggested she try a T-shirt shop or a stationery store instead. "Women are not perceived as having a small business; we're perceived as having a *little* business. It's as though we're doing it for pin money."[7]

Even when women hold top positions, there are still salary differences between men and women. When the United Way fired its president because of his involvement in a scandal, his replacement, a woman, was paid $195,000—less than half the salary of her predecessor. A survey of 1,029 female and male managers employed by 20 Fortune 500 companies found that even when women have the same educational credentials as men, agree to take transfers, and follow all the other rules for advancement, they lag behind in salary: The women's salaries increased 54 percent over the study's 5-year period while men's increased 65 percent.[8] In a survey of 194 mid- to upper-level managers at major companies across the country, Peter Hammerschmidt found that men earned an average annual salary of $80,722 compared to $65,258 for women. After controlling for such variables as age, race, educational degree, sex, type of organization, and management level, Hammerschmidt concluded that only $3,740 of the salary discrepancy was *not* a result of sex discrimination.[9]

Salaries at entry-level jobs also differ by sex. For example, a *Business Week* survey of 3,664 business school graduates found that a female Master's of Business Administration (MBA) graduate from a "top 20" school earned $54,779 in salary and bonuses in her first year after graduation compared to $61,400 for men. Women also had lower starting salaries in the same industries: on the average, men earned almost 30 percent more than women in information-systems management, almost 7 percent more in marketing, and almost 4 percent more in finance.[10]

In many cases, as experience and seniority increase, salary gaps between men and women also increase. For example, many work places now employ women chemists. Nonetheless, only about 1 in 14 women in chemical companies have managerial positions compared to one in five men. Women chemists earn only 88 percent of what men earn, even after controlling for age, experience, and degree.[11]

Most women are still segregated into lower-paying positions. Large numbers of women continue to work in poorly paid jobs such as child care, dental hygiene, and clerical work that remain more than 90 percent female. Women constitute two thirds of the nation's minimum-wage workers, and two thirds of impoverished adults in the United States are women.[12]

Progress in some areas has had a catch-22 effect on employment. For example, Title IX was passed in 1972 to provide girls and women greater accessibility to athletic programs. When male and female departments were merged, however, more than half of the coaching jobs and nearly 85 percent of the administrative posts went to men. As a result, the number of female coaches and female athletic administrators has decreased drastically during the last 20 years, and more male officials are serving in women's sports than ever before. Between 1972 and 1990, the number of women coaches for women's collegiate teams decreased from over 90 percent to 47 percent.[13]

Politics

". . . And speaking of the Year of the Woman," a radio interviewer chirped . . . going effortlessly from our discussion of the past year's feminist revival to a commercial break, "why not make this your year, ladies, to get rid of those extra pounds with the Nutri/System diet plan? . . ." She spoke without irony. Gaining power, losing weight; liberation, liposuction—what's the diff?[14]

Although 1992 was trumpeted as the "year of the woman," women in that year still represented a small minority of the Senate (6 percent), the House (10.8 percent), and state legislatures (about 20 percent). Membership in state legislatures varies quite a bit by region—from a high of about one-third female in such East and West Coast states as Washington, Maine, and Vermont to a low of less than 3 percent in such southern states as Louisiana.[15]

Many nations have larger percentages of women lawmakers than one finds in the United States: Finland, 39 percent; Norway, 36 percent; Sweden, 34 percent; the Netherlands, 29 percent; Iceland, 24 percent; Cuba, 23 percent; Austria, 21 percent; and China, 21 percent.[16]

Female leaders as "uppity hysterics." Female leaders are often targets of putdowns and sexist slurs. For example, when French Prime Minister Edith Cresson criticized Japan's trade policies, Japanese Parliament member Shintaro Ishihara remarked that "we shouldn't be bothered by her. She is just a middle-aged hysteric." The *Los Angeles Times* described Kim Campbell, Canada's first female prime minister, as "a 46-year-old lawyer with a sharp tongue and an unconventional life."[17] Ms. Campbell was described as having a "sharp tongue" because she is witty and quick, and her comebacks are sometimes sharp. Her "unconventional lifestyle" might be attributed to the fact that she is twice-divorced, currently single and childless, and began and quit careers in law and académe and in two political parties. The previous premier of the state of Victoria, Australia, was pilloried for looking "frumpy."[18] Throughout her career, England's Prime Minister Margaret

Thatcher was described as an "iron lady" because she was tough and aggressive. Ann Richards, the governor of Texas, gets as much publicity about her "sharp tongue" as her progressive policies. Except for Congressperson Pat Schroeder's reference to Ronald Reagan as "the Teflon President," we don't hear pejorative comments about male politicians who are bald, adulterous, arrogant, larcenous, lecherous, or dumpy.

The least stereotypical women are the most likely to be criticized by the media and the general public. Consider Hillary Rodham Clinton, for example. After Bill Clinton was elected president in 1992, there was considerable criticism of his wife's potential role as adviser and policy maker. Soon, however, one national poll found that when people were asked "What kind of a job do you think Hillary Clinton will do as First Lady?," those saying "good" or "excellent" increased from 46 percent in April 1992 to 72 percent a year later. Nonetheless, 59 percent did not want Ms. Clinton to be a major adviser to her husband on policy and personnel, and 70 percent preferred that she serve as a "traditional" first lady.[19] Moreover, some polls show that many well-educated men under the age of 30 still believe that women "don't belong" in politics.[20]

Although Hillary Rodham Clinton is the first First Lady who combined traditional and career roles, she is not the first to play an active political role. In the late 1940s Eleanor Roosevelt testified before a congressional committee on the migration patterns of U.S. workers, and in the late 1970s Rosalynn Carter attended cabinet meetings and urged Congress to spend more on mental health programs.[21]

Why are there attacks on Hillary Clinton? Perhaps she did not meet many Americans' perception of women's "proper place." For example, she had once earned more than her husband ($179,920 compared with her husband's $43,667 in 1991), alarmed many people by remarking that she chose to pursue a career instead of staying home to bake cookies, had a "no-nonsense" hairdo and wardrobe, and was seen as "uppity and arrogant" by many voters in Arkansas during the late 1970s, when Bill Clinton ran for governor, because she wanted to keep her maiden name.

Since the gubernatorial and presidential elections, Hillary Clinton has become "more digestible": She took Clinton as her surname, traded the "bold-colored power suits" for "softer, more stylish pastel suits," gave up her "preppy black hair band" for "updated" haircuts, sponsored a tea for congressional wives, and even participated in a bake-off of chocolate-chip cookies with Barbara Bush.[22]

Historians point out that no matter how they performed their jobs, presidents' wives have often had detractors:

> Critics pointed to their extravagance (Mary Lincoln), coarseness (Margaret Taylor), casual entertaining (Dolley Madison), elitism (Elizabeth Monroe), prudishness (Lucy Hayes), gaiety (Harriet Lane), excessive grief (Jane Pierce), advanced age (Martha Washington), and youth (Julia Tyler). When wives appeared to exert some influence on their husbands or on government, they were charged with exercising "petticoat government" (Edith Wilson), running their

husbands' careers (Florence Harding), putting words into the president's mouth (Eleanor Roosevelt), and "getting people fired" (Nancy Reagan).[23]

Education

One of the most often-cited statistics to "prove" that women are making great progress is that they now make up more than 50 percent of college students. The statistic is accurate; the conclusion is wrong.

A report based on hundreds of empirical studies of elementary and secondary education concluded that "young women in the United States today are still not participating equally in our educational system."[24] The study found that teachers pay less attention to girls than to boys, that even girls who do well in mathematics and science classes are not encouraged to pursue these careers, that many school textbooks still ignore or stereotype girls and women, that some tests are still biased against girls, and reports of sexual harassment of girls by their male classmates are increasing.

Some observers note that there is a "gender-sorting machine" in schools that steers girls and young women into outdated female roles despite the guidance provided by well-intentioned parents and progressive teachers.[25] Even after young women earn exceptional grades in math and science classes in the middle school, by the time they graduate from high school, they are outnumbered 2 to 1 in computer classes and score 50 points lower than boys on the math portion of the Scholastic Aptitude Test (SAT). One of the results of the lower scores is that girls believe they are less able than their grades indicate and, less intelligent than boys. Consequently, they are less likely to aspire to "super-elite" colleges.[26]

Many women—students, faculty, or even college presidents—are still facing serious inequities in higher education. Although women make up more than half of college students nationwide, many of the educational resources are targeted at men. For example, a study by the National Collegiate Athletic Association found that men receive more than two thirds of athletic scholarship money and three quarters of the sports budgets.[27] Greater competition between men and women has also resulted in greater sexism. On some law school campuses, for example, women are reporting more hostility from male law students. Some of the increasing animosity may be due to the economic recessions and shrinking job markets. On the anniversary of the death of a feminist law professor at the New England College of Law, the *Harvard Law Review* published a parody of an article she had written entitled "A Postmodern Feminist Legal Manifesto." The parody was entitled "She-Manifesto of Post-Mortem Legal Feminism," signed Mary Doe, Rigor-Mortis professor of Law, and was described as having been written "from beyond the grave." Twenty-one law professors signed a protest letter that said the parody was a symptom of a much wider problem: "the *Review*, like much of the law school," has an environment that is hostile to women. Other law professors argued that students' free speech, however antifemale, should not be condemned.[28]

The proportion of women among Ph.D. recipients has increased—from 10 percent in 1962 to 37 percent in 1992.[29] Yet many of these women are not enjoying the same rewards as men. Although almost one third of full-time faculty are women, only 15 percent are in the highest "professor" ranks. In the elite group of 8 Ivy League universities, women make up 7 percent to 13 percent of professors. Many departments do not have a single female full professor.[30] Not only do women faculty earn less than men, but the gap has been increasing. For example, during 1980–1981, the average salary of full-time faculty nationwide was $24,499 for men and $19,996 for women. Women were earning 82 percent of what men earned. By 1992, the gap increased to 80 percent ($46,848 for men and $37,534 for women).[31]

Women are much less likely to be hired into tenure slots or to get tenure. In the field of economics, for example, among the 30 top-ranked graduate programs, women account for just over 3 percent of the full, tenured professors. At the top 10 math departments in the United States, there are 300 tenured men and *only 2 women.*[32]

At the highest administrative levels, colleges and universities are hiring a few more female presidents. Women represent a meager 12 percent of all presidents, up from 5 percent in 1975. Over 40 percent of these serve at community colleges where salaries are lower, budgets are tighter, and there are considerably fewer perks and resources. According to the director of the American Council on Education's office on women: "When over half the undergraduates are women, and when by the year 2000 over half the Ph.D.'s will go to women, to find only 12 percent in the top post says to me something is seriously wrong.[33] Dr. Judith Rodin, who took office at the University of Pennsylvania in 1994, is the first woman to head an Ivy League institution. More typically, female presidents believe that they are more likely to be funneled into the toughest presidential jobs either because fewer men apply for them or because women have fewer options than men: "Women are left with a difficult choice: Take on the presidency at a troubled institution, or be offered none at all."[34]

Mass Media

Although there has been some progress, many women have second-class status in the print media and limited or stereotypical exposure in movies and television.

The print media.   The influence of women in journalism has not matched their larger presence in the field. At U.S. newspapers, one third of the work force is female. About half of the new employees are female, but women hold only 15 percent of the executive positions. Among publishers and general managers, only 5 percent are women. One observer has noted, "The overall employment of women as newspaper managers continues to grow in tiny increments . . . even though women have made up a majority of journalism school undergraduates since 1977."[35]

The situation of minority women journalists has been even worse. Although minority women journalists have been active in the United States since the nineteenth century, their numbers in mainstream media are still minuscule. A study by the American Society of Newspaper Editors found that 51 percent of U.S. daily newspapers employ *no* people of color in their newsrooms. Women of color make up 7 percent of the newspaper work force. They were 3 percent of the executives and managers at newspapers and constituted only 6 percent of news-editorial employees—up one percentage point from a 1990 study.[36]

Although a few of the talented African American women are hired by some major newspapers, their lack of support, low salaries, and restrictions on articles can be devastating. Jill Nelson, an African American journalist who quit the *Washington Post,* described her job as "volunteer slavery":

> I'm just tired of being here, of justifying myself every day, of fighting with ignorant caucasians, of the whole trip. It's not any one thing or person, it's the institution. . . . I don't think the *Washington Post* is interested in or ready for someone like me, or the type of writing I do, and it's not worth it anymore. I'm tired.[37]

Coverage of and by women is also low. For example, a survey of three major U.S. news weeklies—*Newsweek, Time,* and *U.S. News & World Report*—showed a slight increase in the number of female by-lines but, between 1989 and 1990, a decline in the number of references to and photos by women.[38] Another study found that only 11 percent of the people quoted in major newspapers were women, and only 24 percent of the photographs included women, usually with their families. The prestigious *New York Times* was "dead last" in paying, employing, and featuring women.[39]

Television and movies. The high visibility of such television celebrities as Barbara Walters, Diane Sawyer, and Connie Chung suggests that women broadcasters are standard fare. This is not the case. At the major networks (including CNN and PBS) in 1990, women correspondents reported only 15 percent of the news stories—a decline of 1 percent since 1989. A survey of network evening newscasts found only 5 women among the 50 most prominent network reporters, and only 6 percent in the top news media jobs. An estimated 97 percent of TV anchors over age 40 are men. The only place women outnumber men is on the bottom rung, as beginning reporters or in advertising sales.[40]

The situation of women of color in broadcast news is even worse. Of the total number of stories on network news, including CNN and PBS, only 2 percent are filed by women of color. They are estimated to be 3.2 percent of television news directors and 2.8 percent of radio news directors. The survey of the 50 most prominent reporters mentioned earlier found *no* women of color.[41]

Although there are many women movie stars, there are few notable women's roles and even fewer women's films (where the movie deals with women's problems from a female perspective). In the early 1990s, there were a few exceptions, such as *Fried Green Tomatoes, A League of Their Own,* and *Thelma and Louise,* which were commercial hits. Perhaps the most controversial was *Thelma and Louise.* Some observers felt that this was a "women's film" because Thelma and Louise shot a rapist, took their revenge on an offensive trucker, and eluded law-enforcement officers (i.e., they, not men, took control of their lives and made the decisions).[42] Many women cheered as Thelma and Louise played out many women's fantasies of avenging their attackers.

Similarly, little boys get more movie roles than little girls. As the box entitled "No Girls Allowed in Hollywood" shows, most of the recent films have featured boys.

NO GIRLS ALLOWED IN HOLLYWOOD

According to journalist Bruce Westerbrook, girls' parts in Hollywood films are minuscule while boys "can do anything." Some examples of recent popular films that featured boys include the following:
- in *Free Willy,* a boy tames and trains a killer whale
- in both versions of *Home Alone,* a young boy outwits adults
- in *Searching for Bobby Fischer,* a boy becomes a chess champion
- in *The Mighty Ducks,* boys become hockey champions
- in *Rookie of the Year,* a boy becomes a baseball champion in the major leagues
- in *Last Action Hero,* a boy is a sidekick to Arnold Schwarzenegger's super-cop
- in *The Man Without A Face,* a boy becomes best pal to his tutor
- in *Forever Young,* two boys rescue the hero from a deep freeze
- in *The Sandlot,* boys find an ally in a big-leaguer
- in *Lost in Yonkers,* two brothers change a mean grandma
- in *Sleepless in Seattle,* the determined matchmaker is a boy.[43]

One of the biggest sources of sex-role stereotyping is music videos. In a study of sex-role stereotyping of 182 Music Television Videos (MTV), Steven Seidman found that both male and female characters were shown in sex-typed roles. Male characters were adventuresome, aggressive, and violent, while females were affectionate, dependent, nurturing, and fearful. A large percentage of female characters wore revealing clothing as well as initiated and received sexual advances more often than males. Female characters were typically presented as "sex objects" or as "second-class citizens" in the working world:

> The distributions for some occupations were striking. For example, 98 percent of the soldiers, 94 percent of the security and police personnel, 91 percent of the photographers, 90 percent of the athletes, and all scientists, politicians, and business executives and managers were males, whereas 89 percent of the hair stylists, 83 percent of the dancers, and all fashion models and telephone operators were females.[44]

Men's activities typically get more media attention than do women's accomplishments. For example, it was about the same time in the early 1990s that "Magic" Johnson, the basketball star, resigned from the National Basketball League, General Colin Powell resigned from military service, and Toni Morrison won the Nobel Prize in Literature.

Who got the least coverage? Magic Johnson's press conference got generous air time, was replayed for several days, and attracted numerous articles and editorials. Even General Powell got more publicity than Toni Morrison. Some people might argue that none of this is sexist because, among other things, Magic Johnson and General Powell were already "celebrities" and many (male) Americans are more interested (or journalists assume that they are more interested) in sports and war heroes than in the contributions of scholars or scientists. Since the media are dominated by men and men's issues, however, glossing over women's accomplishments can become a self-fulfilling prophecy. Strikingly, Toni Morrison's major accomplishments got almost *no* coverage in the mass media.

Sexual Harassment and Violence

As later chapters show in detail, such problems as stalking, rape, sexual harassment, and wife battering are still widespread. During the last 10 years some jurisdictions have been more progressive in changing rape laws and prosecuting wife batterers. For the most part, however, many women and their children are still defenseless against attackers. (This is true overseas as well as in the United States. In London, a judge put a man on probation even though he admitted trying to have sex with an 8-year-old girl. The judge remarked that the girl was "not entirely an angel."[45]) Swarthmore College "punished" a student who stalked and intimidated a freshman woman by trying to transfer him (and paying his tuition!) to Columbia University (which denied admission because of low grades).[46] When Paula Coughlin pressed charges against the Navy pilots who assaulted her and other women during the naval aviators' Tailhook convention in Las Vegas in 1991, the immediate reaction of her superiors was denial. None of the officers involved has been court martialed. The Government Accounting Office, the investigative arm of Congress, found that *97 percent* of the female students at the nation's military academies have experienced sexual harassment.[47]

Although Republican Senator Robert Packwood of Oregon has been accused of sexual harassment by more than two dozen women, there have as yet been no political or legal sanctions for his actions. In fact, corporate officials, prominent politicians, and labor groups have made generous donations to hire one of the most prestigious law firms in Washington, D.C. to defend Packwood.[48] According to a Labor Department study, women account for only 7 percent of on-the-job fatalities, but 40 percent of their work-place deaths are from *murder*.[49] Large numbers of women are exposed to crime by working late at night. In the last few years, however, increasing numbers of ex-husbands and ex-boyfriends have walked into offices during the daytime and have shot women in front of dozens of witnesses.

We note examples of violence in other countries as well. Many people were shocked when Japan recently admitted that an estimated 200,000 women (primarily Korean and Filipino) were forced into sexual slavery for its soldiers between 1932 and 1945. The political rationale for forcing these "comfort women" into slave brothels was to satisfy the desires of conquering Japanese soldiers and thus discourage rape and keep down the incidence of venereal disease. After considerable pressure from women's groups, in 1993 the male-dominated Japanese government finally acknowledged that virtually all the women were recruited against their own will, were kept "in misery", and "in a coercive atmosphere." Although some of the women are demanding compensation, a government representative refused to admit the acts constitute a war crime and said that Japan would continue to "consider seriously how best to show remorse."[50]

Many people were outraged by both the existence of "comfort women" and Japan's refusal to admit full culpability. In addition, there has been little public outcry even though thousands of girls and women have been raped by Croat and Serbian soldiers in the Bosnian war in Europe during the early 1990s. Many have been gang raped or raped repeatedly while held hostage.

BACKLASH IN THE NINETIES

Many Americans still feel that women's place is in the home. In a recent survey of thousands of students entering 392 2-year and 4-year institutions, for example, over 25 percent agreed with the statement that "married women's activities are best confined to home and family."[51] And 1 out of 5 of the college women agreed that women should still be "confined" to home and family.

In her book, *Backlash,* Susan Faludi describes the 1980s as the "backlash decade" that produced "one long, painful, and unremitting campaign to thwart women's progress."[52] Donna Jackson describes the backlash as "retrosexism"—a "new wave of sexism" that increasingly views and treats women as objects.[53]

Sources of Backlash

Where is the backlash coming from? According to Faludi, from almost everywhere: government officials, Hollywood films, popular psychology manuals, the fashion industry, academics, and even "liberated" women. Publications from *The New York Times* to *Vanity Fair* to *Nation,* she says, "have issued a steady stream of indictments against the women's movement:"

> They hold the campaign for women's equality responsible for nearly every woe besetting women, from mental depression to meager savings accounts, from teenage suicides to eating disorders to bad complexions.[54]

Some of the attacks are even coming from highly visible women. Kathleen Sullivan, a former network news anchor, was fired from her job in 1990—presumably because she was slightly overweight, temperamental, and had prematurely gray hair during her twenties. She has recently done a series of commercials for Weight Watchers®. Some of her critics have included Katie Couric, co-host of NBC's *Today* show, and CNN reporter Judy Woodruff, both of whom have questioned Kathleen Sullivan's future credibility as a journalist.[55] The more important question is why capable female journalists who are a few pounds overweight are fired from their jobs while men who are *extremely overweight* keep their jobs.

In such recent family television shows as *Full House, Empty Nest,* and *Blossom,* mothers have been "killed off or have gone away to find themselves" even though 86 percent of single parents in this country are mothers, not fathers. One male writer suggested that killing the wives off might be wish fulfillment by men who are angry about mothers working outside the home.[56] Even the commercials on many of these shows are reverting to dated stereotypes where women choose domesticity over a career:

> Consider a recent credit-card commercial, in which a woman's boyfriend, upon hearing that she's considering a better job offer in another city, suddenly offers a diamond ring, asking her to forgo her job opportunity for him. The commercial closes with the woman smiling tearfully, the job now forgotten, the ring sparkling.[57]

Some of the most violent backlash has been in the area of reproductive rights. In the early 1990s, several physicians who performed abortions have been shot and killed, there were several attempted murders, kidnappings, bombings of women's health clinics, and continuous harassment of women who are seeking abortions. In Mississippi, for example, antiabortion activist Roy McMillan uses a variety of intimidating techniques:

> Mr. McMillan was at his usual post outside the clinic wearing a gold cross and a T-shirt with a full-color picture of an aborted fetus. He carried a human embryo in a small vial of formaldehyde and was prepared to thrust it toward the car windows of women driving into the parking lot. Periodically, [he] noted the cars' tag information and called out the names of the counties where the drivers had come from. He has used license numbers to trace the homes of three young women seeking abortions. He said he had visited all three homes—two where the parents of pregnant teenagers listened sympathetically to his entreaties, a third where, he said, a couple "all but threw me out. They wanted their grandchild dead."[58]

While men are often at the forefront of the pro-life movement, they are rarely visible in movements supporting children's rights, pressing for welfare reform, or advocating tougher laws against rape, wife battering, incest, or sexual harassment. Many men are crusading to control women's reproduction but are disinterested in girls *after they are born.*

Reasons for the Backlash

There are many reasons, most of them overlapping, for the male backlash against women. Indicting women, and especially feminists, sells newspapers and magazines. Typically, most feminist work goes unnoticed. Two recent books that appeared to be critical of feminist perspectives (Katie Roiphe's *The Morning After* and Camille Paglia's *Sexual Personae*) received widespread and uncritical praise from journalists, however. Similarly, *Mother Jones,* a magazine that usually supports feminism and women's rights, had been largely ignored by the "mainstream" press until it published an article that harshly criticized women's studies programs. Books (such as Warren Farrell's *The Myth of Male Power*), which argue that men and not women are the "oppressed" group, often receive enthusiastic pre-publication judgments on the front pages of book-review sections in such influential newspapers as *The New York Times* and the *Washington Post.*

Attacking women makes some people rich. A few years ago, misogynist comic Andrew Dice Clay made a reputation and a fortune by calling women "pigs" and "sluts." Such radio hosts as Rush Limbaugh and Howard Stern ridicule women, especially feminists and lesbians, or they glorify only those who are mindless sex objects or pro-life activists. Both talk shows are among the most popular in the nation. Some black rappers have skyrocketed to fame with songs that call women bitches and whores and describe shooting, raping, sodomizing, or torturing women. Madonna's money-making book, *Sex,* has numerous photographs of women in sadistic poses. In the preface, Madonna writes "Some women want to be slapped around . . . I think for the most part if women are in an abusive relationship and they know it and they stay in it, they must be digging it."[59] This outrageous interpretation is contradicted by much research showing that women often stay in abusive relationships because of fear or economic reasons, not because they "dig it." Exploiting or otherwise degrading women is often "good business."

Why are misogyny and antifeminism so popular? Although it is beyond the scope of this chapter to summarize the extensive literature that provides explanations, three reasons can be noted briefly: deeply ingrained attitudes about women's and men's "proper" roles, fear of losing status or resources, and the persisting institutionalization of gender inequality.

Ingrained attitudes about women's and men's "proper" roles.   Most children internalize sex stereotypes between the ages of 2 and 5. A recent study found that children "seem to be as stereotypically sex-typed as those of yesteryear."[60] Even when girls have professional mothers as role models and do well academically, by the age of 11 or 12 they have learned that "good girls" attempt to please everyone, are too nice to express anger, and put their own needs last.[61]

In 1993, the Ms. Foundation organized the first annual "Take Our Daughters to Work Day" to help raise girls' self-esteem. An estimated 1 million mothers and daughters participated in the event. Although it is certainly worthwhile for girls to see where and how their mothers work, it is interesting that we don't feel we have to raise boys' self-esteem, that there is no counterpart activity such as mothers taking their sons to work, or organizing a "Teach Our Sons Domestic and Child-care Day" in which fathers and sons participate. Many of our efforts, however laudable, are still focused on changing women's rather than men's roles.

Fear of losing status, power, or resources.   In the early 1990s, there was an explosion of books about men and the "men's movement." For example, Robert Bly's *Iron Men* (a treatise on what American men lack) and Sam Keen's *Fire in the Belly* (a book that argues that men can find themselves only by separating from women) were best-sellers.[62] Hundreds of men's groups formed workshops, conferences, retreats, informal meetings, and support groups to discuss the meaning of manhood, fatherhood, communication, and the breakup of marriages or long-term relationships. Many people have praised the men's movement because the participants discussed such "feminine" issues as emotional ties and challenged stereotypically male roles of success, achievement, and power. But the men's movement for the most part is a backlash by a small group of privileged white men who are more concerned about losing their positions than in attaining gender equality:

> This men's movement has a lot of things wrong with it. It's over-intellectualized and over-hyped, its drum-beating lunatic fringe has been given far too much press, some of it is an angry backlash against feminism, and it involves only a fraction of the male population—and almost everyone in the movement is a white upper-middle-class heterosexual.[63]

Some men have supported the women's movement because it has taken some of the pressure off their being the sole economic providers for their families. Yet they are reluctant to share some of the domestic work and child care demanded by their fatigued partners that cuts into their leisure time (as we will document in later chapters). Also, many men feel nervous about the increasing numbers of women who are demanding a piece of the pie. As a male colleague stated, "I'm all for women's equality, but not if she gets the job and I don't." One of the most revealing comments of feeling threatened by women was President George Bush's statement that "I am delighted with some of the [Democratic party] women that our [Republican party] Senate candidates are going to be taking on because they will be easier to beat."

Men are not alone in trying to abort women's rights. In a study of the consciousness of gender inequality in the United States, Great Britain, West Germany, and Austria, Nancy Davis and Robert Robinson found that U.S. women were *much less likely* than their European counterparts to support government intervention to reduce gender inequality. The researchers speculated that one reason for this difference is that some American housewives may be opposing efforts to increase gender equality in the work place because such efforts devalue and threaten their status as full-time homemakers or might erode their husbands' earnings.[64]

Women who are doing well are especially likely to get little sympathy when they experience discrimination. One woman, who considered suing a prestigious Wall Street firm for sex bias when she was repeatedly passed over for promotion despite her first-rate performance, said she went to her lawyer with documented proof that less-qualified men were being promoted. The lawyer advised her not to sue. "He said I had a solid case, but he couldn't picture a judge or jury shedding any tears for a plaintiff who made 'only' $220,000 a year."[65]

Institutionalization of sex inequality.   The problems of sexism are more than individual problems. They are imbedded in the organizations and institutions of this society. Institutionalization refers to the process by which people learn the shared expectations about the rights and duties of specific social roles that have been built into established patterns of behavior in such institutions as the family, education, economy, and political systems. Sex inequality has long been sewn into the basic fabric of our institutions, values, and gender roles.

Gender roles—the rights, responsibilities, expectations, and relationships of women and men—permeate all aspects of our lives. They are difficult to change. Even in the countries with the most generous parental-leave policies, for example, many fathers are reluctant to take advantage of unpaid leave, even when they want to develop closer relationships with their children. They fear, often justifiably, that they will be ostracized by their relatives and friends, demoted at work, or both.[66]

In a study of 12 countries (Austria, Denmark, Finland, Great Britain, Israel, Japan, the Netherlands, Northern Ireland, Norway, Sweden, the former West Germany, and the United States), Patricia Roos found "substantial" cross-cultural occupational sex segregation: Men predominate in administrative and managerial occupations as well as in high- and medium-prestige production jobs while women predominate in high-prestige clerical, low-prestige sale, and low-prestige service occupations; occupations held mainly by women are low paying across industrial societies; and incumbents in traditionally female occupations are underpaid relative to their average educational achievement.[67] Even countries with the most enlightened social policies for child-care and equal-employment opportunity have not produced gender equality in public life, in the work place, or in the home.[68] Thus, it is difficult to dispel the effects of patriarchal control that shape many women's work and domestic lives.

Some aspects of sex inequality have improved. There is, however, a great deal of evidence that sex inequality is still a major problem and may even be increasing in some areas. As this chapter has shown, many women still face discrimination in employment, education, politics, and the media. Perhaps because women have made modest gains, the backlash, which includes women, seems to be intensifying. Those with the most power—judges, Fortune 500 companies, prestigious higher education institutions, and media makers—are also the most resistant to women's (and some men's) demands for greater sex equality.

The next chapter discusses, more specifically, women's place in a still-sexist society.

NOTES

1. Saundra Torry, "Study Finds Sexual Harassment Prevalent in Western U.S. Courts," *Washington Post,* August 5, 1992, p. A2. Throughout this book some references to newspapers, magazines, newsletters, and wire service releases are taken from Mead Data Central's computerized database called Nexis. In those cases only the first page of the source is provided in the database, and our references reflect this fact.

2. Materials from Rodney Peterson, Campus Compliance Officer, Office of Human Relations Programs/Office of the President, University of Maryland at College Park, June 1993.

3. Richard O'Mara, "Church of England OKs Female Priests," *Baltimore Sun,* November 12, 1992, pp. 1A, 10A.

4. Laura Sessions Stepp, "Bishops Back Ordination Ban on Women," *Washington Post,* April 9, 1992, pp. A1, A8.

5. See Shari Rudavsky, "A Status Report on the Glass Ceiling," *Washington Post,* August 12, 1992, p. A19.

6. Cited in Frank Swoboda, "Looking for a Way to Break the 'Glass Ceiling'". *Washington Post,* September 29, 1990, p. A15.

7. Anetta Miller with Karen Springen and Dody Tsiantar, "Now: The Brick Wall," *Newsweek,* August 24, 1992, p. 55.

8. Cited in Meryl Gordon, "Discrimination at the Top," *Working Woman,* September 1992, p. 70.

9. Cited in *Working Woman,* "An Extra $11,724 for the Guys," September, 1992, p. 21.

10. Monica Roman, "Women, Beware: An MBA Doesn't Mean Equal Pay," *Business Week,* October 29, 1990, p. 57.

11. Ivan Amato, "Profile of a Field: Chemistry; Women Have Extra Hoops to Jump Through," *Science* 13 (March 1992), pp. 1372–1373).

12. U.S. Department of Commerce, *The Black Population in the United States: March 1990 and 1989.* Bureau of the Census, Current Population Reports, Series P-20, no. 448, Washington, DC: Government Printing Office, 1991.

13. R. Ann Casey, "Title IX and Women Officials—How Have They Been Affected?" JOPERD (March 1992), pp. 45–47; Vivian Acosta and Linda Jean Carpenter, "As the Years Go By—Coaching Opportunities in the 1990s," JOPERD, March 1992, pp. 36–41.

14. Susan Faludi, "Looking Beyond the Slogans," *Newsweek* 120:26, December 28, 1992, p. 31.

15. Cited in Naomi K. Cohen, "Shaking Off Legislative Typecasting," *The Journal of State Government* 64, April/June 1991, pp. 57–59.

16. *Baltimore Sun,* "Number of Women in Parliaments Drops," September 12, 1993, p. 5A.

17. *Baltimore Sun,* "Canada Selects Woman to be Prime Minister," June 14, 1993, p. 3A.

18. Comments through WMST–L (Women's Studies List).

19.   Kenneth T. Walsh and Thomas Toch, "Now, the First Chief Advocate," *U.S. News & World Report,* January 25, 1993, pp. 46–50.

20.   Stephen Earl Bennett and Linda L.M. Bennett, "From Traditional to Modern Conceptions of Gender Equality in Politics: Gradual Change and Lingering Doubts," *The Western Political Quarterly* 45 (March 1992), pp. 93–111.

21.   See, for example, Betty Boyd Caroli, *First Ladies* (New York: Oxford University Press, 1987) and Carl Sferrazza Anthony, *First Ladies: The Saga of the Presidents' Wives and Their Power* (New York: W. Morrow, 1990).

22.   Susan Baer, "More Digestible Hillary Now Offers Cookies," *Baltimore Sun,* July 16, 1992, p. 10A.

23.   Caroli, *First Ladies,* p. xxi.

24.   American Association of University Women Educational Foundation, *How Schools Shortchange Girls,* Washington, DC, 1992, p. 84.

25.   See, for example, Joanne M. Schrof, "The Gender Machine," *U.S. News & World Report,* August 2, 1993, pp. 42–44.

26.   Phyllis Rosser, *The SAT Gender Gap: Identifying the Causes,* Washington, DC: Center for Women Policy Studies, 1989.

27.   Douglas Lederman, "NCAA Officials Try to Counter Charges of Sex Bias in Sports," *The Chronicle of Higher Education,* April 15, 1992, pp. A43–A44.

28.   Michele N-K Collison, "Angry Protests over Diversity and Free Speech Mark Contentious Spring Semester at Harvard," *The Chronicle of Higher Education,* May 6, 1992, pp. A39–A40.

29.   Paula Ries and Delores H. Thurgood, *Summary Report 1992: Doctorate Recipients from United States Universities,* Washington, DC: National Academy Press, 1993, p. 19.

30.   Anthony DePalma, "Rare in Ivy League: Women Who Work as Full Professors," *The New York Times,* January 24, 1993, p. 1. For a discussion of Canadian faculty, see Paula J. Caplan, *Lifting a Ton of Feathers: A Woman's Guide to Surviving in the Academic World* (Toronto: University of Toronto Press, 1993).

31.   U.S. Department of Education, National Center for Education Statistics. *Digest of Education Statistics: 1993,* Washington, DC: Government Printing Office, 1993, p. 234.

32.   Paul Selvin, "Does the Harrison Case Reveal Sexism in Math?" *Science* 252 (June 18, 1992) pp. 1781–1783.

33.   Courtney Leatherman, "Colleges Hire More Female Presidents, but Questions Linger About Their Clout," *The Chronicle of Higher Education,* November 6, 1991, pp. A19–A21.

34.   Ibid.

35.   Maurine H. Beasley and Sheila J. Gibbons, *Taking Their Place: A Documentary History of Women and Journalism* (Washington, DC: The American University Press, 1993), p. 268. A new study by Advertising Women of New York shows that men are paid considerably more than women in the fields of advertising, broadcasting, and publishing. The salary gap starts at about $7,000 at the beginning of women's careers and reaches a median difference of almost $32,000 after 20 years (see Peter Caranicas, "Who's Come a Long Way?: A New York Study Finds Persistent Sexual Discrimination in the

Communications Industries," *Back Stage Shoot,* May 14, 1993, pp. 1, 10, 28).

36. Cited in Beasley and Gibbons, *Taking Their Place,* p. 307.

37. Jill Nelson, *Volunteer Slavery: My Authentic Negro Experience* (Chicago: Noble Press, Inc., 1993), p. 238.

38. Cited in Beasley and Gibbons, *Taking Their Place,* p. 286.

39. Ibid.

40. Ibid. *See also,* Beasley and Gibbons, *Taking Their Place,* p. 269.

41. Beasley and Gibbons, *Taking Their Place,* p. 307.

42. Judy Gerstel, "The Women Stars Are There, but Where Are the Movie Roles for Them to Shine in?" *Baltimore Sun,* August 15, 1993, p. 3e.

43. Bruce Westerbrook, "It's Still 'No Girls Allowed' in Hollywood," *Baltimore Sun,* December 20, 1993, p. 6D.

44. Steven A. Seidman, "An Investigation of Sex-Role Stereotyping in Music Videos," *Journal of Broadcasting & Electronic Media* (Spring 1992), p. 212.

45. Richard O'Mara, "Britons Shake Their Head over Judges' Far-Out Rulings," *Baltimore Sun,* June 14, 1993, pp. a1, 4a.

46. Mary Jordan, "Swarthmore Confronts Sexual 'Intimidation,'" *Washington Post,* January 11, 1994, pp. a1, a4.

47. See *Baltimore Sun,* "Service Academy Sexism Held Rampant," February 4, 1994, p. 8a.

48. Donna St. George, "Packwood's Pals Help with Cash," *Baltimore Sun,* November 19, 1993, pp. 1A, 19A.

49. Cited in *Baltimore Sun,* "Murders Cause 40 Percent of Deaths of Women in Workplace, Survey Says," October 2, 1993, p. 3a.

50. John E. Woodruff, "Japan Admits Using Women Sex Slaves," *Baltimore Sun,* August 5, 1993, pp. 1a, 15a.

51. Reported in *Chronicle of Higher Education,* "This Year's College Freshmen: Attitudes and Characteristics," January 30, 1991, pp. A30–A31.

52. Susan Faludi, *Backlash: The Undeclared War Against American Women* (New York: Crown Publishers, Inc., 1991), p. 454.

53. Donna Jackson, "The Return of Sexism," *New Woman* 22:1, January 1992, pp. 80–85.

54. Faludi, *Backlash,* p. xi.

55. Alice Steinbach, "Sullivan Loses Pounds as Others Lose Their Heads," *Baltimore Sun,* January 15, 1994, p. D1.

56. Jackson, "The Return of Sexism," p. 83.

57. Ibid., p. 81.

58. Fawn Vrazo, "Mississippi Abortions Drop 50% with 'Delay' Law," *Baltimore Sun,* October 1, 1992, p. 3A.

59. Madonna, *Sex* (New York: Warner Books, 1992).

60. Kay Bussey and Albert Bandura, "Self-Regulatory Mechanisms Governing Gender Development," *Child Development* 63:5 (October 1992), pp. 1236–1250.

61. See, for example, Lyn Mikel Brown and Carol Gilligan, *Meeting at the Crossroads: Women's Psychology and Girls' Development* (New York: Ballantine

Books, 1992).

62. Robert Bly, *Iron John: A Book About Men* (New York: Vintage Books, 1992); Sam Keen, *Fire in the Belly: On Being a Man* (New York: Bantam Books, 1991).

63. Neely Tucker, "Manhood: Hits & Myths" *Washington Post,* November 10, 1992, p.C5.

64. Nancy J. Davis and Robert V. Robinson, "Men's and Women's Consciousness of Gender Inequality: Austria, West Germany, Great Britain, and the United States," *American Sociological Review* 56 (February 1991), pp. 72–84.

65. Anne B. Fisher, *Wall Street Women* (New York: Alfred A. Knopf, 1990), p. 88.

66. See, for example, Hilda Kahne, "Progress or Stalemate? A Cross-National Comparison of Women's Status and Roles," in *Women's Work and Women's Lives: The Continuing Struggle Worldwide,* eds., Hilda Kahne and Janet Z. Giele (Boulder, CO: Westview Press, 1992), pp. 279–301; and Linda Haas, *Equal Parenthood and Social Policy: A Study of Parental Leave in Sweden* (Albany: NY: State University of New York Press, 1992).

67. Patricia A. Roos, *Gender and Work: A Comparative Analysis of Industrial Societies* (Ithaca: NY: State University of New York Press, 1985).

68. See, for example, Janet Z. Giele, "Promise and Disappointment of the Modern Era: Equality for Women," in *Women's Work and Women's Lives: The Continuing Struggle Worldwide,* eds., Hilda Kahne and Janet Z. Giele (Boulder, CO: Westview Press, 1992), pp. 3–27.

CHAPTER TWO
WOMAN'S PLACE IN A SEXIST SOCIETY: SOCIETY, ORGANIZATIONS, AND INDIVIDUALS

The *Wall Street Journal* once featured a front-page story about a New York City group called the Baker Street Irregulars, prominent men dedicated to reliving the adventures and spirit of Arthur Conan Doyle's detective, Sherlock Holmes. They hold annual dinner parties for men only, with a predinner toast to "the woman," a woman specially chosen for the occasion, who, after the toast, is sent away. These male aficionados of Holmes, the bachelor, believe that Holmes had a distaste for women. Heading its story with "To a Sherlockian, Coolness to Women Is an Elementary Canon" and providing a critical insight into yet another good-old-boy ritual, the *Wall Street Journal* article both demonstrated and reinforced the antifemale aspects of much male togetherness in this society. The sex discrimination faced by women is a critical feature of a society that is so male dominated that few analysts, journalists, or researchers can fathom its deep roots.[1]

Many people, including many college students, are convinced that sex discrimination is no longer a serious problem in the United States. Even the most informed college students sometimes become visibly impatient when we introduce such "ancient history" as sex discrimination and male dominance into our course lectures.

After all, students argue, things have really changed in the last few decades: "My boss has told me several times that the company has to hire more women." "If there were sex discrimination, I wouldn't have been accepted into the management training program." "I can be anything I want to be."

These views are not surprising, for they can be found among such prominent writers and advisers to recent U.S. presidents as George Gilder and Phyllis Schlafly. In *Wealth and Poverty,* the influential conservative George

Gilder has argued that there is no need for affirmative action because (1) it would seem genuinely difficult to document the idea that America is still oppressive and discriminatory, and (2) discrimination has already been effectively abolished in this country.[2] Sex discrimination is explicitly described by Gilder as a "myth," and affirmative action is seen as unnecessary. Phyllis Schlafly, another prominent conservative advocate, has argued vigorously in recent years that sexual harassment is not a serious problem in this country. Schlafly advocates the Ozzie-and-Harriet family image, with the woman at home with the kids and the man bringing home the paycheck, even though she herself spends most of her time traveling and lobbying for conservative causes.[3] Schlafly has attacked such progressive changes as federal affirmative action regulations, which she views as hurting the traditional mother in the ideal family by allegedly giving her husband's job to a woman and by "obsoleting the role of motherhood."[4] In the 1980s and 1990s, Schlafly has become an outspoken opponent of the woman's right to choose abortion.

Schlafly, who established the politically right-wing Eagle Forum, was an important player in the development of the 1992 Republican platform. Interestingly, during the 1992 presidential campaign the news media discovered that Schlafly's son John was gay. Yet Schlafly is well known for her vocal opposition to the "lifestyles" of gay and lesbian Americans. Indeed, one reason for her adamant hostility to the Equal Rights Amendment is that she fears it would permit gays and lesbians to marry.[5] She has also denounced a proposal for AIDS education as the "teaching of safe sodomy."[6] Nonetheless, she has defended her son John's "coming out of the closet," even while she denounces homosexual rights on the lecture circuit.

Although the views of Gilder and Schlafly are among the most reactionary of the views on sex roles, many powerful and rank-and-file Americans share them. We will now examine these reactionary views more closely at the societal, organizational, and individual levels.

THE SOCIETAL LEVEL

We can first note some broad trends at the societal or national level. At the societal level there have been some significant advances for women in this society. We have seen, for example, modest changes in the token numbers of women who are important decision makers in corporate, governmental, and judicial work places. In 1981, Sandra Day O'Connor became the first woman ever to serve on the U.S. Supreme Court, and in 1993, Ruth Bader Ginsburg became the second. It is significant that Ginsburg, unlike the conservative O'Connor, is a feminist and a pioneer in litigation on behalf of women's rights.[7] Still, in most areas of this society the changes have usually been only token victories. The momentum of the late 1960s and early 1970s, which was directed toward expanding employment and educational opportunity for women, slowed significantly between the mid-1970s and the mid-1990s. Governmental policymakers and private-sector decision makers have become preoccupied with matters other than sex discrimination. By the 1990s, many were viewing the women's movement not as a local movement but as a small group of women's lobby organizations in Washington, D.C. For example, one writer has described the largest group, the National Organization for Women (NOW), as little more than a direct-mail information organization, with only a modest number of activists and organizers.[8] While we think this view is greatly exaggerated—there are many grass roots efforts being made by NOW groups today—it is true that NOW does not get the national media coverage that it did in previous decades.

Younger generations of women have not, as yet, been actively recruited in large numbers into these major activist organizations. Yet there are new groups constantly emerging. One of these is the Women's Action Coalition, a group that emerged after the Anita Hill hearings and that is oriented to more active resistance strategies. Moreover, by the early 1990s there were more women in Congress, but in the 1980s and early 1990s there were still significant cuts in programs for women. Major legislation on behalf of women was usually stalled by the male members of Congress.

The Presidential Level

Presidents Ronald Reagan and George Bush publicly opposed the Equal Rights Amendment (ERA). In 1983, Reagan intentionally destroyed the U.S. Commission on Civil Rights, an organization long effective in the fight for better conditions for America's women and minorities. He replaced two politically moderate members of the Commission with new members sympathetic to right-wing views of the situations of women and minorities in U.S. society. The Commission abandoned its traditional role of studying federal government programs to see if they are discriminatory. As Martha Burk, writing in *Nation* magazine, put it, "Reagan-appointed judges gutted Title VII of the 1964 Civil Rights Act, regulatory agencies such as the Equal Employment Opportunity Commission (EEOC) were effectively dismantled, enforcement of anti-discrimination laws was stopped and meanspirited anti-woman policies were the order of the day."[9] Reagan's heir, George Bush, continued this conservative tradition of working against women's rights. The dismantling of many civil rights agencies throughout the 1980s created serious problems for Congress and the White House in the 1990s. As yet there has been no major rebuilding of these agencies to protect the work place and other opportunities for women. Even in the mid-1990s, neither the President nor leading male members of Congress have come out strongly for legislation on pay equity or on the equal rights amendment, still two major goals of the women's movement.

Many analysts have viewed President Bill Clinton as more sympathetic to women's issues than his Republican predecessors. He signed the Family and Medical Leave Act and appointed a few more women to important government positions, including the first woman, Janet Reno, ever appointed to the position of U.S. attorney general. However, only four of his top 15 political appointments were women, in spite of his being supplied with numerous names of highly qualified women by some women's groups. Clinton's pro-choice stance fueled the hopes of many that he would take major steps to protect women's abortion rights, but as of late 1994 he had taken only a few modest steps and seemed reluctant to press for major new women's rights initiatives.[10]

The Courts

There has been uneven progress in the federal court system. There are still hundreds of sections of the U.S. legal code and of state laws that are riddled with sex bias or sex-based terminology in conflict with the ideal of equal rights for women. In the 1980s and early 1990s, a conservative Supreme Court demonstrated a halting move away from equal rights. In 1984, for example, the Supreme Court ruled that an entire college is not subject to civil rights laws protecting women, even if one of its programs receives major federal aid.[11] Title IX of the 1972 Educational Amendments prohibits sex discrimination in "any educational program or activity receiving federal financial assistance." Yet the administrators at Grove City College, a private college in Pennsylvania, argued that the college should not be covered by Title IX because the only federal aid it received went directly to students and also that it did not discriminate in any programs against women. The Court ruled that the college was covered by Title IX, but only for the specific federal aid program involved. This decision signaled a retreat from a broad protection of women's rights in educational institutions. During the Reagan and Bush administrations the Department of Education did not work aggressively to enforce Title IX in regard to colleges and universities.

After the *Grove* ruling, Title IX was significantly weakened. However, in 1988 the U.S. Congress did pass the Civil Rights Restoration Act to broaden Title IX to again cover all programs at colleges that received any federal aid. In addition, an important 1992 Supreme Court decision on sexual harassment declared that a student could collect compensatory damages for sex discrimination under Title IX.[12]

Title IX remains as a legal requirement that athletic opportunities for women in higher education be proportional to their numbers. Today, however, college women do not have equal participation with men in college athletic programs. In 1991–92 there were about 186,000 male athletes in 21 NCAA sports, but only 96,467 women in 16 NCAA sports. This male/female athlete ratio is even worse at many larger colleges and universities. Yet, the times may be changing. Under pressure for gender equity and facing major budget crises, many college athletic administrators are considering dropping some of the male sports that do not produce money and replacing them with certain women's sports. In order to meet the legal requirements for gender equality, many colleges may have to cut down football programs and sponsor more major sports for college women.[13] (Because of threats to large football programs, some universities have threatened to pull out of the NCAA.) For two decades there has been snail-like progress in improving the gender balance in college athletics. Numerous Title IX lawsuits—at universities as diverse as the University of Texas, Brown, Colgate, Colorado State, and Auburn—are forcing many college athletic programs to expand sports opportunities for college women much more rapidly than in the past.[14]

Affirmative Action

From the late 1970s to the present, there has been a marked backing away from positive programs designed to upgrade women in U.S. society. In contrast, between the late 1960s and the mid-1970s, much legislation and many judicial decisions, executive orders, and administrative orders generated requirements for result-oriented programs to promote women and minorities in employment. Called "affirmative action," these "goals" programs have suffered from many outside attacks, especially from white men. Many critics of such programs assume that "goals" and "quotas" are synonymous, that "preferential treatment" is being given to so-called "unqualified" women and minority job applicants, and that affirmative action programs violate promotions based on tradition, "merit," and seniority. Much of this debate has been misplaced. Most female and minority jobseekers have the necessary credentials. (It also seems odd to us that no one ever speaks of "unqualified white male applicants.") It is often the case, moreover, that company executives and governmental officials have drawn up only "paper tiger" affirmative action plans that are not seriously implemented.[15]

Because many affirmative action officers are poorly trained, lack significant enforcement powers, and are not supported by top executives in their organizations, they may not be taken seriously by other managers or they may actually function to slow down gender and racial desegregation of their organizations. Some affirmative action programs may involve a poorly constructed affirmative action plan issued with fanfare but weakly enforced. A number of observers, reacting to organizational pressures for affirmative action have noted that more effort has often been put into paperwork than into aggressively finding women for historically male jobs and positions.

Some corporations are actively recruiting women and minorities into better-paying positions. The president at Coca-Cola, Donald R. Keough, has argued that the shift in the political climate against affirmative action does not "slow us down at all. We just don't pay attention to the politicians."[16] Under strong leadership, the Xerox corporation has substantially increased the proportion of women and minority workers in its work force since 1980. Major firms have emphasized enhancing cultural diversity rather than traditional affirmative action approaches. For example, in some companies bonuses are provided to managers who increase diversity as well as productivity.[17] In cases such as Coca-Cola and Xerox, the demands of doing international business have created the business necessity of establishing a more diverse management structure. However, apart from a handful of top firms, there has been much business retrenchment in regard to affirmative action. According to the head of one Urban League group in Mississippi: "They're sliding backwards because no one is really putting any pressure on them."[18]

Today, the attacks on affirmative action for women consistently fail to link patterns of discrimination to the need for affirmative action remedies. Most critics of affirmative action focus on the operation and effects of the programs and ignore the background and context of sex discrimination. An adequate defense of affirmative action requires a thorough problem–remedy approach, since it is the discriminatory problem that requires the remedy. Equal opportunity and affirmative action efforts make sense only if one understands clearly the problems of individual and institutionalized sex discrimination. Those who attack affirmative action usually do not believe that massive discrimination still exists. Prominent white male leaders not only reject most serious affirmative action efforts but also argue that discrimination has been all but abolished in this country. Some decline in blatant sexist attitudes and some decline in blatant forms of discrimination are taken by many male commentators as signs that discrimination is dead—or so near death as to require little further organizational or governmental intervention.

Two decades into equal opportunity and affirmative action programs, few systematic or fundamental changes can be seen in most major institutional sectors of this society. White males overwhelmingly dominate upper-level and middle-level positions in most major organizations, from the Department of Defense, to large corporations, to state legislatures, banks, and supermarket chains. The dominant national concern has shifted away from patterns of sex (and racial) discrimination.

The Resurgence of the Beauty Standard in American Culture

Beyond the governmental level, we see today a broad trend in reemphasizing traditional aspects of woman's place in our patriarchal society. In their analysis of fashion, Lauer and Lauer show that, historically, women's fashions changed in response to men's perceptions of feminine beauty. To accentuate a small waist and a large bosom, nineteenth-century women corseted themselves even though corsets crushed ribs, weakened the lungs by making breathing difficult, and crowded internal organs, which sometimes ceased to function properly.[19]

From the early 1900s to the present, most fashions have showcased women's bodies, sexuality, or femininity. During the 1920s and 1930s, "flappers" showed a lot of leg. During the 1950s, billowy skirts, several layers of petticoats, tiny waists, and cleavage were "in." The miniskirts of the 1960s and the 1990s have revealed more body than clothing. During the late 1960s activist women, in what came to be called the "women's liberation movement," often reacted negatively to standard definitions of beauty based only on physical appeal; many refused to wear cosmetics, endorsed natural hairstyles that did not necessitate monthly visits to beauty salons, and wore clothes that did not accentuate their bodies.

Since the 1960s there has been a renewed emphasis on women looking "beautiful." Most women are still judged primarily by their physical attractiveness, whereas men are mostly judged in terms of their achievements. We still live in a society where more money is spent on women's looks than on all social service programs for the needy. Americans spend billions of dollars on cosmetics, beauty books, cosmetic surgery, designer clothes, beauty spas, and exercise tapes.

Being attractive to men is still a major goal of most women. Because a woman's looks are treated as her primary asset, the older a women gets, the more anxious she becomes about aging. As the baby boom cohorts are moving into their forties, the cosmetics industry is launching campaigns that create the "older woman's" need to be beautiful and glamorous and is promoting products that will meet those needs. Many women are still afraid to age gracefully:

> [Cher] looks much younger at forty-six than she did at forty, as do most actresses of her generation, for whom face-lifts are virtually routine. These actresses are changing cultural expectations of what women "should" look like at forty-five and fifty. This is touted in the popular literature as a liberating development for older women . . . . But in fact Cher, Jane Fonda, and others have not made the aging female body sexually more acceptable. They have established a new norm—achievable only through continual cosmetic surgery—in which the surface of the female body ceases to age physically as the body grows chronologically older.[20]

"Looks" have a major impact in this society, even though many Americans might admit that talent, intelligence, achievements, and effort should be accorded more importance in assessing a woman's contribution.

Beauty pageants remain a major national example of the heavy emphasis on the bodies of women. In the early 1990s Canadians abandoned several of their major beauty pageants, including the Miss Canada contest, because of feminist pressures and declining profits. Many in the Canadian public seem no longer interested in such pageants. As one *Toronto Star* editorial put it, "Judging a parade of unmarried bathing beauties like cows at a nationally televised cattle auction is a pastime that is passe."[21] In contrast, only a fifth of the respondents in a recent U.S. poll felt that the Miss America pageant is "degrading and insulting to women," and two thirds said they would be proud if their daughter wished to enter such a pageant.[22]

The Mass Media

Another sign of the lack of continuing progress at the societal level is the treatment of women in the mass media. Essential to modern capitalism is widespread advertising, with sexist ads being so commonplace they cannot be avoided. Women appear less frequently in ads than men, are much more likely to be seen in home rather than work settings, and are more likely to be in ads for food, home, beauty, and clothing products. Growing numbers of women have moved into the work place, but there has not been a corresponding increase in the occupational portrayals of women in magazine ads. Ads for women continue to accent the beautiful-body theme (modeling, fashion, cosmetics, beauty aids) and the housewife theme (parenting, cleaning, cooking). In the 1970s, the mass media briefly gave some attention to women other than housewives and secretaries. Some advertising presented models in pantsuits or pinstriped business suits who looked like the stereotype of the "new business woman." Yet, in the 1980s and 1990s, advertising moved away from this business-woman emphasis to more traditional models, such as women in low-cut gowns or bikinis or in poses showing heavy dependence on "their men."

Cigarette ads also exploit women. The R. J. Reynolds Tobacco Company started a series of advertisements for Dakota cigarettes that specially targets women. The female Dakota smoker is shown to be "leaning on a taller male companion, whose arm is around her neck." This is a subtle indication of her dependency. She wears modern western clothes, with "a suede coat, a paisley vest, white jeans and a T-shirt, and a hip belt decorated with a number of dangling keys."[23] Her clothes, long hair, and "cool" sunglasses signal that the Dakota woman is the female counterpart to the rugged Marlboro man, but her own personal identity comes from her close ties to men. She is a "feminized version of frontier values; her looks, life-style, and behavior embody the feminine rather than the masculine American dream."[24] According to the analysis of researcher Barbara B. Stern, the Dakota ads show women as sexually open to and dependent on men. This is a modern version of the sexist ad message of the past. The Dakota woman is the opposite of the self-reliant and independent Marlboro Man.[25] Individualistic femininity means vulnerability—the need for protection, dependence on, and subordination to men.

Compared to most other consumer products, ads for some American beers are among the most sexually exploitative and demeaning to women. In recent years there has been an increase in sexism in beer advertising, with much of it directed at young men. One recent article put it this way: "Young, leggy, sex kittens are back. So's the happy homemaker (now the 'neo-traditionalist'). So's the unhappy single woman obsessed with fears of aging."[26]

Celebrated sex discrimination cases are discussed in the news media, but usually for a short time. Cumulative patterns of discrimination, the deep problems of discrimination for women, are ignored—as though the media also accept the view that women no longer suffer from much sex discrimination. An example is the case of Christine Craft, a woman newscaster who sued a Kansas City TV station that fired her because station researchers said local viewers saw her as too old and unattractive and "not deferential enough to men" when on the air. In the mid-1980s, after a long court battle, she was awarded $325,000 in damages by a Missouri jury. Her case received extensive national publicity for a few days, but no systematic analysis of the discriminatory conditions faced by women professionals like her was conducted by the media. A federal appeals court overruled the jury decision and rejected Craft's sex discrimination charge. The appeals court ruled that the TV station had not defrauded Craft by promising "no makeover or substantial changes" in appearance when she was hired but then requiring her to spend hours with clothing and "appearance" consultants. The appeals court ruled that Craft had to prove that her employers intended to change her appearance.[27] Recently, as we discussed in Chapter 1, Kathleen Sullivan was fired as a news anchor because she was slightly overweight and had locks of prematurely gray hair that she didn't dye.

Violence Against Women and Children

The 1980s and early 1990s have seen an increase in gendered violence against women and girls in the United States. Activists working against male violence sometimes view it as part of a larger pattern of the societal promotion of, or winking at, such violence. Today, video stores are full of movies that revel in showing extreme violence against women, including the infamous "slasher" movies. The founder of one group working to reduce male violence put it this way: ". . . themes of violence toward women run through our entire culture, from film to television to advertising. To think there's no connection between the violent images men are watching and the violence they are committing would be naive."[28] For many years, there have been complaints by thoughtful analysts about the way women are portrayed as sexual objects on television and in ads generally. Sometimes women are pictured as "asking for" a slap or other physical violence, which some men view as necessary to keep them "in their place." Activists point out that stereotypes of women as whiners or nags are often used by woman batterers to justify their actions.[29] The perpetuation of such images in advertising feeds into sexual harassment at many levels.

THE ORGANIZATIONAL LEVEL

At the level of specific organizations and institutions, some progress was made in the 1960s and early 1970s in upgrading the position of women workers, but there has been backtracking in major areas in the last two decades. Today, male decision makers in many public and private organizations are willing to hire women into historically male positions, but all too often only in token numbers. Let us look briefly at some examples of organizational problems.

Old-Boy Networks in Organizations

A key problem is that the men who dominate particular organizations, private and governmental, tend to perpetuate their own kind. Diana Kendall has suggested that there may be a weird "sociobiology of organizations where a person wants to foster another person who will assist him while he is still in the organization and will carry on just as he did when he retires, dies, etc. This may be a way in which people leave their 'mark' on an organization—by leaving someone else there who is very much like themselves. The woman and/or minority group member does not fit this model that rules organizations."[30]

This pattern is still strong in many public and private organizations. Women (and minorities) somehow fall outside the critical old-boy networks. Corporations are frequently dominated by the good-old-boy network, a type of male tribalism. Such networks can function during and after work hours. Women employees are often handicapped by not being part of after-hours events, such as having drinks at a bar or going on a golf outing. At these times, important advice is passed along by older managers to rising young employees about how organizations work. Because women are excluded from these informal networks, they may not get the critical information necessary for organizational advancement.

Much business is conducted on elite private golf courses, yet until recently few women managers and professionals have been permitted to move into this male business arena. One female executive at Presbyterian-Orthopaedic Hospital in North Carolina said, "I view playing golf as part of professional development at this point. If you're in business and you can't play golf, you're at a disadvantage."[31] Many women have been discouraged from developing their interests in golf or have faced outright exclusion or demeaning rules of restriction at golf and country clubs. Some of these traditionally male places reserve the good playing times for men or refer to women golfers as the "ladies." As this book goes to press, however, a few business women are suing private clubs to get equal golf privileges.

The like-reproduces-like feature of organizations is reinforced by other problems. Women moving into organizational worlds where few have gone before are often more honest and forthright than men and expect the business world to be fair and meritocratic. It is difficult for these women to accept the dishonesty and unfairness of the business world, including cases where the boss takes credit for a woman's work or promises a woman subordinate a promotion he does not intend to give (see Chapters 5 and 6). Another example of sex discrimination at the organizational level was documented in one study of middle-level male managers, who tended to promote older, less aggressive women for management positions. At many levels, boat rockers do not do well in modern corporations. Women's rights advocates, no matter how business-like, are usually considered boat rockers. As Lawrence Schwimmer puts it, "If management perceives you to be a boat-rocker, you may never get the opportunity to move up to the higher ranks."[32]

Many women who try to move up the organizational ladder are rejected. As a result, they then may send out negative messages to other women in the organization and, through interviews in the mass media, to women outside the organization. Since they become "fed up" with trying to make it in an organization, they communicate negative feelings to other women, including friends and relatives. This in turn reduces the motivation of other women to try to penetrate the corporate system.

In recent years, a number of women's organizations have been created to provide women in white-collar and business jobs with more business and information networks of their own. For example, since the early 1980s the group called Professional Women in Construction and Allied Industries has worked to bring together hundreds of women managers and business owners in a variety of construction firms into one organization and to provide "lucrative networking opportunities and professional support."[33]

Other Blatant Discrimination in Organizations

Blatant sex discrimination is still common in many areas in most organizations. The chauvinistic attitudes of male executives and managers remain a major barrier to women in business. One problem is that male managers often resist sending single female employees on business trips with married male employees. Another is the assumption that women cannot handle technical fields as well as men. Yet another problem is recurring sexual harassment. Sexual harassment is the "unsolicited nonreciprocal male behavior that asserts a woman's sex role over her function as a worker."[34] A key aspect of sexual harassment on the job is its reinforcement of other types of sex discrimination. Work becomes a prize men give to women if women permit harassment. Like rape, this sexual harassment is usually pervaded with stereotypes of working women as sex objects, including the notion that most women intentionally invite the harassment.

Sexual harassment is still common in many workplaces. In the mid-1990s, an outside consulting firm found that the National Institutes of Health near Washington, D.C., had a group of senior men who offered women employees job advancement and other benefits in return for sexual favors. The report found widespread sexual harassment and noted that the network "thrived boldly and obviously for several years, and went unchallenged until recently."[35] Since the report, there has been considerable debate over the scale and scope of the gender discrimination at this prestigious health research facility. Of course, the private sector has similar problems. A recent survey of women managers at 1,500 major companies found that six in ten reported some type of sexual harassment in their places of employment. Of these, just 14 percent reported the acts, and less than one percent filed an official complaint or lawsuit.[36]

The impact of blatant and subtle sex discrimination can be seen in the limited number of women employees who rise to middle and upper levels of influence and decision making. A "glass ceiling" blocks the upward mobility of many women employees in major corporations. A recent survey found that women made up just 99 of the 1,315 members of the boards of directors of Fortune 100 firms, and another study reported that women made up less than 3 percent of the top 6,500 executives in Fortune 500 firms.[37]

Women lawyers have similarly reported that it is difficult to do well in the upper reaches of the legal profession. Cynthia Jacob, a partner at a major firm in New Jersey, has stated that top corporate officials, mostly older men, "are not used to turning to women for help. I think there is a considerable resistance on the part of corporate management to women attorneys, particularly in the courtroom."[38] The large corporations seem to be the most reluctant to hire and promote women lawyers. Without access to such experience women lawyers are seriously handicapped in their careers. In addition, a recent survey of the most influential people in the music record business by the *Los Angeles Times* found only one woman, Madonna, on the top-40 list. Few women were even mentioned for the list of those who are powerful. The president of the National Academy of Recording Arts and Sciences put it this way: "There's no question that the music business—as well as the entire entertainment industry—is still very much a good old boy network."[39] He added that he expected no change in the near future.

THE INDIVIDUAL LEVEL

At the level of individual women and men we see continuing problems as well. While many individual women, and some men, have broken substantially with the old sex-role patterns, there has also been some backtracking among women and men in regard to a range of personal and family issues. Today many women and men are still uninformed about the range and character of continuing gender inequality. Many seem to look past institutionalized sexism to their own individual concerns. Indeed, many seem to be more conservative about sex-role expectations than in the past.

The Success Ethic

Popular books emphasize individualistic themes, views that take blame off the patriarchal system. Many women have been so bombarded with the individualistic success ethic proclaimed in best-selling books that they have accepted the proposition that their own failure or success is primarily of their own making. For example, in *Having It All: Love-Success-Sex-Money,* Helen Gurley Brown, the creator of *Cosmopolitan* magazine, advised women on how to get ahead: dress "pretty," diet to be sexy, loving clothes is not a sin, love his entire body, get a job in order to get in touch with the better type of man, starting as a secretary is a good way to make it, "nice" girls finish first, don't be aggressive, sexual harassment isn't so terrible (tolerate it if you can), try to be a woman, and don't be afraid of having sex with the boss. A basic theme in the book is that being successful is up to the woman; that women should accept sexist roles and defer to men; that barriers such as sexual harassment are not very serious; that if women don't succeed, they should try and try again; and that if women fail, it is probably their fault.[40]

In the 1990s, even Gloria Steinem, a longtime leader in the women's movement, published a book, *Revolution from Within: A Book of Self-Esteem,* in which she calls on women to search within themselves for answers to the sexism imposed from the outside.[41] As one reviewer put it, "In place of the relational feminists' emphasis on distinctively female characteristics, Steinem, like the early feminists, focuses on self-completion, reclaiming women's strong, independent, assertive side. But she too has joined the growing chorus urging that the political be personalized."[42] This renewed emphasis among some women on the personal and the individual is dismaying but not surprising. The societal backlash, aging, fatigue, and the individualistic ethic are difficult for many individual women to overcome.

The Child-rearing debate.   The 1990s have seen a continuation of women doing most of the child rearing in individual American families. Most women feel that it is *their* responsibility to do the lion's share of child rearing. Societal pressure creates and reinforces this feeling. Some scholars have recently reinvigorated the argument that until women give up trying to be "super-women"—that is, both top-notch mothers and super employees—they cannot be the full equals of men.[43] Professor Mary Frances Berry, the head of the U.S. Commission on Civil Rights, has noted that full gender equality is impossible so long as society expects women to do most of the child rearing. The very substantial energy that child rearing and other home work require makes it impossible for women to contend for workplace advancement on a par with their male peers, for the latter typically do not have such domestic responsibilities. In Berry's view, for significant improvements to occur, men must take over an equal share of the child-rearing chores.[44]

The Resurgence of Femininity in Everyday Practice

In the last decade or two, we have seen periodic emphases on femininity among women. Susan Brownmiller has noted this emphasis, especially among many better-off women, on baubles and beads, on high heels, makeup, and high-priced dresses. Brownmiller raises questions about the new individualized emphasis on femininity, which she attributes in part to the failure of many women to get good jobs outside the home and to intensified competition among women for the "available men." In the intensive competition for men, women as individuals often undergo expensive, painful, unnecessary, and sometimes unsuccessful cosmetic surgery to be more attractive.[45]

In *The Beauty Myth*, Naomi Wolf argues that the "beauty backlash" is destroying women physically and depleting them psychologically. The beauty myth undermines women's self-confidence and occupational advances by focusing on their idealized physical appearance:

> During the past five years, consumer spending doubled, pornography became the main media category . . . and thirty-three thousand American women told researchers that they would rather lose ten to fifteen pounds than achieve any other goal. More women have more money and power and scope and legal recognition than we have ever had before; but in terms of how we feel about ourselves *physically*, we may actually be worse off than our unliberated grandmothers.[46]

The persisting concern among the majority of women and most advertisers with "feminine" clothing—sexy clothes, hose, and high heels—is symbolic of the retreat from progress for women. There has been an increased emphasis on dresses for women workers. One journalist put it this way: "It's representative of a resurgence of unabashed femininity in the '90s."[47] While a focus on clothes can have a positive side, an excessive preoccupation with appearance among many women both reflects and reinforces the sexist roles in society. It distracts women and men from much more important issues, such as equity in jobs, education, and politics.

There is also the obsessive concern of many women about their weight and about dieting. Today, there is an emphasis in some advertising on models of beauty who are very thin, what some have called the "waif" look: "Waif-like models who barely weigh 100 pounds in combat boots began showing up on magazine covers everywhere. Voluptuous models . . . suddenly shared runways with skinny newcomers."[48] In recent years, models have often been portrayed with vacant or helpless looks. The dependent childlike female is again being peddled by the fashion industry, and this reinforces the excessive concern that many individual women have about their own bodies. Many doctors, eating disorder researchers, and women's rights advocates have been very critical of this "waif" trend in magazine and fashion models. The fear is that this emphasis on excessive slimness could increase dieting fads and the incidence of anorexia and bulimia. This omnipresent super-thin image makes many women feel inferior. Leslie Katz has noted the image and its impact: "She's tall, thin and leggy, with blond hair, blue eyes, and a tiny nose. She stares at us from billboards, magazines, and television screens."[49] One can imagine how most American women, who do not fit this idealized image, react to it and how they may internalize negative images of themselves as a result.[50]

Most women employees consider traditional femininity a valuable asset in the world of work. For example, a successful female vice-president in a fine arts college was very proud of the "feminine" characteristics that, she believes, helped her be upwardly mobile:

> When I was on the faculty, I purposely negotiated between the faculty, especially the men, who are always squabbling. . . . I'd comfort the losers and praise the winners. . . . I made sure, too, that I never aligned myself with the feminist faculty. . . . Giving a lot of small, classy parties didn't hurt.

PROGRESS AND PRESSURE

Why did the changes for women that began in the 1960s slow down by the 1970s and regress during the 1980s and 1990s? There are a number of reasons. They include a false sense of security among women and sympathetic men about the progress and achievements of the 1960s and 1970s. Some critics have cited a lack of aggressive leadership in some women's organizations. But much more important has been the resistance of a male-centered society even to modest gender-role changes. The conservative political groups that rose to power in the 1980s and early 1990s intentionally rolled back many gains made by women. The difficulties encountered in trying to penetrate a male-dominated society have significantly reduced the expectations of many women. Some women have accepted limited progress in nontraditional employment. Others have retreated from the male world, some into extreme femininity. Many women have lowered their expectations and have accepted more traditional gender roles because they feel powerless to do otherwise, not because they prefer subordinate roles or inferior jobs.

The good news is that many historically male-dominated organizations and institutions have become less sexist under pressure from lawsuits and other protests by women acting alone or in groups. However, most U.S. organizations and institutions are so male oriented and male dominated that these changes are modest and too easily reversed. Men who control organizations do not have to work hard to perpetuate sex discrimination when most organizations and institutions have been structured that way for a very long period of time. Women may have made their way into some entry positions in many such organizations, but it is much harder, if not impossible, for them to get into the top positions, the core, the "inner sanctum." Virginia Woolf once wrote that women have served many centuries as "looking glasses possessing the magic and delicious power of reflecting the figure of man at twice its natural size." Women have challenged and are challenging their looking-glass function in this society, but they are a long way from shattering the glass.

NOTES

1. Lee Barton, "To a Sherlockian, Coolness to Women Is Elementary Canon," *The Wall Street Journal,* January 6, 1984, p. 1.
2. George Gilder, *Wealth and Poverty* (New York: Basic Books, 1981).
3. "How Long Till Equality?" *Time,* July 12, 1982, p. 29.
4. Spencer Rich, "Schlafly: Sex Harassment on Job No Problem for Virtuous Women," *Washington Post,* April 22, 1981, p. A2.
5. Laura Blumenfeld, "Schlafly's Son, Out of the Closet," *Washington Post,* September 19, 1992, p. D1.
6. Richard Cohen, "Schlafly's Silence," *Washington Post,* September 24, 1992, p. A29.
7. Tony Mauro, "Ginsburg Nominated; 'Thurgood Marshall of Gender Equality Law'; 'Consensus Builder' Slated for High Court," *USA Today,* June 15, 1993, p. 1A.
8. Martha Burk, "Is Bill Clinton a Feminist?" *Nation,* February 8, 1993, p. 154.
9. Ibid.
10. Ibid.
11. "Supreme Court Rules Anti-Sex Bias Law Covers Only College Programs that Get Direct U.S. Aid," *Chronicle of Higher Education,* March 7, 1984, pp. 1, 19–25.
12. David Barton, "Increasingly, Women Athletes Go to Court—and Win," *Houston Chronicle,* June 27, 1993, p. 12.

13. Mike Dame, "Inequality of the Sexes," *Orlando Sentinel,* August 1, 1993, p. C1; see also Jane Gottesman, "Gymnastics Rescued at UCLA," *San Francisco Chronicle,* August 21, 1993, p. F2.

14. Dame, "Inequality of Sexes," p. C1.

15. Nijole V. Benokraitis and Joe R. Feagin, *Affirmative Action and Equal Opportunity* (Boulder, CO: Westview Press, 1978), pp. 44–56, 95–115, 154–168.

16. Jonathan Tilove, "We Won't Ditch Affirmative Action," *Orlando Sentinel Tribune,* August 11, 1991, p. G1.

17. Ibid.

18. Quoted in ibid.

19. Robert H. Lauer and Jeanette C. Lauer, *Fashion Power: The Meaning of Fashion in American Society* (Englewood Cliffs, NJ: Prentice-Hall, 1981), pp. 209–215.

20. Susan Bordo, *Unbearable Weight* (Berkeley: University of California Press, 1993), pp. 25–26.

21. "Beauty Takes a Bath," *Toronto Star,* January 7, 1992, p. A123.

22. George Gallup and Frank Newport, "Few Americans Think Miss America Pageant Degrading to Women," *The Gallup Poll Monthly,* September 1990, pp. 53–54.

23. Barbara B. Stern, "Feminist Literary Criticism and the Deconstruction of Ads: A Postmodern View of Advertising and Consumer Responses," *Journal of Consumer Research,* 19 (March 1993), p. 556.

24. Ibid.

25. Ibid.

26. Jeffry Scott, "Selling with Sexism," *Atlanta Journal and Constitution,* November 24, 1991, p. H1.

27. Joseph A. Reaves, "Fired Announcer Taps Grass-roots Support," *Austin American Statesman,* January 15, 1984, p. A6; "Woman TV Announcer Loses Jury Award," *Austin American Statesman,* June 6, 1985, p. E1.

28. Bob Hohler, "Some See Seeds of Abuse in Culture," *Boston Globe,* October 13, 1992, p. 21.

29. Ibid.

30. Diana Kendall, personal communication.

31. "Women Execs Fight 'Glass Ceiling'" *The Business Journal-Charlotte,* June 7, 1993, Section 1, p. 16.

32. "Women Executives: What Holds So Many Back?" *U.S. News & World Report,* February 8, 1982, p. 64.

33. Beth Reinhard, "Women's Group Provides Support," *Chicago Tribune,* May 4, 1991, Zone W, p. 18.

34. Lin Farley, *Sexual Shakedown* (New York: McGraw-Hill, 1978), pp. 14–15.

35. Veronica T. Jennings, "Sex Drove Promotions at NIH Unit, Report Says," *Washington Post,* May 8, 1993, p. A1.

36. Chris Swingle, "Sexism Still an Obstacle," *USA Today,* June 30, 1993, p. 1B.

37. Dottie Enrico and Deana Bunis, "Crack in Glass Ceiling Develops After Pressure; Deloitte & Touche Sees the Light after Study," *Newsday,* April 28, 1993, p. 41.

38. Linda Bean, "Women Who Make Rain Without Thunder," *New Jersey Law Journal,* August 9, 1993, p. 4.

39. Chuck Philips and Robert Hilburn, "The Ole Boy Network Plays On," *Los Angeles Times,* November 29, 1992, p. 58.

40. Helen Gurley Brown, *Having It All: Love-Success-Sex-Money* (New York: Simon & Schuster, 1982), pp. 16–60.

41. Gloria Steinem, *Revolution from Within: A Book of Self-Esteem* (New York: Little, Brown, 1992).

42. Karen Lehrman, "The Feminist Mystique: New Books by Gloria Steinem and Susan Faludi Fail to Advance Women's Issues," *New Republic,* March 16, 1992, p. 30.

43. Mary Frances Berry, *The Politics of Parenthood* (New York: Viking, 1993).

44. These views are summarized in DeWayne Wickham, "Getting Dads into Child Care," *USA Today,* April 12, 1993, p. 12A.

45. Susan Brownmiller, *Feminists* (New York: Simon & Schuster, 1983), pp. 15–16.

46. Naomi Wolf, *The Beauty Myth* (New York: William Morrow, 1991), p. 10.

47. Elizabeth Snead, "Stylish Dresses Are Suitable for the Office Again," *USA Today,* January 17, 1991, p. 5D.

48. "The Politics of Skinny," *The Buffalo News,* August 11, 1993, p. 7.

49. Leslie Katz, "Jewish Women Face Images of Beauty at Local Confab," *Northern California Jewish Bulletin,* as reprinted in *The Ethnic NewsWatch,* April 30, 1993, p. 31.

50. Ibid.

CHAPTER THREE
BLATANT/SUBTLE/COVERT SEX DISCRIMINATION: AN OVERVIEW

In the mid-1990s, the toy company, Mattel, Inc. introduced Teen Talk Barbie. Each of the Barbie dolls was programmed to say four things, randomly selected from a pool of 270 statements. One of the statements was "Math class is tough." A journalist noted that "It's been 20 years since Barbie has spoken her little plastic mind . . . but math teachers are not amused." The president of the American Association of University Women complained, "Barbie has been a role model for a generation of girls, and now she's speaking and what is she saying? That girls don't do well in math."[1] Many educators were especially concerned because a report published just a few months earlier showed that although fifth-grade girls score as well on standardized math tests as fifth-grade boys, by the seventh grade the girls have fallen behind in math, and by high school, far fewer girls than boys are in upper-level math courses.[2]

In response, a Mattel representative said that the programmed statements were based on interviews with "thousands of children" and that there were other sayings such as "I'm studying to be a doctor," "We should start a business," and "Computers make homework fun." According to the Mattel representative, all these sentiments send the message that it's important to be proficient in math. Despite protests from many well-educated and influential women, Mattel did not remove the offensive statement.

Even in the mid-1990s, we are still bombarded with gender-role stereotypes. This overview chapter catalogues the gender stereotypes and sex discrimination that most of us encounter on a daily basis.

TYPES OF SEX DISCRIMINATION:
DEFINITIONS AND ILLUSTRATIONS

As we use the term in this book, *sex discrimination* refers to the unequal and harmful treatment of people because of their sex (i.e., biological differences between males and females, which include hormones, chromosomes, and anatomical characteristics). Sex discrimination is usually internalized and institutionalized (see chapter 1). Broadly viewed, it is the socially organized set of attitudes and practices that deny women the opportunities, freedoms, and rewards that this society makes available to men. Modern sexism involves both antifemale prejudices and stereotypes and the *power* men have to implement them in the everyday practices of discrimination. When the discriminatory practices of men pervade all aspects of a society such as the United States, we can speak of *institutionalized* sexism.

Although both men and women can be targets and victims of sex discrimination, a vast literature shows that sex discrimination in the United States is overwhelmingly a matter of men targeting women. Being a woman is frequently a better predictor of discrimination and inequality than such variables as age, religion, intelligence, achievements, or socioeconomic status. Although men may be discriminated against because, for example, of their education, religion, race, or political affiliations, they are seldom treated unequally *because* they are men. Quite to the contrary, being a man may neutralize or override racial, age, sexual orientation, or religious discrimination. At many points in their lives, all women, on the other hand, will be treated unequally simply *because* they are women and regardless of other variables. Women are more likely than men to face many layers of sex-related obstacles. They often encounter a double, triple, or even quadruple "whammy" because of their race or ethnicity, age, social class, *and* sex.

Women encounter blatant, subtle, and covert sex discrimination on a daily basis. After providing some working definitions and examples of each of these types of serious antifemale discrimination, we will suggest some dimensions across which discrimination varies and discuss why many Americans accept gender inequality. Although the different types of sex discrimination often overlap or occur simultaneously in real life, they are presented separately here for analytical purposes.

Blatant Sex Discrimination

Blatant sex discrimination refers to the unequal and harmful treatment of women that is typically intentional, quite visible, and easily documented. It may or may not be illegal under existing U.S. laws. Examples of blatant sex discrimination include sexual harassment, sexist language and jokes, physical violence (rape, incest, wife abuse), and other forms of obviously unequal treatment in the family, employment, politics, religion, law, and other areas.

Blatant discrimination has immediate harmful results that can be easily documented and that can be remedied. Its effects can be seen, for example, in the disparate distribution of economic rewards by sex. Nationally, for example, women who worked full time year-round in 1991 earned 74 percent as much as men; women had median earnings of $18,928 compared to $25,542 for men.[3] Women who have completed four years of college earn about the same as men who have completed only high school ($28,017 and $26,653 respectively).[4]

The practices that constitute blatant discrimination are obviously unequal and discriminatory. Consider women in the sports media. One of the most important equity issues today is women's access to locker rooms. If a female sportswriter cannot get immediate access to athletes after a game or practice, she may miss deadlines and will likely be "scooped" by the competition. In 1978, Time, Inc. sued and won the right to allow *Sports Illustrated* reporter Melissa Ludtke to enter the New York Yankee clubhouse to interview players. Since the 1978 federal court ruling, the number of women in sports journalism has increased to around 500, but complaints about the harassment that female journalists encounter on a daily basis have not disappeared. In 1990, reporter Lisa Olson of the *Boston Herald* charged that several New England Patriots exposed their genitals and made lewd remarks while she was trying to conduct a postgame interview. A month later, *USA Today* football reporter Denise Tom was barred from the Cincinnati Bengals' locker room by coach Sam Wyche, who stated, "I will not allow women to walk in on 50 naked men." *USA Today* sent a protest letter to the National Football League (NFL) demanding enforcement of the league's 1985 policy of equal access to players for female journalists.[5]

The sports arena also provides examples of the immediately harmful economic consequences of blatant sex discrimination. According to a recent National Collegiate Athletic Association (NCAA) study of average salaries in Division 1, a men's basketball coach earns $88,984 compared with $45,847 for a women's basketball coach. These base salaries do not include such perks as shoe contracts and radio or television deals that men's coaches usually get. In college tennis, a sport where the exposure and fan interest in men's and women's teams is about equal, the salary gap is smaller: $26,612 for a men's tennis coach compared to $23,802 for women. Gymnastics was the only college sport in which women coaches earned slightly more (instead of considerably less) than their male counterparts—$32,187 versus $31,340.[6] Since women usually do not have access to the private meetings where decisions about salaries are made, it may be difficult to prove conclusively that these differences are intentionally discriminatory. However, the fact that women get slightly larger salaries, on the average, in only 1 sport out of 15 clearly signals that salary inequality in sports is not isolated or accidental. The inequality is so widespread that it is obvious that people (mostly men) are consciously discriminating in regard to salaries and other rewards.

There is much direct, explicit, and "up-front" sexism that talented women encounter on a daily basis. For example, a 32-year-old assistant professor of math at Princeton University left for another college. According to the professor, "There's a perception in the math community that I'm taking an enormous step down for no reason." Being at Princeton, however, was "something of a nightmare:"

> While in the hall, one junior faculty came up to me and said, "I feel bad about it, but I really do feel women are genetically inferior in math.". . . . Other junior faculty would say similarly upsetting things. . . . Eventually . . . I just locked myself in my office and didn't come out for 4 years.[7]

Telling a colleague that "women are genetically inferior" in any discipline is ignorant, but, more important, it is quite direct and intentional. Some male faculty members feel it is all right to tell women that they're genetically inferior because it's an accepted "fact" in a particular department, group, or subculture.

Some blatant discrimination may seem harmless to unreflective men. While many men consider such everyday behavior as sexist remarks and jokes as acceptable, many women feel intimidated or humiliated. A few years ago, for example, women delegates in Maryland tried to pass a law requiring that public buildings provide equitable restroom facilities for women. Their efforts resulted in silly newspaper stories and lewd jokes, but no laws. When a first-term female legislator complained that there was no nearby bathroom for women, the (male) Speaker presented her with a fur-lined toilet seat in front of the entire House of Delegates.[8] While most of the male legislators thought the incident was hilarious and "all in good fun," many women felt embarrassed and outraged.

Subtle Sex Discrimination

Subtle sex discrimination refers to the unequal and harmful treatment of women that is typically less visible and obvious than blatant sex discrimination. It is often not noticed because most people have internalized subtle sexist behavior as "normal," "natural," or customary. However liberated we might like to be, many of us—men and women alike—often feel deep down that women are *really* not as good, capable, competent, and intelligent as men—especially in prestigious, competitive, and traditionally male-dominated jobs. For example, when a male faculty member becomes chairperson of a department, he is typically congratulated, encouraged, and reinforced in his "promotion." A female faculty member, on the other hand, is quite likely to get such spontaneous (and sincere) comments as, "Didn't anybody else [i.e., men] in the department want the job?" Sometimes, of course, men also get such comments. The tone and message are quite different, however. For men, there is a playful ribbing about giving up the more important roles of teaching and research to "push paper." Despite the teasing, the man is supported and reinforced. For women, however, the comments raise questions about their administrative competence or ability. Thus, whereas men are kidded because "aren't you *too good* to be doing administration?" the message to women is "Are you *good enough* to be doing administration?" Similar experiences have been reported by women administrators and managers in the private sector.

Subtle sex discrimination can be relatively innocent or manipulative, intentional or unintentional, well intentioned or malicious. As Chapter Five will show, although subtle sex discrimination can be documented, it is usually not as easy to prove as is blatant sex discrimination because many people do not perceive subtle sex discrimination as serious or harmful.

Subtle sex discrimination is often more complex than it appears: What is discrimination to many women may not seem discriminatory to many men. For example, a judge said he thought he was being "nice" when he complimented female lawyers in court on their appearance. When one of the women finally complained, he was surprised: "He never realized that this didn't do much for her credibility with clients, who were looking for a tough litigator, not a cute companion."[9]

Many people point to the increasing numbers of women in such professions as law, medicine, and engineering as indicators of occupational equality. We rarely hear, however, that the most influential, prestigious, and lucrative positions are still overwhelmingly male or that the few women at the top suffer from subtle discrimination. There is an occasional article about the "glass ceiling" or the "brick wall," but they are infrequent and are often relegated to the "soft" back sections of the newspaper.

Covert Sex Discrimination

Covert sex discrimination refers to the unequal and harmful treatment of women that is hidden, purposeful, and, often, maliciously motivated. As Chapter 6 will show, there are several forms of covert sex discrimination. Regardless of the form it takes, covert sex discrimination refers to male behavior that consciously attempts to ensure women's failure, such as in hiring or other employment situations.

Many employers have become shrewd at circumventing sex discrimination laws. The Pregnancy Discrimination Act of 1978 requires companies with 15 or more employees to treat pregnancy as they would any other medical disability. Because of a weak economy and improved maternity leave benefits (especially at large organizations and many state agencies), unprecedented numbers of women work during pregnancy and return to work within six months.[10] However, because many employers *expect* that the woman will not return or that she will not be as productive as before, even large companies with leave policies use a variety of ploys to replace pregnant workers:

> A manager restructures a department in a way that just happens to eliminate the pregnant woman's position, or a supervisor suddenly starts documenting problems with the woman's job performance, paving the way for a demotion or a layoff.[11]

A major problem, as we will see in Chapter 6, is that covert sex discrimination is very difficult to prove or document.

Summary

The three types of sex discrimination can be seen as lying along a continuum of general visibility, from high to low. They also vary on such dimensions as intent, degree of harm, documentation, and remedies. Table 3.1 suggests several generalizations. First, although the three types of discrimination (blatant, subtle, covert) are different, there is some overlap of characteristics across the categories. All three types of discrimination can vary in degree of harm, yet unintentional discrimination does not mean that it is less harmful.

Second, a single institutional setting can involve several types of sex discrimination. For example, since its passage in 1976, several large financial institutions, such as Household Finance Corporation, have been sued for violating the Equal Credit Opportunity Act. Some of the violations—requiring the spouse's approval for a loan, for example—are blatant discrimination. Other loan and credit discrimination is more subtle.[12] For example, some financial institutions still do not inform their customers that if they volunteer information on income from alimony, child support, or public assistance, the applicant will probably be defined as "financially unstable" and rejected as a "bad risk." Purposely not telling consumers that they are not required to give information on sex, marital status, and some sources of income can be a form of sex discrimination. Using such information to screen out women who are not supported by a man's "stable" income is covert discrimination.

Finally, because subtle and covert discrimination are more difficult to prove, remedies are harder to implement. Thus, it is especially important to recognize and document both of these types of inequality.

LEVELS OF SEX DISCRIMINATION

Sex discrimination and inequality can operate at four levels—individual, organizational, institutional, and cultural.

TABLE 3.1. Sex Discrimination Typology

TYPE OF DISCRIMINATION			CHARACTERISTICS		
	VISIBILITY	INTENT	DEGREE OF HARM	CAN BE DOCUMENTED	CAN BE REMEDIED
Blatant	High	Usually intentional	Very severe to mild	Always	Definitely
Subtle	Varies	Intentional and unintentional	Very severe to mild	Often	Often
Covert	Very low	Intentional	Very severe to mild	Rarely	Rarely

Individual Discrimination

At level one—individual discrimination—the unequal behavior occurs on a one-to-one basis and is targeted at specific people. It may be direct and face-to-face, indirect and impersonal, or indirect but personal. For example, a recent controversy at Converse College, a private women's college in South Carolina, involved discriminatory attacks on the campus's first female president. Dozens of older alumnae criticized her hiring of a black woman as dean of students—a choice they called "unnecessary" for a college where only about 8 percent of the students are black—and accused her of creating a supportive atmosphere for lesbian students. Moreover, the new female president was singled out by the alumnae as personally inferior in comparison with past presidents:

> . . .[she] is short, with short gray hair that is not in the least bit attractive, and wears godawful clothes . . . [whereas] past presidents were dignified, wonderful men who had high morals and wonderful backgrounds.[13]

In rare cases, individual discrimination can operate independently of one discriminator's prejudice. In some cases, an employer who is genuinely not sexist may be reluctant to hire a woman because a masculine subculture encourages the degradation of women.[14] He may fear retaliation from other men. More commonly, however, individual discrimination is motivated by prejudice or a general hostility toward women. For example, in a study of 208 female instructors employed at a major university, Elizabeth Grauerholz found that many women professors experienced a variety of behaviors, mostly from male students, which ranged from sexist comments to sexual assault. Even though faculty members have clearly defined authority, the women professors' higher status did not protect them from such intimidating or disrespectful behavior as sexist remarks, obscene phone calls, sexual advances, and informal terms of address.[15]

Organizational Discrimination

Sexism also occurs because the practices, rules, and policies of formal organizations, such as corporations or government agencies, are sometimes different for men and women. For example, one of our respondents, a female physician employed at a nationally known pharmaceutical company, noted that in interdepartmental memos and introductions to outsiders, women physicians are often called by their first name (or even "Miss" and "Mrs.") while the men are always addressed as "Dr." In addition, women routinely have smaller budgets than men in achieving the same objectives and they get fewer rewards when they are successful. In a study of major U.S. law firms, Stephen Spurr found that women were about one half as likely as men to achieve partnerships even though they did not significantly differ from men in academic distinction, the rank of their law schools, or productivity.[16] A chief resident in psychiatry at The New England Medical Center in Boston said that women are unwelcome in "nearly all the environments in which I have worked or studied, from college and medical school classrooms to hospitals to media corporations."[17]

Sex discrimination may be built into routine procedures to lower an organization's financial costs. Large public hospitals often serve as both major trauma centers and the only source of medical care for the poor. Because most urban hospitals are underfunded and understaffed, large numbers of patients must be treated as expeditiously as possible. In the case of battered women, patients are usually not asked about the relationship to the assailant or the history of abuse. By "medicalizing" the injuries, hospital personnel reinforce whatever feelings of helplessness and isolation the woman may already feel and do not address preventive measures.[18]

Discrimination is often unchallenged because unequal treatment has been built into routine practices and philosophies of male-dominated organizations. Female Veteran Administration hospital employees recently appeared before a congressional subcommittee to testify on a range of sexual harassment complaints, including such retaliatory actions as unwanted job transfers, reduced responsibilities, and punitive work schedules. The president of the National Association of Women Veterans said that "a basic disrespect and lack of esteem for women in general" have allowed sexual harassment to flourish within the military and the Department of Veterans Affairs.[19]

Organizations often reveal long-term patterns of sex discrimination. In 1992, a prison scandal in Georgia uncovered widespread abuse of women prisoners by male guards and wardens. The recurring abuses included rape, forced abortions, women prisoners left stripped and bound for weeks, and inmates being taken off the grounds to work as prostitutes. Some of the allegations went back to 1979, and similar abuses have been reported in California, Ohio, Minnesota, Michigan and New York.[20] Thus, all of these examples suggest that women in a variety of organizations encounter discrimination that is recurring and socially sanctioned. Whatever the formal rules may require in such organizations, the informal, male-dominated networks shape everyday policies and procedures. The informal networks often become the *real* organizational structure in such organizations.

Some organizational practices discriminate by not providing equal opportunities because of sex. In a study of retail sales clerks, for example, Joan Talbert and Christine Bose found that women's wages are lower than those of men because women are routinely not given the opportunities to increase their salaries.[21] Women are generally segregated into jobs that are highly routinized and outside of locations that have high salaries (such as specialty stores, suburban stores, and departments servicing high-status customers). Hiring men into "big ticket" departments means that women are excluded from positions that result in high commission rates: Women sell pots and pans, while men sell refrigerators and kitchen cabinets; women sell such accessories as lamps, throw pillows, and sheets, while men sell furniture and expensive appliances.

Institutional Discrimination

At level three—institutional discrimination—we see sex discrimination occurring on a routine and repeated basis in family, political, economic, educational, military, and religious institutions. Institutional sex discrimination is by definition pervasive and overlapping.

Sexism is pervasive.   Educational institutions illustrate the pervasiveness of sex discrimination. Treating girls (and women) as inferior starts in the lower grades and continues throughout professional education. Throughout the educational process, girls and boys have very different experiences.[22]

Let's consider, briefly, some examples of sexism in high school and higher education. In a study of 21 boys', girls', and coeducational high schools, Valerie Lee and her associates found sexist incidents—usually initiated by teachers—in all three types of schools. Just one of many recurring examples is the following:

> [In a coeducational chemistry class] . . . the male teacher was describing an experiment involving measuring liquids. His discussion was directed to the boys. A girl in the front row asked for clarification of the use of the graduated cylinder. As her inquiry was ignored, she repeated her question. The teacher, clearly exasperated with the student, tossed the water in the graduated cylinder onto the girl and her desk. The entire class laughed, which was not controlled by the teacher. An after-class conversation with this teacher revealed an attitude that girls weren't suited to "do" science.[23]

The most severe forms of sexism occurred in boys' schools, and especially in English classes where teachers (who were typically male) encouraged discussions and essays that described men degrading women. The researchers felt that several of the selective girls' schools showed a subtle and "pernicious" form of sexism by fostering academic dependence and nonrigorous instruction:

> We found what seemed to be an attempt to make Calculus palatable by trivializing formulas, mathematical language, and procedures. We considered this a serious example of sex-role stereotyping—talking down to girls, setting expectations that Calculus was only acceptable to females if wrapped in a nontechnical package.[24]

Institutionalized sexism persists as high school girls become college women. Between 1969 and 1971, a number of Ivy League universities and other selective liberal-arts colleges became coeducational (such as Trinity, Brown, Colgate, Princeton, Yale, Dartmouth, and the Wesleyan universities). Female students at such formerly all-male institutions have a long list of complaints: the curricula don't reflect the contributions of women; faculty members don't always treat women equally; the health and safety needs of women are ignored; and the institutions don't hire enough female faculty members and administrators.[25] Moreover, women who graduate from women's colleges are *twice* as likely as female graduates of coeducational institutions to earn doctoral degrees. They made up 42 percent of the women members of the last Congress and 15 of the 50 leading corporate women—even though women's colleges graduates account for only 5 percent of all college-educated women.[26] In women's colleges, the students find a much more supportive environment where they can excel because there is less sexism.

Technology is becoming an increasingly important facet of our lives. Many of us depend on home computers, FAX machines, answering machines, electronic mail, and other technological "miracles" to do our work. The computer technology does not always include women, however. Boys are more likely than girls to have access to home computers and programming courses, while girls are more likely to have had introductory or word-processing programs. When both males and females are exposed to computer-programming languages, male students are more likely to have learned Fortran (which tends to be used in the sciences), while female students are more likely to learn Pascal (which tends to be used in business settings).[27] This gender-differentiated behavior in computer usage is evident even in women's' colleges that have recently become coeducational:

> It was encouraging to find gender equity in students' use of the three campus computer rooms. However, given the history and demographics of the college, it was discouraging to have found any evidence of gender inequity or of stereotypic gender tracking with regard to the use of computers (i.e., women using word processing software and dot matrix printers and men using desktop publishing software and laser printers). Formerly the college was exclusively a women's institution. The data reported here were collected during the Fall semester of the college's third year of transition to co-education, when male students were only 17 percent of the entire student population. Therefore, these findings demonstrate that the technological gender gap can emerge even in a predominately female environment. . . .[28]

Although the percentages of women attending and graduating from professional schools have increased, some recent graduates argue that a general disrespect for women has been built into many curricula. Adriane Fugh-Berman, who graduated from the Georgetown University of Medicine, feels that many of the medical students learned misinformation and demeaning attitudes toward and about women. Some of her examples illustrate widespread blatant, subtle, and covert sexism in medical education:

- On the first day of classes, an anatomy professor remarked that their elderly cadaver "must have been a Playboy bunny" before instructing us to cut off her large breasts and toss them into the thirty-gallon trash can marked "cadaver waste." Barely hours into our training, we were already being taught that there was nothing to be learned from examining breasts. Given the fact that one out of nine American women will develop breast cancer in her lifetime, to treat breasts as extraneous tissue seemed an appalling waste of an educational opportunity. . . .
- Teaching rounds were often, for women, a spectator sport. . . . I have seen a male attending physician demonstrate an exam on a patient and then wade through several female medical students to drag forth a male in order to

teach it to him. This sort of discrimination was common and quite unconscious: The women just didn't register as medical students to some of the
doctors.

- "Why are women's brains smaller than men's?" asked a surgeon of a group
  of male medical students in the doctors' lounge (I was in the room as well,
  but was apparently invisible). "Because they're missing logic!" Guffaws all
  around.
- In a required course on human sexuality, only two of the eleven lectures focused on women, and of the two lectures on homosexuality, neither mentioned lesbians. We learned that oral sex is primarily a homosexual practice,
  and that sexual dysfunction in women is often caused by "working." In the
  women-as-idiots department, we learned that when impotent men are im-
  planted with permanently rigid penile prostheses, four out of five wives can't
  tell that their husbands have had the surgery.[29]

Sexism is overlapping.   Besides pervading institutions, sex inequality
overlaps across institutions (both in the private and public sectors). Consider
what happens in many marital dissolution cases when sexist family, economic,
and legal practices intersect.

When wealthy men like Johnny Carson, Donald Trump, and Lee Iac-
cocca were divorced, their alimony payments made headlines because their
wives received millions of dollars in the settlements. In real life, fewer than 15
percent of divorced women are awarded alimony, and only 3 percent actually
receive any payments.[30] Many women who have been full-time housewives
most of their lives and experience divorce in their forties or fifties are especially likely to become poor. Often, the (usually male) judges have unrealistic
ideas about the employment potential of older homemakers or women with
young children and about women's hardship in supporting children because
many have low-paying jobs. Some judges base their decisions on the erro-
neous assumptions that all women remarry after divorce and that they will be
taken care of by another man.

Judges often give mothers custody of children because they are seen as
"natural" caretakers and nurturers. Many judges admit that child support is
usually set at amounts below those specified by state guidelines and that the
nonpaying parent (typically the father) is rarely forced to comply. One national survey found that—largely because mothers support their children—
divorced men had incomes of 17 percent above need, but divorced women
had incomes 7 percent below need.[31] Nearly half of all men neither see nor
support their children after a divorce.[32] About a fifth of fathers have never
provided any form of assistance, such as child-support payments, paying for
clothes, buying presents, taking the children on vacations, paying for routine
dental care or uninsured medical expenses, helping with homework, or attending school events.[33] According to one study, two thirds of noncustodial
parents (who are usually fathers) contribute more toward car payments than
to child support.[34] Often, women give up on enforcement because the legal
costs may be higher than the support and because mothers, especially those
in low-paying jobs, would be jeopardizing their employment because of the
repeated court appearances.

Over 90 percent of mothers get custody of the children. Fathers are far more successful in custody disputes than is commonly perceived, however. A study by the Massachusetts Supreme Judicial Court found that fathers who actively seek custody obtain either primary or joint physical custody in more than 70 percent of cases. Custody awards often punish women who breach the stereotype of the ideal mother, because, for example, she works outside the home or has had a sexual relationship outside marriage. In contrast, men are usually not penalized for extramarital sexual liaisons. There is also a growing tendency to award custody to the wealthier parent. Given women's and men's unequal earnings, fathers who want to raise their children are increasingly more likely to get custody than are mothers.[35]

Although divorce is an agreement between two people in principle, in reality women's lives (more so than men's) during and after divorce are shaped by many other institutions—political, legal, and economic.

Cultural Discrimination

At level four—cultural discrimination—sex discrimination and inequality are built into our literature, art, music, language, morals, customs, beliefs, and ideology. When anthropologists and sociologists speak of culture, they are referring to the norms, values, religion, knowledge, language, artifacts, and symbols that make us human, shape our communication, and define a generally agreed-upon way of life. In art, we see women as seductresses (Bellini, Titian), as sex objects (Rubens, Renoir), as masses of distorted sex organs (Picasso), and as grotesque molls (Lindner).[36] In an examination of how popular culture has distorted the images of women in fiction, television, motion pictures, fashion, magazines, and advertising, Kathryn Weibel found that women have been portrayed primarily in domestic, housewifely, and consumer roles over the past century and a half despite women's increased participation in the labor market.[37]

DIMENSIONS OF SEX DISCRIMINATION

Blatant, subtle, and covert discrimination can vary on four dimensions: cumulative or episodic, deliberate or unintentional, public or private, and formal or informal.

Cumulative or Episodic

Some discriminatory barriers are cumulative—they grow and snowball. Yet others are episodic—they flare up and subside on a short-lived basis. In terms of the former, for example, one study found that school superintendents' sex-role stereotypes have long-term and incremental implications. Because women are expected to perform family responsibilities, they will be excluded from consideration in jobs that are "financially rewarding, have prestige, or may be critical for professional advancement."[38] Rejecting women from such jobs in the present will affect their *future* long-term salaries and promotions. Moreover, even when there are no gender differences in educational attainment, field of study, and other qualifications, many women receive lower starting salaries than men when they are hired. The salary disparity at the time of hire plays a major role in shaping job promotions and opportunities in subsequent years.[39]

Episodic discrimination may be situation-specific but does not have to be limited to only one type of situation. For example, management might institute dress codes for women (but not men) and only in certain positions (for receptionists but not for women working in mail rooms). Since it is situation-specific, episodic discrimination does not imply an absence of widespread sex discrimination. Quite to the contrary, episodic discrimination can be pervasive and deep-rooted. For example, a maintenance department (staffed predominantly by men) may refuse a secretary's request to shampoo the office rugs because "the guys are too busy" or may respond only if the secretary is attractive or seen as potentially sexually accessible. If the issue is pursued by the secretary's supervisor, the secretary is told by the maintenance supervisor that "I'm tired of you secretary types always telling me what to do." Such reactions are not penalized within a work environment that is pervaded with persisting sexism.

Deliberate or Unintentional

As we discussed earlier, there are many accounts of consciously motivated, malicious, and deliberate discrimination—especially against women in traditionally male-dominated jobs—in both blue-collar and professional occupations. Women's participation has been discouraged through unionized sabotage, practical jokes, sexual harassment, social isolation, open hostility, hazing, vulgar teasing, wrong directions/instructions, and exclusion from training programs.[40]

Also common is discrimination that may be due to ignorance, insensitivity, provincialism, misinformed kindness, or misguided favors. In terms of the last two behaviors, for example, most women faculty members are often automatically assigned women-related responsibilities that impede their professional progress and development. They are given extracurricular sex-stereotyped tasks (such as counseling women students, providing community service on women's issues, and being a "women's representative" on myriad faculty committees) that infringe on the time needed for research, publications, and professional growth. Many women are automatically expected to perform a variety of extra duties just *because* they are women and irrespective of their abilities or interests.

Public or Private

A number of our respondents noted that public and private stances on discrimination in public and private settings can be quite different:

> Our office manager has told several of us, in private conversations, that she gets very angry when the men refer to secretaries as "girls." She also makes a big point of correcting some of us when we say "he" rather than "he or she." But she's never done this with any of the bosses. She just smiles, nods, and says, "Yes, sir." (Secretary in manufacturing)

Similarly, men may be private feminists and public chauvinists:

> One of my best friends at work is the chair of the communications department. He's the first, when a bunch of us are talking informally, to correct men about comments like "Can we invite our wives (rather than "spouses") to the dinner?" to criticize male faculty for their leering and sexist asides about coeds, and to use "the student," "the faculty member," and "they" instead of "he," "him," or "his." When we're at public functions, though, and especially if male administrators are present, he never corrects the deans or the president, laughs heartily at dirty jokes (even when women faculty are present), and talks about his wife and daughter in very derogatory, demeaning ways. (Female faculty in an English department)

A public-private schism may reflect political motivations. By castigating discriminatory behavior privately but participating in discrimination publicly, men may be trying to play both sides—especially if the group membership does not overlap.

Whether the offensive behavior is private or public, it hurts and alienates women. Two decades ago, it was rare to find a female chief of staff anywhere in Congress. Today, one out of every four chiefs of staff in the Senate and one of three in the House are women. Yet the larger number of female staff has not necessarily diminished the number of disparaging comments made about women. According to a professional staff member on the international development subcommittee of the House Banking, Finance and Urban Affairs Committee,

> Oh, yes, there are the jokes about women, jokes about female body parts, there are humorous put-downs of women, and sometimes derogatory comments, but done in a light, joking way so as to make it difficult to raise an objection without being thought of as a wet blanket.[41]

According to this staff member, the backroom culture and good-old-boy "spirit" of Capitol Hill sends women the message that "you are outsiders here."

Formal or Informal

As we discussed earlier, formal sex discrimination exists in such areas as pension payments, insurance rates, and prosecution of sex crimes. Even when organizations have gender-neutral formal rules and procedures, however, their informal application may be discriminatory. A 22-month study of the U.S. Naval Academy by the General Accounting Office (GAO) found that female students were held to tougher disciplinary standards than their male counterparts. Although most men believed that women were either treated equally or better by honors and conduct boards, this was not the case. Women were more likely than men to be charged with honor offenses (such as lying, cheating, and stealing), 6.1 percent of the first-year women compared to 0.8 percent of freshmen men were convicted of such serious conduct offenses as drunkenness, and the cases brought against women were less likely to be dropped. The GAO found that a significant percentage of white male students felt that women don't belong at the Naval Academy.[42]

ACCEPTANCE OF INEQUALITY

Whether the behavior is conscious or inadvertent, intentional or unintentional, many people reinforce sexism (1) by not being aware of sex discrimination; (2) by internalizing sex stereotypes; (3) by ignoring sexism because they seek acceptance by male peers or bosses; and (4) by not doing anything about sex discrimination because they are afraid of rejection or reprisal. Since women are products of and participants in their culture, it is not surprising that they often collaborate in sexist behavior.

Lacking Awareness of Widespread Sex Inequality

Many Americans, male and female, are not aware of the pervasiveness of sex inequality. Students in middle schools and high schools rarely hear about sexism or sex inequality in classes. Even in college, many students are suspicious of national data that document sex inequality. For example, even though only 2 percent of all secretaries, stenographers, and typists are men, their weekly earnings are *still* higher than those of women! (See Table 3.2.) When many of our students—including women—see such data, some of the common reactions are, "Well, the Bureau of the Census must be wrong," "That was last year; what about this year?" or "This certainly won't happen to me!"

Even highly educated men and women are often ignorant of sex inequality. Few people are aware, for example, that women routinely pay more and get less as consumers. Many of us are familiar with stories about women being overcharged for car and home repairs and undergoing unnecessary surgery. As Frances Whittelsey notes, however, women are charged, on the average, over 27 percent more than men to dry clean a basic white cotton shirt and 25 percent more for a basic shampoo, cut and blow dry, and women rarely get free alterations when they purchase expensive clothes in department stores that don't charge men for alterations.[43]

Violence against girls and women is commonplace, but we rarely talk about it. A recent issue of *Parade* magazine was devoted to "What Kids Say." Although important, the only topics covered were sex education and safety at school and in the neighborhood. With the exception of a handful of high school programs and an occasional talk show, young people seldom hear about date/acquaintance rape, incest, courtship violence, or battered

TABLE 3.2.   Median Weekly Earnings of Full-Time Workers, by Selected Occupations and Sex, 1990

	NUMBER OF WORKERS (IN THOUSANDS)	%	MEN MEDIAN WEEKLY EARNINGS	%	WOMEN MEDIAN WEEKLY EARNINGS
Elementary school teachers	1,311	15	$575	85	$513
Cashiers	1,081	21	231	79	210
Secretaries, stenographers, and typists	3,689	2	387	98	341
Registered nurses	1,181	6	616	94	608
Waiters and waitresses	596	25	266	75	194

Source: Bureau of Labor Statistics, unpublished data, 1991

spouses. Social scientists regularly find a correlation between pornography and violence against women.[44] Yet, nearly half of those renting the 410 million adult video tapes each year are either individual women or women accompanying men. The muteness of women on many issues reinforces a widespread perception that sex discrimination is acceptable.

Internalizing and Disseminating Sex Stereotypes

By the time they reach high school, many girls and boys have internalized sex stereotypes. According to a 15-year-old boy (whose response is representative), sexism is a myth:

> I think a lot of women use their sex as an excuse. A woman goes to get a job, and if she doesn't get it, they'll blame the company, saying they're sexist. And really—I've talked about this with my dad—a lot of times it's just that the male is more qualified.[45]

His source, not surprisingly, is his dad. Many stereotypes and prejudices are learned primarily in the family and from the media.

Sex stereotypes are reinforced throughout adult life. In a study of television commercials, Stephen Craig found that sex stereotypes are rampant. During daytime television, when the audience is mostly women, products and settings generally involve cooking, cleaning, child care, or maintaining an attractive physical appearance. Men are portrayed as the primary characters in less than half of the commercials. When they do appear, it is generally in a position of authority and "patriarchal dominance," such as celebrity commentator, husband, or professional. Commercials aimed at the weekend male audience are quite different. Products and settings are generally associated with life away from the home and family, and the commercials frequently exclude women and children. The ads and the sports programming in which they appear stress male stereotypes such as physical strength and ruggedness, aggressiveness, competitiveness, and daring. Commercials for alcohol, automobiles, and trucks still play up to male sexual fantasies by featuring young, attractive, bikini-clad women.[46]

Some well-educated women purposely "play dumb" because of organizational pressure. Because competitiveness is prized in male attorneys, women attorneys often tone down their forcefulness because they will be labeled as "unfeminine" or as "unpleasant associates."[47] A fear of rejection or being fired may result in women's setting less ambitious goals. For example, women in math may submit their best work not to the leading journals but to lesser publications:

> Sue Geller, a math professor at Texas A&M and head of a committee on the status of women sponsored by seven national math organizations, surveyed more than a dozen editors of math journals. "I've been told by a number of (male) editors [at the less prestigious journals] that they have found their best papers written by women," says Geller. "In many cases they asked, 'Why didn't [these women] submit to more prestigious journals?'"[48]

The point is that many female researchers have internalized sex-role stereotypes, see themselves as inferior, and don't compete.

Seeking Acceptance by the Group

Although we hear a lot of rhetoric about individuality, in reality U.S. culture rewards conformity and punishes deviation. If women work in male-dominated jobs, they may be especially anxious to fit in. Women may ignore sexual harassment because they want to be accepted by their male colleagues, especially if the men are the majority. A 23-year-old woman who works aboard a Navy vessel said she is harassed every day ("Nice butt;" or the men wag their tongues at her and ask if she got laid during shore leave). She has never reported such behavior because "it doesn't bother me. I don't have a chip on my shoulder. . . . Most of the other women do." Another woman on the same ship stated: "There's more conflict between women and women than between women and men. With women there's jealousy about how much you know and rivalry about prettiness." Another woman, a hull technician, said the guys refer to her breasts as flotation devices, but she never filed a complaint:

> "If you write someone up, everybody would be like, 'Oh, she's a bitch,' and no one would talk to you again. . . . Some women are bitches."[49]

Because many women want to "fit in," they often accept sexual discrimination. Note, too, women's criticism of each other's behavior as they vie for men's acceptance.

Avoiding Reprisal or Rejection

Many women don't try to move up from their current positions because they expect to be rejected. The reason is that most organizational settings are controlled by men. For example, women coaches say that they have to "walk on water" to be successful, that the "old-boy network" is so strong they have difficulty moving up in current positions, much less new ones, and that women have become discouraged with the lack of openness of job-search committees or feel they will be hired as tokens rather than being taken seriously.[50]

Although some men and women are personally liberated, they are often unwilling to fight public battles because they want to avoid conflict and are afraid to be stigmatized as "bra burners" or "wimps" or to be excluded from all-male (or all-female) discussions and recreational activities. In the sciences, some women are isolated and lack mentorship from older male colleagues that the younger male scientists often enjoy. Others are denied tenure or promotion because of entrenched attitudes that women are not as good at science or are less committed to research due to family responsibilities.[51]

In other cases, women don't report blatant discrimination because they fear reprisal. A young woman, an officer, said that an instructor in the Naval Academy forced her to lift up her skirt and grabbed her. When she told her father, a Navy man, he warned her "don't be a whistle-blower in the military." She remembered her father's advice and didn't do anything even after someone slipped notes under her cabin door while she was serving a tour of duty aboard a navy vessel: "I see you. I'm going to grab you. I'm going to [expletive] you." She was so shaken up, she was afraid to sleep at her apartment during shore leave.[52]

On Capitol Hill, women chiefs of staff who earn less than similarly-qualified men rarely complain, even privately, because they risk being labeled "difficult," "whiners," or "troublemakers." Those who protest publicly may find themselves ostracized by the lawmakers or coworkers. Even worse, they might find themselves unemployed or unemployable on Capitol Hill. As one senior female House aide stated, "It's like quicksand. The more you yell, the deeper you sink."[53]

The internal and external pressures to maintain rigid sex stratification within and outside the home are functional for men and the business sector. For many men, sex discrimination results in less competition in the work place and more leisure time because they are free of domestic responsibilities. Business and industry profit from discrimination in several ways. Wives donate much free time, effort, and energy to the company by doing supportive work that allows husbands to give most of their time to the company. Moreover, persuading women that their work is not important justifies paying them low wages and salaries. Finally, sex-segregated labor markets ensure male dominance in the economic sector, which, in turn, influences men's and women's unequal participation in religious, legal, military, and political sectors.

A number of researchers have documented the continuous processes and hazards of sex inequality. The next three chapters discuss in more detail how sex inequality works through blatant, subtle, and covert sex-discriminatory mechanisms.

NOTES

1. Kevin Sullivan, "Foot-in-Mouth Barbie," *Washington Post*, September 30, 1992, pp. A1, A11.

2. *The AAUW Report: How Schools Shortchange Girls: A Study of Major Findings on Girls and Education* (Washington, DC: American Association of University Women Educational Foundation, 1992).

3. U.S. Department of Labor, *Employment and Earnings.* Bureau of Labor Statistics (Washington, DC: Government Printing Office, 1991).

4. U.S. Department of Education, National Center for Education Statistics, *Digest of Education Statistics: 1993* (Washington, DC: Government Printing Office, 1993), p. 392.

5. Leslie Whitaker, "Trouble in the Locker Rooms," *Time*, October 15, 1990, p. 97.

6. Ibid., p. 2C.

7. Paul Selvin, "Mathematics: Profile of a Field: Heroism Is Still the Norm," *Science* 255, March 13, 1992, p. 1382.

8. Thomas W. Waldron and Laura Lippman, "It's a Man's World at the State House," *Baltimore Sun*, March 22, 1992, pp. 1A, 12A–13A.

9. Example cited in Saundra Torry, "Study Finds Sexual Harassment Prevalent in Western U.S. Courts," *Washington Post*, August 5, 1992, p. A2.

10. *Family Planning Perspectives Digest*, "Two-Thirds of Women Now Work During Their First Pregnancy; Half Return to Work Within One Year," 22:4 (July/August 1990), pp. 184–185.

11. Diane Harris, "You're Pregnant? You're Out," *Working Woman*, August 1992, p. 50.

12. See Leslie Maitland Werner, "Loan Company Settles U.S. Bias Case," *New York Times*, November 1, 1984, p. 23.

13. Cited in Courtney Leatherman, "President's Hair Style, Clothing, Marriage, and Handling of 'Moral Issues' Rile Older Alumnae of Converse College," *The Chronicle of Higher Education*, December 16, 1992, p. A18.

14. Keith Russell Ablow, "Sexist Remarks," *Washington Post*, Health Supplement, December 10, 1991, p. 9.

15. Elizabeth Grauerholz, "Sexual Harassment of Women Professors by Students: Exploring the Dynamics of Power, Authority, and Gender in a University Setting," *Sex Roles* 21:11/12 (1989), pp. 789–801. See also, Anne Statham, Laurel Richardson and Judith A. Cook, *Gender and University Teaching: A Negotiated Difference* (Albany, NY: SUNY Press, 1991), for similar findings.

16. Stephen J. Spurr, "Sex Discrimination in the Legal Profession: A Study of Promotion," *Industrial and Labor Relations Review*, 43: 4 (April 1990) pp. 406–417.

17. Keith Russell Ablow, "Sexist Remarks," *Washington Post, Health Supplement*, December 10, 1991, p. 9.

18. Carole Warshaw, "Limitations of the Medical Model in the Care of Battered Women," in *Violence Against Women*, eds., Pauline B. Bart and Eileen Geil Moran (Newbury Park, CA: Sage Publications, 1993), pp. 134–146.

19. "Sex Harassment in VA Centers Alleged," *Baltimore Sun,* September 18, 1992, p. 25A.

20. "Ga. Probes Years of Abuse of Female Inmates at State Prison," *Baltimore Sun,* December 31, 1992, p. 20A.

21. Joan Talbert and Christine E. Bose, "Wage-Attainment Processes: The Retail Clerk Occupation," *American Journal of Sociology* 83 (1983), pp. 403–424.

22. See, for example, Linda L. Lindsey, *Gender Roles: A Sociological Perspective,* 2nd edition (Englewood Cliffs, NJ: Prentice Hall, 1994; Hilary M. Lips, *Sex & Gender: An Introduction,* 2nd edition (Mountain View, CA: Mayfield Publishing Company, 1993); Claire M. Renzetti and Daniel J. Curran, 2nd edition, *Women, Men, and Society* (Boston: Allyn and Bacon, 1992); and Margaret L. Andersen, *Thinking About Women: Sociological Perspectives on Sex and Gender,* 3rd edition (New York: Macmillan Publishing Co., 1993).

23. Valerie E. Lee, Helen M. Marks, and Tina Byrd, "Sexism in Single-Sex and Coeducational Secondary School Classrooms," Mimeographed paper, July 28, 1993. (Also presented at the American Sociological Association meetings, 1991.), p. 26.

24. Ibid., p. 22.

25. Michele N-K Collison, "20 Years Later, Women on Formerly All-Male Campuses Fight to Change Their Institutions' 'Old Boy' Images," *The Chronicle of Higher Education,* December 12, 1990, pp. A23–A24.

26. Mary S. Hartman, "Mills Students Provided Eloquent Testimony to the Value of Women's Colleges," *The Chronicle of Higher Education,* July 5, 1990, p. A40.

27. Katherine Canada Frank Brusco, "The Technological Gender Gap: Evidence and Recommendations for Educators and Computer-Based Instruction Designers," *Educational Technology Research and Development,* 39:2 (1991), pp. 43–51.

28. Ibid., p. 45.

29. Adriane Fugh-Berman, "Tales Out of Medical School," *The Nation* 254:2, January 20, 1992, p. 55.

30. U.S. Bureau of the Census, *Marital Status and Living Arrangements: March 1990.* Current Population Reports, Series P0-20, no. 450 (Washington, DC: Government Printing Office, 1991).

31. Lynn Hecht Schafran, "Overwhelming Evidence: Reports on Gender Bias in the Courts," *Trial,* 26, February 1990, pp. 28–35; see also, Sarah M. Singleton, "Gender Bias Skews Justice for Women," *Trial* 26, February 1990, pp. 39–43.

32. See S. A. Hewlett, "The Feminization of the Work Force," *New Perspectives Quarterly* 7:1, Winter 1990, pp. 13–15.

33. J. D. Teachman, "Contributions to Children by Divorced Fathers," *Social Problems* 38:3, August 1991, pp. 358–370.

34. Cited in Sarah M. Singleton, "Gender Bias Skews Justice for Women," *Trial,* 26, February 1990, pp. 39–43.

35. Schafran, "Overwhelming Evidence . . ."

36. Marie Richmond-Abbott, *The American Woman* (New York: Holt, Rinehart and Winston, 1979), pp. 71–95. For a recent discussion of "woman-hatred"

in the work of famous painters and sculptors, see Marilyn French, *The War Against Women* (New York, Summit Books, 1992), especially pp. 162–165.

37.   Kathryn Weibel, *Mirror, Mirror!* (Garden City, NY: Anchor Books, 1977). See also Angela G. Dorenkamp, John F. McClymer, Mary M. Moynihan, and Arlene C. Vadum, *Images of Women in American Popular Culture* (New York: Harcourt Brace Jovanovich, 1985).

38.   J. Frasher, R. Frasher, and F. Wims, "Sex-Role Stereotyping in School Superintendents' Personnel Decisions," *Sex Roles* 8 (1982), p. 267.

39.   Barry Gerhart, "Gender Differences in Current and Starting Salaries: the Role of Performance, College, Major, and Job Title," *Industrial and Labor Relations Review* 43:4, April 1990, pp. 418–433.

40.   See, for example, Terry Metherby, ed., *Conversations: Working Women Talk About Doing a Man's Job* (Milbrae, CA: Les Femmes Publishers); Gena Corea, *The Hidden Malpractice: How American Medicine Treats Women as Patients and Professionals* (New York: William Morrow and Co., 1977); and Brigid O'Farrell and Sharon L. Harlan, "Craftworkers and Clerks: The Effect of Male Co-Worker Hostility on Women's Satisfaction with Non-Traditional Jobs," *Social Problems* 29 (1982).

41.   Richard Morin, "Female Aides on Hill: Still Outsiders in Man's World," *Washington Post,* February 21, 1993, p. 18.

42.   David Hess, "Naval Academy's Female, Minority Mids Fare Worse," *Baltimore Sun,* May 22, 1992, pp. A1, 11A.

43.   Frances Cerra Whittelsey, *Why Women Pay More* (Washington, DC: Center for Study of Responsive Law, 1993).

44.   Wendy Melillo, "Can Pornography Lead to Violence?" *Washington Post. Health Supplement,* July 21, 1992, pp. 10–12.

45.   Lynn Minton, "Fresh Voices: What Do You Think of Feminism?" *Parade* magazine, January 20, 1991, p. 14.

46.   Stephen R. Craig, "The Effect of Televison Day Part on Gender Portrayals in Televison Commercials: A Content Analysis," *Sex Roles* 26: 5/6 (1992), pp. 197–211.

47.   Harriet Zuckerman, Jonathan R. Cole, and John T. Bruer, eds., *The Outer Circle: Women in the Scientific Community* (New York: Norton, 1991).

48.   Selvin, "Mathematics . . . ," p. 1383.

49.   Laura Blumenfeld, "They're on Board the Ships, but It's Still a Man's World," *Washington Post,* September 22, 1992, p. B4.

50.   R. Vivian Acosta and Linda Jean Carpenter, "As the Years Go By—Coaching Opportunities in the 1990s," *JOPERD,* March 1992, pp. 36–41.

51.   Ann Gibbons, "Two-Career Science Marriage," *Science,* March 13, 1992, pp. 1380–1381.

52.   Blumenfeld, "They're on board the ships . . . ," p. B4.

53.   Morin, "Female Aides on the Hill . . . ," p. A18.

CHAPTER FOUR
HOW BLATANT SEX DISCRIMINATION WORKS

Blatant sex discrimination includes those discriminatory actions directed against women that are quite obvious to most observers and are highly visible. They can be illegal or legal under current civil rights laws. But illegal or legal, such discriminatory practices are well-institutionalized in the United States. Blatant discrimination is today widespread and can be found in all of this society's basic institutional arenas. As we will see in this chapter, it can be found in the family, in dating practices, in the workplace, in housing, in colleges and universities, and in law and politics.

SEX DISCRIMINATION BEGINS AT HOME

Most adult Americans get married at some point in their lives, although many also get divorced. In all family systems there are critical roles and sets of rights and duties tied to specific positions in families. Wife and husband, mother and father, are social roles with specific expectations. In U.S. society, a woman as wife is usually expected to act in certain subordinate ways as a consequence of her role. She has certain traditional and legal duties and rights, many of which reflect clear-cut subordination and discrimination. There are exceptions, with a growing number of women and wives filling nontraditional roles, such as college professor and construction worker, but most women still play out traditional gender roles in their lives, inside and outside the home.

Sexism in Making Decisions

Decision making in the U.S. family is still typically patriarchal, in spite of jokes about women "wearing the pants." Modern marriages are set within a larger society with its conventional female and male roles stratified in terms of power, resources, and benefits. Research indicates that the husband's power in the family typically derives to a substantial extent from his job, income, and position in the outside world. While over the last few decades there has been an increase in the number of wives who earn more than their husbands, today more than two thirds of wives have less in the way of economic and political resources than their husbands. In the minority of cases where the wife has greater economic resources than the husband, there is greater potential for her to have more say in the family decision making. Nonetheless, in most of the latter families the sex-role division remains relatively traditional.

Who gets the burden of child rearing? One feature of family life that accents the unequal power of the husband is the childbearing and child rearing cycle. Mothers still have the primary responsibility for parenting.[1] Single mothers rarely get much help from fathers. A substantial number of wives quit work outside the home when they have their children, at least for a time. Having to quit work reduces their resources, and thus their power in the family. Other wives continue working as much as they can before and after the child is born. Child care originally came under the auspices of the wife because of her biological role in bearing and breast-feeding infants. But, with bottle feeding, it has become possible for men to take over the total child-rearing function, although most still have not done so.

Even today, taking responsibility for child care is still a major aspect of the prevailing definition of a woman's family role. This means that, just when many women are no longer hemmed in by frequent childbirth or the need to nurse infants, they are pressured by sex-typed role definitions to remain as the major socializers of the children. Fathers have become more involved in child care and housework than a generation back, but the changes have been modest. In some families, husbands and wives work alternate shifts and thus husbands can alternate with their wives in providing childcare. However, our family ideology has become more egalitarian than our actual behavior. Even when fathers take care of their children, their involvement is often secondary; it is done while watching television or doing chores. The wife often provides more care, and more intimate care.[2]

The Man's "Right" to Sex

Perhaps the most taboo-ridden dimension of the traditional woman's role is sexuality. In regard to sexual intercourse, husbands have historically had a legal or traditional "right" to insist on intercourse, and a wife has a duty to submit even if she does not want to do so. This view is changing, but only slowly. Today, under some circumstances, a wife can charge her husband with rape in many states. However, in "only 20 states is marital rape the same offense as raping a stranger. . . . in the 30 other states, a wife can charge her husband with rape only under narrow circumstances, making it difficult . . . for married women to prosecute their husbands."[3] Moreover, in all states it is difficult for a husband to be convicted for forcibly raping his wife because of the traditional view of a husband's right to intercourse.

In addition, inside and outside the home, women are often treated as sexual objects, as things or commodities. The commodity character of women can be seen in the language many boys and men use, such terms as "broad," "ho" (whore), and "babe." The attitudes of husbands and boyfriends are significantly shaped and reinforced by cultural pressures outside the home. We have noted previously that television programs, movies, mass media advertising, and the cosmetics industry frequently present women as sex objects, to be manipulated for the pleasure of men. As we discussed in Chapter 2, beer commercials often use sexy models, the so-called "busty blondes." Other ads also use sexuality to sell. Alluding to a male term for female breasts, one ad for Bamboo Lingerie showed two door knockers positioned side by side.[4] Similarly, an ad for name-brand jeans in one major magazine pictures a tough biker next to his motorcycle holding a naked woman. Another jeans ad has a man carting a screaming woman, who on the next page appears to have been raped in the back seat of a car. Thus, sexuality is sometimes coupled with aggression or violence against women.[5]

VIOLENT DISCRIMINATION AGAINST WOMEN

Men Target Women at Home

Whether inside the home or outside, perhaps the most blatant discrimination is the widespread violence directed against girls and women because of their gendered status. Violence directed by men against their spouses or partners is the most common cause of injury to women. More women are injured by domestic violence than are hurt in auto accidents, rapes, or muggings combined. Each year, millions of women are attacked by mates or partners, and nearly a third of female homicide victims are killed by spouses or boyfriends. Federal government data show that nationwide a woman is beaten every 18 seconds. We should note, too, that threats of violence, including stalking and limiting a woman's physical freedom, are also part of the culture of gendered violence shaping the lives of U.S. women.[6] Men as well as women can be the victims of domestic violence, but women make up the large majority of the serious cases of family violence. The battering of women tends to be more severe than that of men because of the greater size of men and the use of weapons. One major reason for the battering is the failure of women to submit to the desires or authority of their male partners.

There are many more cases of wife battering than are reported to government agencies. For example, some 34,000 battered women in Minnesota seek help annually, but knowledgeable officials estimate that at least 43,000 women are battered there annually. The first battered women's shelter opened in 1974, and today there are more than 1,400 such shelters. The growing number of battered women's shelters has increased the likelihood of women reporting violence against them.[7]

It is only in recent years that wife battering has been taken seriously by male police officials and officers. Police officers, who were once all male and are still mostly male, have often overlooked wife battering, especially by affluent and influential men. Batterers have often not been arrested because police considered the violence to be "only a family dispute." Yet, because of the work of the battered women's movement in recent decades, violence against wives and other women is now a criminal act in every state, and the perpetrators of violence are more likely to be arrested. Speedy arrest has been found to be the most effective deterrent to men who batter; it seems to shock them into a realization that what they are doing is a crime.[8]

Rape Outside and Inside the Home

Forcible rape is defined by the police as sexual intercourse forced by a man upon a woman against her will. The U.S. Department of Justice has estimated that a large proportion of all rapes are not reported to police, although the willingness of women to report rape has increased over the last two decades. Because of increased reporting and an increase in the number of rapes, the number of rapes reported to the police climbed dramatically from 28,000 in 1967 to more than 70,000 in 1990. The rate of rapes per 100,000 population jumped from 22.5 in 1972 to 42.8 in 1992. Still, the actual numbers are much higher; estimates based on the 1990 National Crime Victimization Survey suggest that there are at least 130,000 forcible rapes annually.[9]

Rape, attempted rape, and other sexual assaults have been reported in all branches of the U.S. military. In Chapter 1, we noted events at the Navy's Tailhook Association convention in Las Vegas in 1991. Lieutenant Paula Coughlin has given an account of being sexually and physically assaulted by numerous male pilots at a Las Vegas hotel. A Navy investigation found that more than two dozen women, including numerous officers, had been attacked. The investigation led to reprimands for some aviators, and eventually to the early (by a few months) retirement of the Navy's top admiral, but there were no prosecutions for the sexual assaults. Later, women serving in several military branches testified before the Senate Veterans Affairs Committee that they had been sexually assaulted in ways similar to Coughlin.[10] Given the weak punishment of the male offenders and her difficult position, Coughlin soon resigned her commission in the Navy.

Rape can happen to any woman—from a 12-month-old infant to an 80-year-old woman. It can involve wives or daughters. An estimated 61,000 wives are the victims of rape by husbands each year in the United States. In addition, the sexual abuse and rape of girls by male relatives—fathers, stepfathers, uncles, and brothers—are widespread problems in the United States. *Incest* is usually a matter of a male relative forcing a girl (less often a boy) to submit to sexual abuse or rape. Until the 1970s, there was little discussion of incest in the United States. Apparently, most Americans thought it was rare. However, recent studies have shown that the majority of sexual assaults target children or teenagers and that incest is very common. Studies have shown that sexual molestation is a major cause of serious psychological problems; some 44 percent to 70 percent of psychiatric patients in several studies were found to have been molested as children.[11] Studies of a number of samples of women in the last decade have found child sexual abuse victimization rates ranging from 22 percent to 45 percent of the women studied.[12] A 1990s estimate by one expert puts the figure at about one third of all women nationally—with only half ever reporting the abuse to anyone.[13]

Child sexual abuse, including child rape, is extremely underreported. In one study of 1,200 college students, 26 percent reported having been victims of child sexual abuse before the age of 13, yet only 6 percent of the victims reported their attacker.[14] As children and later as adults, the victims of such sexual abuse are shamed into silence because U.S. society is unwilling to protect children from male molesters. In her research sociologist Carol Rambo Ronai has pointed out that this societal neglect helps to perpetuate the continued abuse of the young victims.[15]

Rape is the most widespread of the violent crimes committed on campuses across the United States. The most recent federal report of crime on campuses found that there were more than 1,000 rapes on campus in just one year.[16] Given underreporting, the actual number is likely to be at least 2,000. An estimated 85 percent of these are "acquaintance rapes" or "date rapes," that is, coerced sexual intercourse by a male acquaintance.[17] There is some resistance to defining sexual violence by a date as a rape because of the ideal image of college dating, a romantic involvement with the perpetrator, cultural acceptance of male aggression during courtship, false stereotypes about rapists (for example, the image of a stranger attacking late at night), and the embarrassment of the administrators of colleges and other educational institutions in dealing with date rape. The most comprehensive study yet done of rape on campus was directed by psychologist Mary Koss. She surveyed 3,187 women and 2,972 men on more than 30 college campuses and found that one quarter of the women had been the victims of rape or attempted rape and that over half the rapes took place on dates. *One in 12 of the male students* admitted committing acts that met the legal definition of rape.[18] In an early 1990s study of women students at Kent State University, about 1 out of 8 reported being victims of rape, again mostly at the hands of acquaintances.[19] While some conservative authors, such as Katie Roiphe in her controversial book *The Morning After,* have argued that these data are greatly exaggerated, no one has presented any research data contradicting the view that there is a widespread prevalence of date and acquaintance rape.[20]

Some of the female readers of this book will have experienced a date rape incident like the one that Robin Warshaw recounts in her book, *I Never Called It Rape.*[21] A young college student named Lori was asked out on a double date with Eric and his roommate Paul and the latter's girlfriend Amy. The two couples were going to have a barbecue party at the house where the men lived. However, when Lori arrived at the house, she discovered that the other couple had cancelled out on the party. She and Eric ended up being alone. After some food, and some drinking on Eric's part, Eric kissed Lori as they sat on the couch. The phone rang, and after Eric answered it he came back and, as Lori told it later,

> He grabbed me from behind and picked me up. . . . He laid me down [on a bed] and kissed me. . . . He starts taking off my clothes and I said, "Wait—time out! This is not what I want, you know." But Eric said that Lori owed him for the dinner. After she went to the bathroom, Eric seized her, put her on the bed, and disrobed her:
>
> I'm yelling and hitting and pushing on him and he just liked that. He says, "I know you must like this because a lot of women like this."
>
> Then Eric forced her to have intercourse. Afterwards, Lori was in great pain, and crying. After Eric finally took her home in his car, she got into her bed there:
>
> Everything that I could possibly put on I think I put on that night—leg warmers, thermal underwear—everything imaginable. . . . For two weeks I couldn't talk. People would talk to me and I felt nothing. I felt like a zombie. I couldn't cry. I couldn't smile. I couldn't eat. . . . I thought that it was my fault. What did I do to make him think he could do something like that?

Lori did not go to the police, but did finally go back to work at a restaurant where she was employed. Eric came to the restaurant and harassed and teased her with taunts like "I guess you didn't get enough." Eventually Lori dropped out of college and moved to another town in order to get away from Eric's harassment and the pain of the date rape.

Sadly, Lori's experience is not unusual. Many men expect sex in return for a nice evening, and the use of alcohol on the part of men like Eric makes this type of date rape easier to carry out. This case also shows the typical pattern of seduction by stages, and the casual air of the man after the attack, as though he did not get the message. He even came by to see Lori at the restaurant, apparently to get her to date him again. We see here too the woman wondering whether the rape was her own fault, a reaction that is fostered by the casual way many in this society view such rapes. Most significant in this type of blatant sex discrimination is the tremendous price that women pay. Not only was this young woman hurt psychologically in ways she will never forget, but also the pain and fear generated in her changed her life's plans. The huge waste that sexism brings is clearly indicated in cases of date rape.

Few rapists are convicted. Studies in selected cities in the 1980s put the prosecution rate at low figures of 14 percent to 17 percent of all rapes. One recent estimate is that "less than 40 percent of reported rapes result in arrest, and only three percent of these in convictions."[22] The same report estimated that at least 12.1 million American women have been victims of rape. At least that many more have been victims of attempted rape. Informed estimates suggest that, depending on the year and place, 30 to 70 percent of all rapes are not reported. This statistic is ironic in that there is a view among many men that women rush to false accusations of rape, a belief sometimes used to justify excessive evidence requirements in rape cases. Yet a victim of assault or robbery does not, under the law, have to prove that he or she resisted or that the act involved the use of physical force. The fear of men that women freely accuse their male dates or lovers of rape is not supported by research studies.[23]

Under pressure from women's rights groups, numerous state legislatures have changed their rape laws. Since the 1970s, many state laws have been changed to get rid of the requirement that women prove they fought back physically or the requirement that extensive evidence corroborating the woman's story be presented. In some states the term "rape" has even been replaced by "sexual assault" to make it easier for victims to report what has happened to them. Most states have passed shield laws preventing the prior sexual experience of the rape victim from being introduced as evidence in a trial. Yet these changes have come on a piecemeal basis. Most importantly, in many areas there is still a lack of vigorous enforcement of the rape laws.

Numerous rape studies have demonstrated that rape is typically not a crime of sexual passion but rather a crime of violence directed against women. Such violent actions are an extreme extension of the values of a sexist culture that encourages in many males, both the young and the old, an aggressive orientation toward subordinating women sexually and otherwise. Today, the pornography industry has become very successful by using violence against or domination of women in its magazines and films. On occasion, for example, music groups such as 2 Live Crew and some of the "gansta" rappers have extolled rape or other antifemale violence as a way of keeping women "in line." Rape creates a fear for many women that infects their daily lives. The fear engendered in women by the threat of rape is similar to the fear of wife beating. Both fears have broader social consequences in pressuring women to accept subordination and degradation across a number of institutional areas.

DISCRIMINATION: EMPLOYMENT OUTSIDE THE HOME

Blatant employment discrimination is widespread in the United States and can be found in almost every workplace, be it private or public. We give emphasis to the workplace here because it is the place where women are increasingly spending very large portions of their lives.

Segregating Women Workers

The proportion of women in the work force has risen steadily for several decades. By the early 1990s, women made up nearly half of the civilian labor force, with *three quarters* of the women between the ages of 25 and 55 working outside the home. In 1992, there were about 100 million women over the age of 16, and 58 million of them were employed outside the home.[24]

Women's reasons for working in the paid labor force have sometimes been trivialized; some authors in the popular media and some men feel that women, particularly married women, work only for "extra (pin) money" or for personal fulfillment rather than economic necessity. Even the successes accompanying the women's movements since the 1960s have been unable to eradicate negative attitudes toward women's work, attitudes that support this society's entrenched patriarchal system and reduce the decent-paying jobs available to women.[25]

Today, most women in the labor force are employed in traditional occupations. Many U.S. occupations are gender-typed; they are predominantly male or female in composition. The segregation of job categories by gender reflects to a substantial degree institutionalized patterns of blatant discrimination. For example, in a typical office building of a major corporation the workers tend to fall into four broad categories:

1. The managers—mostly male
2. The secretarial staff—almost entirely female
3. The technical staff—mixed, with better-paying positions dominated by males
4. The janitorial staff—dominated by minority workers, many of whom are minority women

Gender segregation is commonplace in all types of corporate and governmental organizations, so much so that it seems to many Americans to be the "natural order of things." Yet this job sorting is *not* natural; it is an unnatural order reflecting the historical and contemporary institutionalization of gender discrimination. Job categories have been intentionally segregated. For example, as late as 1920 most clerical work in the United States was done by men, and as recently as 1950 about 40 percent of clerical employees were male. By 1980, however, only 20 percent of all clerical employees were male.[26] In the 1990s, this pattern continues, with about a fifth of clerical jobs being held by men. Moreover, in some of the major subcategories within the official census bureau category called "clerical" (or, most recently, "administrative support including clerical") the male proportion is much less. For example, in a previous chapter we noted that only *2 percent* of secretaries, stenographers, and typists are male workers. Male clerical workers are most common among clerical supervisors, computer equipment operators, and personnel or order clerks. This shift over the twentieth century was substantially intentional and resulted in a decline in wages paid to certain clerical employees such as secretaries. Today, men work in far more types of occupations than women, who are heavily concentrated in a few dozen of the 500 or so major job categories in the United States.

The Occupational Gap

Table 4.1 shows the percentage of women workers in selected major occupational categories charted by the U.S. Bureau of Labor Statistics for employed persons.[27] While there have been increases in the proportions of

TABLE 4.1.   Percentage of Women Workers in Selected Major Occupational
Categories (1992)

	PERCENTAGE OF WOMEN
Engineers	8.5
Lawyers and judges	21.4
Librarians	87.6
Physicians	20.4
Dentists	8.5
Registered nurses	94.3
Dental assistants	98.6
Elementary school teachers	85.4
Executives, managers, administrators	41.5
Sales workers, retail and personal service	65.5
Secretaries, stenographers, typists	98.4
Receptionists	97.3
Precision production, craft, and repair	8.6
Transportation and material moving	8.8
Food service workers	59.0
Private household (maids, servants)	95.9

women in nontraditional job categories in the last decade (for example, engineers), the longitudinal data show slow changes in traditional job segregation. The proportions of females remain low among engineers, lawyers, physicians, and craft workers. Women are also rare among top capitalists and in the middle and upper-managerial levels in big corporations. In recent years, some media and scholarly commentators have suggested that women are moving up and are closing the occupational gap with men. Yet the gap is actually closing slowly, in part because the movement of women into traditionally-male jobs has been equaled or exceeded by the movement of new women workers into the traditional female-typed jobs. Today most women work in jobs that are mostly female, and relatively few women are found in the traditionally male categories with the highest earnings.

Because of segregation and discrimination in employment patterns, women as a group receive less pay than men do. According to the U.S. Labor Department, 70 percent of minimum-wage workers are women. In 1991, the median income of all women 15 years old and over in the paid labor force ($10,476) was just over half that of their male counterparts ($20,469). Among full-time, year-round workers 25 years old and over, women's median income ($22,045) was only 70 percent that of men ($31,613), and the median incomes of African American women ($14,660) and Latino women ($11,591) were even lower.[28]

Gains in educational and employment opportunities in recent decades have narrowed the gap in men's and women's earnings very little. In the mass media, successful women often "serve to mystify the reality of the majority of women, leading many to think that women are doing better than they are and others to aspire to goals that are achievable only for the very few."[29]

TABLE 4.2.   Comparison of Incomes of Full-time, Year-round Male and Female
              Workers (1991)

EDUCATION	MEN	WOMEN	PERCENT
Less than 9 years	$17,623	$12,066	68%
High School			
1–3 years	$21,402	14,455	68%
4 years	$26,779	18,837	70%
College			
1–3 years	$31,663	22,143	70%
4 years	$40,906	29,087	71%
Professional degree	$73,996	46,742	63%
Doctorate degree	$57,187	43,303	76%

Comparable Pay for Comparable Work?

It is commonly said that market capitalism pays people what they are worth. Yet job evaluation studies looking at the skill, effort, responsibility, and productivity of jobs suggest that this is a myth. Regardless of their worth in terms of objective job evaluations, women's jobs are usually paid less than comparable men's jobs. In defending this blatant inequality, many employers argue that they are not really discriminating, that women are paid less because they are less qualified in education and experience. Yet when educational level is examined, we find that some of the best-educated women have the worst earnings relative to men (see Table 4.2).[30] In no case do women do better than 76 percent, and that at the doctoral level. Increased education, as can be seen in the case of those with a professional degree, does not necessarily increase women's equality to men in terms of income. The bottom line on gender discrimination is that as a group women earn only about 70 percent of what men earn.

Significantly, during the Kennedy administration, the Equal Pay Act (1963) was passed, and although some employers have moved to implement the law on their own, the federal government has not enforced this law vigorously. The federal law does not require equal pay for work that is comparable but not exactly equal. Still, some states like Minnesota and Massachusetts have state laws that do mandate equal pay for comparable work. Thus, in a 1992 court case dealing with this type of law, a Massachusetts judge declared that the women employees in cafeteria jobs in a Boston-area school system had to be compensated as well as the men who served as custodians.[31] The cafeteria workers, all of whom were women, had gotten only $6.35 an hour, while the men received $11.50 an hour. Wages had to more nearly equalized because the skills required were roughly comparable.

In 1982, the state government of Minnesota adopted an equal-pay-for-equal-work law for workers at all levels of government. A mid-1990s study found that the law had improved women's wages in government by more than 10 percent. A half dozen states now have similar pay-equity laws.[32]

Even the opponents of equal pay for comparable work admit that the "prevailing market" sets lower wages and salaries for women. Because this differential is so widespread, these conservatives argue, it cannot be gender discrimination. Yet differential pay for the same work is by definition gender discrimination of an overt and harmful type. Indeed, a major argument is that it would be too costly to pay women a fair wage equal to comparable male-typed jobs. A new employer or an employer expanding operations usually accepts the prevailing market wage rates for women and the prevailing market segregation of jobs. In other words, employers accept and perpetuate the sexism long built into job markets. Blatant discrimination yesterday means blatant discrimination today. One major goal of many affirmative action programs is to fight such widespread gender discrimination.

SPECIFIC DISCRIMINATORY PRACTICES

What are the specific discriminatory mechanisms that help shape the subordination of women in the job sphere? We will deal with subtle and covert examples in the next two chapters. Here we will examine some of the blatant discriminatory mechanisms.

The Workplace

Recall an issue we discussed briefly in Chapter 3, that of the attempts at exclusion of women reporters in the sports world. We noted that in 1990 reporter Lisa Olson reported that several New England Patriots exposed their genitals and made lewd remarks while she was conducting an interview. Other reporters have faced similar problems. For example, Jennifer Frey of the *Detroit Free Press* requested an interview with Detroit Tigers pitcher Jack Morris. Morris replied, "I don't talk to women when I am naked unless they are on top of me or I am on top of them." Tigers president Bo Schembechler admitted that Morris's comments were out of line, but also said that sending a woman into the locker room showed a "lack of common sense." Sportswriter Jeannie Roberts, formerly of the *Tallahassee Democrat,* said it was not unusual during college football interviews to have jockstraps and towels "accidentally" thrown at her, and her fellow (male) reporters would pretend that they didn't see anything. This harassment makes doing one's job difficult. The hostility toward women sports writers was summed up by Frank Defore, a former senior writer at *Sports Illustrated,* who was named Sportswriter of the Year six times. "We [men] think we need you [women] for procreation and recreation, but we don't need you for sports."[33]

Often, women do not complain about blatant discrimination because "they won't hire women if they think it's one long problem. . . . Plus, you don't want to be perceived as a complainer."[34] According to *Time* correspondent Melissa Ludtke, who won the case that gave women sportswriters access to interview players in 1978:

> The locker-room incidents are a stark and valuable reminder that the battles that I and others waged for equality in the 1970s didn't bring an end to discrim-

ination. They only kept the more overt forms from showing. . . . Stereotypical, outmoded and confining images of women, not at all suited to the reality of their actual lives, still pop up and sting us.[35]

In many work contexts, women are not hired for certain kinds of positions, or are hired in much smaller proportions than men. The problem is often one of blatant *exclusion*. In 1993, for example, the Equal Employment Opportunity Commission instituted legal proceedings in a Miami court alleging that since the mid-1960s a prominent Miami restaurant had intentionally discriminated "against women as a class." In order to screen women out of jobs the restaurant "used word-of-mouth hiring and subjective employment interviews to discourage women from applying for jobs."[36] Exclusion by gender can be found in many workplaces. A major study of Hollywood writers found that "in terms of the number of women writers being hired, there has been little growth over the past 20 years. As of 1991, women accounted for 22–25 percent of those employed in television and 16–17 percent of those working in film. Yet women have consistently accounted for 20–25 percent of the industry's workforce in the last two decades."[37] Women writers generally got much less compensation for their Hollywood work than did the men. This pattern has been found in numerous employment settings, including those of insurance agents (see below).

Even in the U.S. Congress, women have not been allowed to move into better-paying jobs to the degree that men have. One Gannett News Service study found that "women hold three out of five congressional jobs on lawmakers' personal staffs, but they mostly populate the back-office desks in clerical positions. . . . only about one-third of House and Senate administrative assistants—the staff bosses—are women."[38]

In addition, women who made it to the higher-level administrative positions still averaged lower salaries than their male counterparts. The pay gaps persist for women staffers even though on the average they have more experience than the men. Particularly important to note here is that this employment discrimination is actually *legal*, because Congress has (as of mid–1994) exempted itself from federal sex discrimination laws.

Employment agencies may play a role in the sex discrimination faced by women seeking jobs. In a midwestern city, one researcher, posing as an employer, called a dozen employment agencies and asked for a saleswoman "with the right image who will fit in—someone attractive and under twenty-five." Nine of the twelve agencies violated the law by accepting this request to discriminate against older women. Similarly, agencies will take orders based on hair color ("get me a blonde") and "good looks."[39] In the 1990s, the EEOC has filed sex (and racial) discrimination suits against certain employment agencies that discriminate against their own workers or job applicants. Some agencies have developed special code words to allow employers to ask only for certain kinds of workers and to exclude others on the basis of sex or race.[40] Sexism in employment includes the "young woman" preference of some male decision makers. A recent study by the Massachusetts Commission

Against Discrimination sent women job seekers in their twenties and over forty to a number of businesses. Four major firms were found to discriminate in favor of the younger women, who were more likely than the older women to be offered full-time positions with serious promotion chances.[41]

In the early 1990s, women held more than 40 percent of all jobs in corporate America that are called "managerial." However, this label is misleading because many of these jobs, such as clerical supervisors, are not what most people think of as managerial. Indeed, less than 2 percent of senior-level management positions are held by women. Some research on women in the white-collar workplace has found a "glass ceiling"—the several types of intentional discrimination, including salary inequalities and differential promotion criteria, that are used to block the upward mobility of women (see Chapter 1). A number of commentators and researchers have noted how women have to be superwomen to move up in the corporate setting. Stereotyped views harbored by male executives that male workers will not work under women supervisors and that women workers are supposed to "serve" men have hindered promotion opportunities.[42]

Many white women seeking promotions in corporations often encounter this glass ceiling. Yet the barriers confronting women of color are even worse, what some have called the "concrete wall." In regard to promotions, according to knowledgeable management consultants, black women are well behind white women. In the early 1990s, only 3 percent of all corporate managers, and less than 1 percent of those in top management positions, were African American women. In Ella Bell and Stella Nkomo's in-depth study of white and African American women's experiences in management, black women reported receiving less support for career advancement from their bosses, less acceptance by their colleagues, and less authority in their jobs than did their white counterparts.[43]

The established hierarchical structure of contemporary white-collar jobs, such as women in clerical work and men in higher management, makes it difficult for many women in clerical jobs to get promotions to other types of positions. While recruitment from the outside varies from one company to another, it is generally the case that once a woman is locked into certain job tracks, such as secretarial or other clerical lines, it is difficult for her to move into higher-level supervisory and management lines.

In 1992, the State Farm insurance company had to provide more than $157 million to victims in settlement of a major class-action lawsuit, the largest settlement ever for a discrimination case that fell under Title VII of the 1964 Civil Rights Act. The gender discrimination at State Farm reportedly took the form of favoring male over female trainee agents. Beginning in the late 1970s, Muriel Kraszewski, an office manager for State Farm, tried to move up in the company by asking to become a sales trainee, but was told there were no positions available to her, even though less qualified men were being brought into some trainee slots. She filed a court suit in the mid-1980s, which became a class-action suit on behalf of all female applicants who had been turned down. In some situations, as the trial testimony indicated, women were told the company did not hire women as trainees or that they were "too attractive" to be an insurance agent. The company was shown to have an almost all-female clerical work force and an almost all-male agent force.[44] What was most damaging was perhaps the climate created by the fact that State Farm policy was established and maintained almost entirely by male decision makers. Wallach and Bernstein note, "The underrepresentation of women gave rise to an all-male image and attitude that was reflected even in the company's recruitment brochures . . . The pool of prospective applicants, drawn informally from agency managers' and directors' business, social and family contacts, was almost exclusively men."[45] A California federal district court ruled that the State Farm company was in violation of the civil rights law. In damage hearings, some women received large amounts of back pay; and in 1992, a huge general settlement was made to the 1,000 women who had made claims.

In a 1992 court ruling, Lucky Stores Inc. was found to have practiced gender discrimination. The case involved thousands of women employees in California stores who had been "channeled into lower-paid positions."[46] The judge found that "Sex discrimination was the standard operating procedure at Lucky with respect to placement, promotion, movement to full-time positions and the allocation of additional hours."[47] Women had been hired disproportionately in lower-paying areas, often making $5 to $6 less than the men in other departments, and were hired into jobs with fewer chances for full-time work and job advancement.

Today there are many problems of sexism in the U.S. workplace. Women clerical employees can be demoted or fired simply because of their subordinate tie to a particular male manager or professional. When a male boss leaves, his male replacement may fire his inherited secretary, preferring his "own woman." This type of managerial empire building can also involve male employees, but because of the peculiarly patriarchal character of the manager-secretary relationship, women seem to be the most likely victims. For example, a very experienced and respected 54-year-old secretary found the following situation when she got a new boss:

> I liked my job and I worked hard, staying late to get things done. Everyone said how competent I was. My trouble began when I got a new boss, who began to pick at little things, saying I talked too much on the phone. . . . Finally I received a scathing memo from him which made it clear I'd have to quit. I was stunned. I had so much experience and knew so many things about that place. . . . It could have been my age, or the benefits I was getting because of my experience, or it could be he wanted a younger woman to chase around the desk."[48]

Job Conditions: Sexual Harassment

A major example of intentional, well-institutionalized gender discrimination can be seen in studies and surveys of harassment. Sexual harassment is widespread and usually intentional. In a recent survey in Seattle, for example, just under half of the women surveyed, all of whom were working for the city government, said they had been victims of sex discrimination, including sexual harassment. Almost all the black women surveyed (90 percent) indicated that they had experienced racial or gender discrimination.[49]

Even when women feel they have made some progress, they can encounter mixed messages about their contributions because of sexual harassment, which can take many forms. For example, Susan Solomon is an atmospheric chemist at the National Oceanic and Atmospheric Administration in Boulder, Colorado. In 1986, she was the first to propose how chlorofluorocarbons could cause a hole in the ozone layer. Her discovery led to international bans on the use of CFCs and numerous prestigious awards, including the Department of Commerce's gold medal for "impeccable science in the cause of humankind." Nonetheless, in Antarctica, where Solomon led a team of 18 men, she got two distinctly different impressions of how men view women in science:

> We were flown down to the Antarctic on Navy aircraft, and our pilot came swaggering in in his flight suit. He looked at us and said, "Who's in charge here?" And I said, "I am." He was taken aback for a second, but then he said, "Good for you." . . . In Antarctica, we were the first new people that the over-winter team had seen in about 6 months. I was assigned a dorm room, which didn't have curtains, so I tacked up some cardboard and began to get undressed when I heard this squeak in the snow right outside my window. And sure enough, there was a Peeping Tom—welcoming me to Antarctica. So there I was in my bra and long underwear thinking, "I bet this didn't happen to anyone else in my group."[50]

That sexual harassment is now commonplace in the workplace has been revealed in numerous local and national surveys. A recent Korn/Ferry survey of high-level female business executives found that six in ten had been sexually harassed in the workplace.[51] Even women working in religious organizations face serious discrimination. Surveying women rabbis across the country, one research study found seven in ten had to contend with sexual harassment.[52]

Sadly, a job is sometimes a "prize" men give to women workers if the women permit sexual harassment. Like wife battering and rape, sexual harassment and extortion at work are just now coming out of the closet. Sexual harassment has been defined as the "unsolicited nonreciprocal male behavior that asserts a woman's sex role over her function as a worker."[53] More specifically, the EEOC has defined sexual harassment as all unwelcome sexual advances, requests for sexual favors, and other conduct of a sexual nature when (1) submission to such conduct is made a condition of a woman's employment or academic advancement; (2) submission to or rejection of such conduct by a woman is used as a basis for employment decisions or academic decisions affecting the individual; or (3) such conduct has the purpose or effect of unreasonably interfering with a woman's work or academic performance or creating an intimidating work environment.[54]

The mechanisms and practices of harassment include touching, staring at, or making jokes about a woman's body, nonreciprocated requests for sexual intercourse, and actual rape at work. For example, in a 1992 court case a female dispatcher at a Middle Atlantic college presented evidence of sexual harassment by the men in her campus security unit. She charged that her male supervisor had made her employment dependent upon providing quid pro quo sexual favors. According to her testimony, after acquiescing in the harassment to get the job, once she became a permanent employee, she fought the sexual advances, but was still a victim of harassment. The judge agreed that she had made a case that she faced a hostile work environment because of the continuing sexual harassment,[55] but ruled that the college had taken proper action in response to her complaints of discrimination.

A recent survey of 60 women wardens in state prisons found that half had been the victims of sexual harassment and other forms of discrimination. Six in ten had also been present when other female prison workers were victims of sex discrimination.[56] Women working in prisons have faced harassment not only from male prisoners but also from male guards and other male personnel. One female guard at a midwestern facility noted that the male personnel "would pinch you on the behind or talk down to you or act like they owned you. You'd get more respect from the inmates."[57]

Verbal abuse can lead to even more serious abuse. One young file clerk reported that her boss regularly asked her to come into his office "to tell me the intimate details of his marriage and to ask what I thought about different sexual positions." The implications were serious. Physical contact ranges from repeated "accidental" contacts to rape. One woman worker noted that "My boss . . . runs his hand up my leg or blouse. He hugs me to him and then tells me that he is 'just naturally affectionate.'"[58]

Sexual harassment is also a barrier faced by women in college and university environments. Thus, one study of sexual harassment at Harvard University found that one third of the female undergraduates, four in ten of the female graduate students, and half the nontenured female faculty members reported being sexually harassed, with harassment ranging from sexist jokes to sexual assault. Again, most said they had not reported the sexist attacks because they feared reprisals or felt that nothing could be done.[59] In a study of 208 faculty members and 314 graduate students at a West Coast university, Louise Fitzgerald and Alayne Ormerod found that men and women had different definitions of and reactions to sexual harassment. Again, while many men considered such everyday behavior as sexual harassment, seductive behavior, and sexist remarks and jokes as "acceptable or even funny," women felt humiliated, angry, or intimidated.[60] What is seen as normal by many men may be seen as repulsive or menacing by many women. Many men are often out of touch with the damage they do to women.

Men can also be the victims in antifemale discrimination, especially if they engage in nonsexist behavior:

> Jerry Marsden of Berkeley, winner of the 1990 Norbert Wiener prize—the top prize in applied math—says, "I had a female graduate student who wrote a fine thesis. Around the time it was being completed, a graduate student told me that is was 'common knowledge' that I wrote her thesis for her in exchange for sexual favors—which of course was not true."[61]

One of the problems with this type of sexist gossip is that respected male faculty members might be wary of working with talented women graduate students and women faculty because they want to avoid rumors of sexual entanglements. Women, on the other hand, might refrain from working with talented, receptive, and "liberated" male faculty and employers because of the widespread suspicion that women can succeed only by sleeping with influential or powerful men.

OTHER EXAMPLES OF BLATANT DISCRIMINATION

We do not have the space here to describe in any detail the many other types of overt discrimination that women face in such areas as housing, law, and politics, but we can give a few brief examples.

The Case of Housing

Discrimination against women in the housing arena has been commonplace. Recently a woman wrote to the *Los Angeles Times* asking if the discrimination she had suffered in a particular housing search was illegal. When she finally found an apartment near her place of employment, the landlord said he would not let her have the apartment "because women use too much electricity drying their hair." Although this kind of sex discrimination is indeed illegal under existing federal housing laws, it is nonetheless widespread. The fair housing laws are only weakly enforced.[62] In most areas intentional discrimination by landlords and real estate brokers against white women is less common than in the case of women (and men) of color but it remains a serious problem. When it comes to the growing number of single women, both white and nonwhite, who are seeking to buy housing with or without children, discrimination regularly rears its ugly head.

Misconceptions abound in the real estate industry with regard to single female renters or homeowners. Single women are believed to be poor credit risks by many male decision makers; women are stereotyped as having less business sense than men. Their incomes are thought to be unstable, and there is a fear that they will become pregnant and lose their jobs. Late in 1992, a Virginia federal court ruled that a woman had suffered sex discrimination at the hands of a real estate agent who worked for an apartment complex. The apartment was advertised as a decent place to rent at $600 per month. Seeing the listing, the woman, who was a single mother, applied for the apartment, but was rejected by the agent. The apartment was subsequently leased to two men for only $580. Angry over the poor treatment, the single mother sued and won. "According to the court opinion, the agent said that she would not rent to the single mother because she was a woman and because of a bad experience in the past with boyfriends of single women."[63] The jury in the district court decided that this was overt discrimination on the part of the agent but not the landlord. However, when the case was appealed, the higher court ruled that the owner of the apartment complex was also culpable.

In the area of housing it is often low-income women, especially mothers with children, who face the most housing discrimination. A recent field audit study by the Massachusetts Commission Against Discrimination (MCAD) found that low-income women faced gendered discrimination in several different apartment complexes in the Boston metropolitan area. Some testers sent to the complexes by MCAD presented themselves as low-income renters and were refused housing, even though other testers who posed as better-off renters were told housing was available in the same complexes. In this case, social class entered into the equation because the low-income women (who were said to have the federal rent certificates) were considered by the white landlords to be potential problems. An MCAD fair housing official put it this way: "Landlords figure they have to do more when they rent to a person with a Section 8 certificate. The place has to be inspected by the health department and it has to be up to code. . . . Renting to a subsidized tenant does require more from the landlord, but the law forbids discrimination."[64] Many single women, including those separated or divorced, must depend on rental property because of their lower incomes and the difficulties they experience in obtaining mortgage loans.

The Legal and Political Arenas

Women face much discrimination in our political and legal institutions. Few women are appointed or elected to judgeships in the United States. For example, only in the last decade have women been appointed to the U.S. Supreme Court. The only two women *ever* appointed in U.S. history (Sandra Day O'Connor and Ruth Bader Ginsburg) are currently serving. State courts show similar patterns. For example, in Ohio there is only one female justice on the state Supreme Court, and just one on the First District Court of Appeals. In Kentucky, there is not one female justice on the state Supreme Court and only one on the Court of Appeals.[65] Nearby Indiana is even worse, with no female judges on any of the state's major courts. One reporter noted that only "9.5 percent of judges serving the Tri-State area are women, which is just about the national average."[66] In the mid-1990s, three dozen states were reportedly conducting some type of investigation of gender bias in their legal or judicial systems.

In every state in the union, female judges or lawyers have reported sex discrimination in their everyday rounds in the legal system. The U.S. Court of Appeals for the Ninth Circuit has handed down a number of important cases in favor of women who were pursuing sex discrimination complaints. Yet, a research study in the Ninth Circuit revealed that women lawyers often faced serious sexual harassment and other forms of gendered discrimination. Six in ten among the 900 women lawyers surveyed said they had suffered sexual harassment, and 6 percent said this unwanted sexual attention came from male judges. In addition, 37 percent reported that male judges "sometimes cut off presentations by women more abruptly than those of men." And one third reported that "they had seen judges address female lawyers less professionally than men."[67] The problems of women in the law, including both lawyers and judges, are serious not only in the pain that is caused for the victims but also in the corrosiveness of this sexism for a legal system that in theory provides "liberty and justice for all."

The Double Discrimination Faced by Lesbian Women

Lesbians have to deal not only with blatant sex discrimination but also with blatant homophobia. Most Americans are ambivalent about the rights of gay men and lesbians. According to a recent *Newsweek* poll, 78 percent of those sampled said that homosexuals should have equal rights in job opportunities. However, 45 percent said that expanding gay rights is a threat to the American family and values, and 61 percent disapproved of adoption rights for homosexual partners.[68]

Even though the majority of Americans support homosexual job rights in principle, many people are still fired from jobs because of their sexual orientation:

> [Mary] was among a dozen or more gay and lesbian workers fired last year from a Cracker Barrel restaurant, a chain with headquarters in Tennessee. Out of the blue, the company announced that it would no longer employ people "whose sexual preferences fail to demonstrate normal heterosexual values which have been the foundation of families in our society." With no gay anti-discrimination laws on the Georgia books, even the ACLU refused to represent [Mary] in court.[69]

There is no federal law protecting gays and lesbians from blatant exclusion—from losing their jobs, being evicted from their homes, or being denied a bank loan. Even in companies that prohibit gay bashing, the atmosphere among coworkers can be oppressive. For example, a lesbian who worked as an auditor for a major bank said that a colleague would shake her body in a repulsed manner as she passed her desk, and that "any time I walked into the ladies' room and she was there, she would walk out."[70]

In higher education, similarly, many lesbian students feel that they are targets of homophobic discrimination: Many faculty tell "queer jokes," lesbian and gay history courses are omitted from the curriculum, and gay and lesbian students often have no right to hold meetings using campus facilities even when similar student organizations get budgets, meeting spaces, and advertising in the college or university newspapers.[71]

In the United States, gender discrimination continues to take many forms, from blatant to covert, from individual to institutionalized, from economic to political and legal. All forms operate, often in a cumulative fashion, to keep a woman "in her place." We have seen in this chapter that blatant sexist discrimination is still very much a part of a supposedly civilized America. Now we will turn to less obvious, but no less serious, types of subtle and covert discrimination.

NOTES

1. Nijole V. Benokraitis, *Marriages and Families* (Englewood Cliffs, NJ: Prentice Hall, 1993), pp. 304–305.

2. R. LaRossa, "Fatherhood and Social Change," *Family Relations* (1988), 37, pp. 451–457.

3. Jim Hickey, *World News Tonight,* ABC News, November 10, 1993.

4. "Same Old Script? Critics: Sexism Still Thrives in Ads," *USA Today,* March 22, 1993, p. 4B.

5. Jeffry Scott, "Selling with Sexism," *Atlanta Journal and Constitution,* November 24, 1991, p. H1.

6. Patricia Horn, "Beating Back the Revolution," *Dollars & Sense,* December 1992, pp. 12–13, 21–22.

7. Anastasia Toufexis, "Home Is Where the Hurt Is," *Time,* December 21, 1987, p. 68; George Colt, "Stop! For God's Sake Stop!" *Life,* October 1988, pp. 121–131.

8. Colt, "Stop! For God's Sake Stop!" p. 130; "Spouse Beaters: The Handcuff Cure," *U.S. News & World Report,* March 2, 1987, p. 12.

9. U.S. Bureau of the Census, *Statistical Abstract of the United States: 1991,* Washington, DC, 1992, p. 176; Lisa D. Bastian and Marshall M. DeBerry, Jr., *National Crime Victimization Survey Report: Criminal Victimization 1990,* Washington, DC, 1991, pp. 3, 5; see also Irene Lacher, "The Rape Debate," *Los Angeles Times,* October 17, 1993, p. E1.

10. Judy Mann, "Combat in the Professional Zone," *Washington Post,* July 3, 1992, p. E3.

11. Marybeth Hendricks-Matthews, "Caring for Victims of Childhood Sexual Abuse," *Journal of Family Practice,* 35 (November, 1992), p. 5.

12. See Mary Ellen Fromuth, "The Relationship of Childhood Sexual Abuse with Later Psychological and Sexual Adjustment in a Sample of College Women," *Child Abuse and Neglect* 10 (1986), pp. 5–15; Christopher Bagley and R. Ramsay, "Sexual Abuse in Childhood: Psychosocial Outcomes and Implications for Social Work Practice," *Journal of Social Work and Human Sexuality* 4 (1986), pp. 33–47; Diana Russell, "The Incidence and Prevalence of Intrafamilial and Extrafamilial Sexual Assault of Female Children," *Child Abuse and Neglect* 7 (1983), pp. 143–146.

13. Janan Hanna, "Endless Energy and Time Make Volunteer Special," *Chicago Tribune,* December 24, 1992, Northwest Zone, p. 2.

14. Henry Giarretto, *Integrated Treatment of Child Sexual Abuse* (Palo Alto, CA: Science and Behavior Books, 1982).

15. Carol Rambo Ronai, "Multiple Reflections of Child Sex Abuse: An Argument for a Layered Account," University of Florida, unpublished manuscript, 1993.

16. Carol Innerst, "Campus Crime Detailed," *Washington Times,* January 20, 1993, p. A3.

17. Toby Simon, "Sexuality on Campus—'90s Style; Survey Results," *Change* 25, September 1993, p. 50.

18. Robin Warshaw, *I Never Called It Rape* (New York: Harper & Row, 1988), pp. 3–16.

19. "USD Plans Mock Date Rape Trial with Student Actors, Law Students," PR Newswire, February 25, 1992.

20. For the critique, see Katie Roiphe, *The Morning After: Sex, Fear, and Feminism on Campus* (Little, Brown, 1993).

21. Warshaw, *I Never Called It Rape,* pp. 14–18.

22. The data are in Michael Parenti, *Land of Idols* (New York: St. Martin's Press, 1993), as cited in Abbas Milani, "Litany from the Left," *San Francisco Chronicle,* February 13, 1994, Sunday Review, p. 7.

23. Timothy Harper, "Legal View of Rape," *Dallas Morning News,* May 18, 1984, p. C2.

24. Institute for Women's Policy Research, "Research-in-Brief: Are Mommies Dropping Out of the Labor Force? No!" April 1992, pp. 1–2; U.S. Bureau of Labor Statistics, *Employment and Earnings,* Washington, DC, January 1992, p. 162; Barbara Presley Noble, "At Work: The New Equality in Hard Times," *New York Times,* August 8, 1993, Section 3, p. 25.

25. See Dorothy Miller, *Women and Social Welfare: A Feminist Analysis* (New York: Praeger, 1990), pp. 66–130.

26. Evelyn Nakano Glenn and Roslyn L. Feldberg, "Clerical Work: The Female Occupation," in Freeman, Women (1984), pp. 317–320.

27. U.S. Bureau of the Census, *Statistical Abstract of the United States: 1993* (Washington, DC, 1993), pp. 405–408.

28. Ibid, pp. 185–190.

29. Miller, *Women and Social Welfare: A Feminist Analysis,* p. 67.

30. U.S. Bureau of the Census, "Money Income of Households, Families, and Persons in the United States: 1991," *Current Population Reports,* Series P-60, no. 180, Washington, DC, 1992, pp. 94–95.

31. Robert J. Ambrogi, "Comparable Work Must Get Equal Pay, Judge Decides; Ruling Puts Spotlight on Rarely Used State Law," *Massachusetts Lawyers Weekly,* August 24, 1992, p. 2.

32. Carol Kleiman, "Comparable Pay Could Create Jobs," *Orlando Sentinel,* October 13, 1993, p. C5.

33. Cited in Lisa Rubarth, "Twenty Years After Title IX: Women in Sports Media," JOPERD, March 1992, pp. 53–55.

34. Ibid., p. 55.

35. Melissa Ludtke, "They Use Bathrobes," *Time,* October 15, 1990, p. 97.

36. "EEOC Accuses Restauranteurs of Sexual Discrimination," *The Legal Intelligencer,* June 9, 1993, p. 5.

37. Kathleen O'Steen, "White Male Pens Still Busiest; Study Finds Hollywood Lags in Hiring Minority, Female Writers," *Daily Variety,* June 15, 1993, p. 1.

38. Pamela Brogan, "Glass Houses—Study: Strong Gender Bias Exists in Congressional Jobs," Gannett News Service, December 14, 1993.

39. Ellen Cassedy and Karen Nussbaum, *9 to 5: The Working Woman's Guide to Office Survival* (New York: Penguin Books, 1983), pp. 121–123.

40. Bureau of National Affairs, "Today's Summary and Analysis," *Daily Labor Report*, December 14, 1993, p. d2.

41. Karen Levine, "MCAD Charges Businesses with Bias," *Massachusetts Lawyers Weekly,* January 31, 1994, p. 2.

42. J. A. Jacobs, "Women's Entry into Management," *Administrative Science Quarterly* 37 (1992), pp. 282–301; J. Fierman, "Why Women Still Don't Hit the Top," *Fortune,* July 30, 1990, pp. 40–62; A. M. Morrison, R. P. White, E. Van Velsor, and Center for Creative Leadership, *Breaking the Glass Ceiling: Can Women Reach the Top of America's Largest Corporations?* (Reading, MA: Addison-Wesley, 1987).

43. Ella Louise Bell and Stella M. Nkomo, "The Glass Ceiling vs. the Concrete Wall: Career Perceptions of White and African American Women Managers," unpublished paper, October 1992, pp. 16–25.

44. Eric J. Wallach and Richard F. Bernstein, "Discrimination Suit Raises the Stakes; Muriel Kraszewski Charges Sex Discrimination in State Farm General Insurance Co.'s Hiring Practices," Best's Review: Property-Casualty Insurance Edition, November 1992, Vol. 93, p. 72.

45. Ibid.

46. "Lucky Stores Guilty of Bias," *Sacramento Observer,* August 26, 1992, Vol. 29, p. G8. (The Ethnic News Watch.)

47. Quoted in ibid; see also Jamie Becket, "Lucky Promises Changes," *San Francisco Chronicle,* September 4, 1992, p. B1.

48. Cassedy and Nussbaum, *9 to 5*, p. 123.

49. Dick Lilly, "City Staff Survey Finds Harassment," *Seattle Times,* October 8, 1991, p. B3.

50. Virginia Morell, "Speaking Out, Susan Solomon," *Science,* March 13, 1992, p. 1387.

51. "Female Execs See Marketing as Fastest Track," *Sales & Marketing Management,* August 1993, p. 10.

52. "Survey Finds Most Women Rabbis Have Been Sexually Harassed on Job," United Press International, August 28, 1993.

53. Lin Farley, *Sexual Shakedown* (New York: McGraw-Hill Book Company, 1978), p. 14.

54. Ellen Bravo and Ellen Cassidy, *The 9 to 5 Guide to Combatting Sexual Harassment* (New York: Wiley, 1992), p. 24.

55. Steven P. Bann, "Sexual Harassment," *New Jersey Law Journal,* December 14, 1992, p. 59.

56. Susan Kuczka, "Female Jail Guards Fight Against Harassment by Male Colleagues," *Houston Chronicle,* October 17, 1993, p. A5.

57. Ibid.

58. Farley, *Sexual Shakedown,* p. 15; see Catherine A. MacKinnon, *Sexual Harassment of Working Women* (New Haven: Yale University Press, 1979), p. 29.

59. "Fair Harvard, Are You Fair?" *Time,* November 14, 1983, p. 109.

60. Louise F. Fitzgerald and Alayne J. Ormerod, "Perceptions of Sexual Harassment: the Influence of Gender and Academic Context," *Psychology of Women Quarterly* 15 (1991), pp. 281–294.

61. Selvin, "Mathematics . . . ." p. 1382.

62. "Rent Watch: Landlord Must Evict Drug-Selling Tenants," *Los Angeles Times,* February 6, 1994, p. K2.

63. Marc D. Jones, "Sex Discrimination in the Rental of Housing: Caveat Lessor II," *The Legal Intelligencer,* May 24, 1993, p. 6.

64. Alexander Reid, "MCAD Cites 4 Apartment Complexes for Bias Against Subsidized Tenants," *Boston Globe,* October 24, 1991, p. 33.

65. Karen M Lundegaard, "Judging Gender Bias," *Cincinnati Business Courier,* October 4, 1993, Section 1, p. 1.

66. Ibid.

67. Associated Press, "Court that Attacks Sex Bias Is Reported Often Guilty of It," *New York Times,* August 7, 1992, p. A17.

68. Bill Turque et. al., "Gays Under Fire," *Newsweek,* September 14, 1992, pp. 35–40.

69. Bob Cohn, "Discrimination: The Limits of the Law," *Newsweek,* September 14, 1992, pp. 38–39.

70. Bill Turque et al., "Gays Under Fire," pp. 38–39.

71. See, for example, Toni McNaron, "Making Life More Livable for Gays and Lesbians on Campus: Sightings from the Field," *Educational Record* 72:1, Winter 1991, pp. 19–22.

CHAPTER FIVE
HOW SUBTLE SEX DISCRIMINATION WORKS

A few years ago, Dr. Frances Conley, a respected brain surgeon, threatened to resign from her tenured professorship after 25 years at Stanford Medical School. She had put up with years of some of her male colleagues calling her "honey" in the operating room, fondling her legs under the table, and making demeaning or sexual comments:

> Medical students came forward with allegations of subtle sexual harassment and inappropriate comments and behavior by professors, including one alleged incident in which slides of *Playboy* centerfolds were used to "spice up" lectures. "I suddenly realized that things had not changed much," Dr. Conley said. "I had not realized how pervasive the sexism was. I couldn't brush it off. I couldn't pretend to be one of the boys any longer."[1]

Subtle sex discrimination is a slippery concept, difficult to define and measure, but it is very real and can be very harmful. Subtle sex discrimination has the following characteristics: (1) It can be intentional or unintentional; (2) it is visible but often goes unnoticed because it has been built into norms, values, and ideologies; (3) it is communicated both verbally and behaviorally; (4) it is usually informal rather than formal; and (5) it is most visible on the individual rather than on the organizational level.

We recognize that much of the subtle sex discrimination discussed in this chapter may seem rather blatant to some readers. That is, most feminists (both women and men), those who are very conscious of sex discrimination, may feel that some examples presented are pretty blatant. Remember, however, that the majority of Americans (including college students and faculty members) are not feminists, and their lack of sensitivity to subtle discrimination suggests why most do not take countering actions when they encounter such discriminatory practices. From our theoretical perspective both blatant and subtle discrimination entail differential treatment that is seriously damaging to the psyches, opportunities, and lives of the female targets and victims.

Nine types of subtle discrimination mechanisms are discussed in this chapter: condescending chivalry, supportive discouragement, friendly harassment, subjective objectification, radiant devaluation, liberated sexism, benevolent exploitation, considerate domination, and collegial exclusion. Although these mechanisms are not exhaustive, they illustrate some of the ways in which subtle sex discrimination works. In our categories of subtle discrimination, we are deliberately using oxymorons (figures of speech that combine incongruous terms) to emphasize the sexist behavior that seems friendly at face value but has pernicious consequences.

CONDESCENDING CHIVALRY

Condescending chivalry refers to superficially courteous behavior that is protective and paternalistic but treats women as subordinates. Because chivalrous behavior implies respect and affection, many men assume that referring to women as "little girl," "young lady," "little lady," and "kiddo" is a compliment—especially if the woman is over 30. Some women may be flattered by such terms of endearment. Yet, comparable references to men ("little boy," "little man") are considered insulting. Many women also feel that such language is demeaning:

> I find myself, usually in social situations, being embarrassed when men, particularly the older ones, remark about my being a "cute little thing" or say something like "isn't she a doll." I don't understand why they refer to me as if I am five instead of thirty-five! (Administrator in federal government)

A manager complained that "Exxon did an article about me as part of a report, and they described me as 'perky.' That's not how they would describe a man." Similarly, male attorneys don't refer to each other as "honey" in court. As a female security guard at a defense installation noted, men would never think of addressing men in the same ways they do women—for example, "Hey, sweetie, will you do this for me?" or "Be a dear and do this." Note that the sexism in such cases is so built into everyday routines that the men involved usually feel it is normal and natural.

In most cases, men assume that women need, want, or should want protection "for their own good." During a lunch with colleagues, for example, one of the authors was discussing prospective faculty who could fill a dean's position that was about to be vacated. The comments, from both male and female faculty, were instructive:

> Mary Ann is a very good administrator, but she plans to get married next year. I don't think she'll have time to be both a wife and a dean.
>
> Well, Susan has the respect of both faculty and administration, but hasn't she been talking about having children?
>
> Tracy's been a great faculty leader and she's done an outstanding job on committees, but she's got kids. What if they get sick when important decisions have to be made in the dean's office?
>
> Sara has been one of the best chairs in the college, a good researcher and can handle faculty. [A pause] On the other hand, now that her kids are grown, she probably wants some peace and quiet and wouldn't want to take on the headaches of a dean's office. . . .

In effect, and at every point of the life cycle, the female candidates were disqualified from serious consideration because it was assumed that women should stay in positions where their femininity, motherhood, and ability to fulfill wifely duties would remain intact.

Even when women are in positions of authority, their power may be undercut through "gentlemanly" condescension. For example, a dean in a business school complained that some male chairs refuse to take her seriously. When chairs are late in submitting schedules and she calls them into her office, some emphasize her gender and ignore her administrative power: "They do things like put their arm around me, smile, and say, 'You're getting prettier every day' or 'You shouldn't worry your pretty little head about these things.'"

Whether well-intentioned or malicious, chivalrous behavior is discriminatory because it reinforces sex inequality in several ways. First, treating women as inferiors rather than as peers stunts their personal and professional growth:

> At a recent conference, a woman corrections officer reported with some frustration that the men she worked with consistently try to protect the women, even though they all had the same training . . . Because men are conditioned to protect women, they may feel that, in addition to working with the inmates, they have an added responsibility to protect the women officers . . . These feelings can make men and women uncomfortable with each other. Women may feel patronized, as if they are merely being tolerated rather than appreciated and affirmed for their work.[2]

Second, chivalry justifies paying women lower wages or salaries and not promoting them. If a woman is "protected" from challenging assignments, her contributions will probably be ignored. If her contributions are ignored, she will not be promoted. If she is not promoted, she will remain in the lower echelons of the wages/salaries scale. If she is in the lower echelons of the wages/salaries scale, she will be "protected" from challenging assignments. Thus, the cycle continues.

Chivalrous behavior can limit women's opportunities. A number of women we talked to said they were automatically excluded from some jobs because men assume that women won't want to travel, will be unwilling to set up child-care arrangements, and "don't want to be in the public eye." Or, when women already have jobs, they will be excluded from important meetings or not considered for promotions because they should be "protected." Consider the experience of one respondent, a 33-year-old, unmarried store manager:

> [Mary's] male counterparts in the company frequently were invited to out-of-town business meetings and social functions from which she was excluded. These occasions were a source for information on business trends and store promotions and were a rich source of potentially important business contacts. When [Mary] asked why she was not invited to these meetings and social gatherings, the response was that her employer thought it was too dangerous for her to be driving out of town at night by herself. . . .

Protecting women from themselves may be exacerbated for women of color:

> One time I was not allowed to go to a meeting in a [suburban] area. I found out about it later and my boss said "Well, we just didn't think that you'd be welcome in this part of town. We got all of the information and brought it back to you." You know, I really felt bad about that because I should have been allowed to make that decision. (Real estate developer)

Men's belief that women should be protected may result in a reluctance to criticize women:

> A male boss will haul a guy aside and just kick ass if the subordinate performs badly in front of a client. But I heard about a woman here who gets nervous and tends to giggle in front of customers. She's unaware of it, and her boss hasn't told her. But behind her back he downgrades her for not being smooth with customers.[3]

Not receiving the type of constructive criticism that is exchanged much more freely and comfortably between men results in treating women as outsiders rather than as colleagues.

Most of us rarely recognize that chivalry can be exploitative. Women are often seen as too helpless to open their own doors but quite capable of chairing unpopular committees, or women are "protected" from the stress of management and supervisory positions but considered tough enough to train 40 or 50 clerical workers or carry the entire student-advising burdens of a department. As Gloria Steinem is reputed to have stated, women enjoy having a door opened for them, but it shouldn't cost them $5,000 a year.

Condescending chivalry is not limited to everyday, face-to-face interactions. Carol Berkin has identified a number of "dangerous courtesies" by which male historians have been courteous in sometimes acknowledging women's work but have relegated women to peripheral roles rather than incorporating their intellectual and scholarly contributions. Two of these dangerous courtesies are the "paternal parentheses courtesy" and the "intermezzo courtesy":

> The "paternal parentheses" courtesy carefully and often apologetically acknowledges that men's and women's circumstances and experiences differed, sometimes dramatically, in our nation's past. But the implications of those differences are avoided by presenting women as the exception to an interpretive rule. Thus, 1820 to 1860 can remain America's "age of democracy," despite the fact that women did not share in the era's expansion of political rights or economic opportunities.

> The "intermezzo" courtesy, most often found in textbooks and surveys of particular eras or movements, introduces vignettes, biographical sketches, or dramatic moments drawn from women's history—but only as digressions from the central text. Self-contained, often walled off from the rest of the text by bold-faced captions or special designs, these stories-within-a-story remain irrelevant to the main argument as presented.[4]

SUPPORTIVE DISCOURAGEMENT

Supportive discouragement refers to a form of subtle sex discrimination in which women receive mixed messages about their abilities, intelligence, or accomplishments. There are at least four types of supportive discouragement: the woman is encouraged but stereotyped, encouraged but not rewarded, encouraged but excluded, and encouraged but then manipulated or exploited.

Encouraged but Stereotyped

In some cases, women are encouraged to be ambitious and successful but are channeled into educational and job avenues that severely limit their choices. What is ironic is that much of the supportive discouragement occurs in educational institutions.

Recently, *The AAUW Report: How Schools Shortchange Girls* received national attention when it concluded that—from preschool through high school—girls are not getting the same quality or quantity of education as boys. Vocational programs are still largely sex-segregated; biased testing gives an inaccurate picture of girls' and boys' abilities; and both formal curricular materials and informal classroom interaction patterns discourage girls and young women. Even textbooks that were adopted because they demonstrated the greatest sense of gender and racial equity still showed "subtle language bias, neglect of scholarship on women, omission of women as developers of history and initiators of events, and absence of women from accounts of technological developments."[5]

Although, increasingly, girls are encouraged to go to college, stereotypes abound. Sarah Hechtman and Robert Rosenthal had 20 teachers each teach a male and a female student a stereotypically masculine lesson (mechanics) and a stereotypically female lesson (vocabulary). They found that teachers exhibited *more positive behavior* toward the students learning stereotypically appropriate material.[6] In college, professors who adhere to gender-appropriate behavior are most likely to receive positive evaluations from students. The competence ratings of women faculty are higher the more they engage in such activities as personalizing their lectures, acknowledging students' contributions, and generating laughter. The competence ratings of male faculty are higher the more they adhere to a masculine sex-typed style that includes teacher-as-expert lecturing as well as admonishing students.[7] Women faculty are expected to be nurturant and mothering while male faculty are expected to be experts who manage the classroom.

Stereotyping limits all women's options. It is devastating for women of color because they often face a "double whammy." A national follow-up survey of high school students found that traditional sex-role socialization was an important factor in the college behavior patterns of Latinas. Women who delayed marriage and having a family were more likely to go to college and stay in college longer than women who followed traditional sex-role patterns. In addition, young Latinas were more likely than their white Anglo counterparts to be placed into general education or noncollege tracks.[8] Moreover, although athletic scholarships have increased the percentage of black women in some colleges, most black female athletes are clustered in such specific sports as basketball and track and field. They are much less likely than their white counterparts to have attended high schools that offer a greater variety of sports.

Often, reentry women are encouraged to go to college or to pursue graduate degrees, but in such stereotypically female fields as social work, teaching, and nursing rather than in business, engineering, and computer science because "you've got a real knack for dealing with people." Highly educated women are also stereotyped. In many fields of science, women with doctoral degrees who decide to marry and have children are seen as having a weak commitment to work.[9] In contrast, men are usually applauded for combining jobs and marriages.

Encouraged but Not Rewarded

A devastating form of supportive discouragement involves encouraging women to succeed in general but not rewarding their actual achievements. Some of our respondents still remember accomplishments or ideas that were ignored simply because of their sex:

> As a child, I was encouraged to learn my spelling words and increase my vocabulary. I studied and studied during my fourth grade. I received 3 A's and 2 B's. My parents congratulated me but I was let down by their casual response. Yet when my brother won the science fair contest, my dad took him out and bought him 6 racing cars.

> I remember when I was in shop class in high school when my teacher ignored my suggestion for rebuilding a fence. He said the materials weren't readily accessible. Yet, my cousin came in three class periods later and made the same suggestion. His class took a vote and they decided to look for extra wood and then rebuilt the fence that enclosed the school yard. I don't think he wanted to help me and the other girls in my class to search for the material. My cousin's class was all boys.

In *How to Suppress Women's Writing,* Joanna Russ suggests several subtle ways by which women are encouraged but not supported in writing:

> I remember a writing student weeping in my office not because her family opposed her writing but because they thought it would keep her busy until she got married. "Nobody takes it seriously!" A contemporary of mine, who has now published two novels, said bitterly that her father was more impressed by her hobby of macramé (which "takes the brains of a flatworm") than by her first book.[10]

A number of interviewees reported similar instances of general encouragement but lack of support in specific situations:

> I had only my high school diploma and my supervisor often told me that I really had ability and I could go a lot further if I got my degree. I was encouraged and went back to school. When I got my first grades and I had done well and I worked hard, I thanked him for encouraging me and I showed him my grades. And he said, "How many of these teachers are men?" and "Where did you sit in the class?" and "What did you wear?" Yea, can you believe it? It's absolutely, positively true. That's just what he said. All of that encouragement was really kind of overshadowed by that attitude. (43-year-old black social worker)

Many women with Ph.D.s do not fare much better. In mathematics, for example, 22 percent of the Ph.D.s are women (compared to 10 percent a decade ago). Few, however, have tenured professorships at top universities. In 1991, the top 10 departments had approximately 50 men with tenure-track assistant professorships and only 3 women; there were 300 tenured men and only 2 women. In the top 40 schools women made up less than 5 percent of the tenured faculty and many were concentrated at just a few universities. One observer has noted, "The land mines concealed under the surface include a lack of encouragement from faculty members, sexual advances of mentors, and a suspicion on the part of male colleagues that women can succeed only by sleeping with male mathematicians."[11]

Women make up more than 38 percent of all medical students, but few women are in the top echelons of medical programs. Of the 126 medical schools in the United States, *only three* are headed by female deans.[12] Outside of medical schools, women are clustered in pediatrics and other lower-paying specialties rather than in the higher-paid male-dominated fields such as surgery and urology. Some female medical students say their choice of courses and fields has been influenced by the more congenial atmosphere of the specialties with the largest number of women physicians.[13] This pattern of not supporting or rewarding most women also characterizes business and industry.

Encouraged but Excluded

A third form of supportive discouragement encourages women but excludes them from meaningful participation. Some universities formally encourage women's athletic programs but discourage women's participation by not providing competent coaches, by permitting usage of facilities only when they are not being used by men, and by providing only a few scholarships to recruit women athletes. Men receive practice uniforms, women do not. Men typically are provided athletic equipment, whereas women must provide their own materials. Women may receive men's leftovers:

> When I went to college I played on the field hockey team for four years. Each year we were issued practice uniforms that were handed down from football or were too small for the football players. This lasted until my senior year, when the team finally got practice uniforms with "field hockey" on them. We had to store our equipment in an old shed that was also used by the baseball team in the spring. For two years we complained that the shed leaked and that our equipment got wet when it rained. We were ignored. I was quite surprised to see, during my junior year, that a new shed was being built, just in time for the baseball season. It should be noted that the athletic director was also the baseball coach . . . (Doctoral candidate)

When playing out of state, men receive money for meals (women do not), sleep two to a room (women—four to a room), spend the pregame night away (women travel the same day as the game), and travel in buses that have a driver (women travel in vans driven by the women coaches). Male coaches often have courtesy cars (women coaches do not) and have larger offices and more secretarial help. Women athletes must do their own pregame setups, male athletes do not. If games are played during holidays, men athletes stay at motels, whereas women athletes stay at the student health center. Men's athletic programs receive up to 85 percent of the recruitment monies. In a recent lawsuit, a judge noted that Colgate University had treated its male varsity hockey team like "princes" and its female players like "chimney sweeps."[14]

A common complaint is that some women receive an impressive title in lieu of an increased salary, authority, or both. Fancy-sounding titles can be counted—a nice bonus for an organization that wants to appear committed to affirmative action goals. Women are beginning to realize that formal encouragement (a title change) can still result in informal exclusion from decision making. One interviewee, a young woman who was "promoted" into an entry-level management position in a manufacturing company, found her supervisor undercutting her power by using the excuse that "I'm trying to make you a good manager":

> He's had my desk moved so he can watch me from his office. He listens to my phone conversations, yells at me when other division managers are in the office

and tells our secretaries—who are responsible to me, not him—to get his approval before they do the work I assign them. Worst of all, he takes credit for my work. The reports come from him without any mention of my name. Sometimes, he just takes my name off the reports.

Supportive discouragement is especially common in nontraditional student populations. Because of falling enrollments, colleges and universities have initially been very interested in reentry women—developing special recruitment materials, offering scholarships, and expressing interest in the applicant during admissions interviews. Once these students enroll, however, they all too often become invisible. Many reentry women face a number of obstacles (e.g., coordinating child care and family responsibilities; coping with divorce, self-esteem, economic problems) that are not being addressed by educational institutions because the latter do not take these problems seriously.[15] According to a female faculty member, reentry women are often discouraged from participating in academically oriented social functions:

> Faculty (even women faculty) often assume that responsibilities such as child care take precedence over informal learning. . . . Last semester, after one of the evening graduate classes, a faculty member suggested that the students join him for a beer at one of the local pubs to continue a lively class discussion. He looked at the [reentry] woman and said, "We'll miss you, but I realize you have to get back to the kids." She went home to the kids.

Women faculty often speak of feeling isolated in their departments and being excluded from national committees or conferences. A professor in a predominantly male department at a public, coeducational, historically black college said:

> I have been in this department for a long time and it is very male oriented. They do most of the committee work and write most of the joint proposals. Usually the women, including myself, are not invited to participate. Also, all other opportunities are usually awarded by the department chairman or the dean to men in the department. I have turned to writing and research on my own. Having these outlets has enabled me to get along with the men and keeps them from feeling threatened.[16]

Encouraged but Manipulated/Exploited

A fourth type of supportive discouragement encourages women and then manipulates or exploits them. Several women in diverse settings reported receiving support for developing grant proposals, new programs, or services that required much extra effort. When these projects were funded, the women were either given new assignments or the monies were transferred to male-controlled ventures. Consider the experiences of a woman in banking:

> My boss always comes to me for help understanding regulations, but doesn't tell me exactly what he needs them for. Then, when we get into meetings, he brings up the regulations and takes all the credit. . . . I was encouraged to open new ac-

counts of all kinds, be it bonds or Christmas clubs or what have you. In a short span of time, I had opened over a million dollars in new accounts. I felt good. I felt charged. I was very happy. It was a proud accomplishment for me. However, when the annual evaluation was issued, the manager was credited with what was my hard work. It's absolutely infuriating to be exploited. I was outraged!

FRIENDLY HARASSMENT

Friendly harassment refers to sexually oriented behavior that, at face value, looks harmless or playful. If it creates discomfort, embarrassment, or humiliation for the female targets, however, it is a form of subtle discrimination. The three most common forms of friendly harassment are flattery, hostile humor, and psychological intimidation.

Flattery

Flattery is a long-recognized form of seduction, power, and control. During the sixteenth century, Niccolo Machiavelli cautioned the prince to guard against flatterers "who abound in all courts." Using flattery to get one's way is usually associated with women, however. Girls learn early that flattery is effective in getting affection and attention.

Yet men use flattery to persuade and seduce. Because men often use flattery in the workplace and women have been socialized to use flattery in domestic spheres, men's use of flattery has more powerful effects. When women succumb to flattery, the economic costs can be high. An insurance agent said that until she "caught on," male flattery was instrumental in getting her to do the men's work:

> I was in an office with two guys whose productivity was lower than mine. They would often tell me how great my work was, how organized I was, and would ask my help in finishing their reports. I felt sorry for them. So, for a long time, I'd help them with their reports, follow up on clients, and do some of their paperwork. It was only after they were promoted and I wasn't that I realized I had been used.

Women are more vulnerable to flattery than men in work situations for two reasons. First, they have been socialized to be modest, dependent, and accommodating: "Too many women tend to gear their behavior in the workplace to the approval or disapproval of others. They seem to have an excessive need to be liked, to be approved of and loved. . . . Conversely, if they are disapproved of, disliked, unloved, then they are in the same measure 'worthless.'"[17] The more approval women get, the harder they work. The harder they work and the greater the verbal appreciation, the more likely they are to have a positive self-image. The more positive the self-image, the harder they work.

One of the authors gave a talk on subtle sex discrimination to a group of seniors at a private girls' school in Baltimore. Categorically, the girls (who were bright and considered themselves "liberated") all denied the existence of subtle discrimination:

INTERVIEWER: When you're out with a guy, does he talk about you, how you feel, what you want to do, and what you like?
[The students looked around uncomfortably, giggled, and shifted in their seats.]

STUDENT 1: All we ever talk about is him—sports, school, and his trip to the Caribbean during the Christmas break.

STUDENT 2: No, he never asks anything about me or how I feel.

STUDENT 3: I smile and nod a lot, but I don't think there's anything wrong with that.

STUDENT 4: I sometimes get tired of talking about him, him, him . . . but if I don't, he won't like me.

INTERVIEWER: Don't you think your present relationship should include an equal give-and-take in discussing your interests?

STUDENT 1: No, because the guys in college will be different.

STUDENT 2: I don't mind. I plan to be a doctor, and I know I'll be treated as an equal then.

Although these young women seemed somewhat annoyed by their role as flatterers and ego enhancers, they genuinely believed that adult men would be different. In all likelihood, by now many of them have become accustomed to the role of nurturer, listener, and flatterer, and have probably accepted such behavior as normative.

Finally, men sometimes use flattery to disguise sexual harassment. Some of our respondents said that they felt uncomfortable when their bosses or professors made remarks about their "pretty eyes" or "nice figure." In some cases, when the women backed away, the men became angry because "I was only giving you a compliment." Thus, instead of apologizing, men often cover up sexual innuendoes by blaming women for being "too sensitive."

Hostile Humor

Humor and jokes serve a number of functions: They reinforce group solidarity; define the deviant/outsider group; provide a safety valve for discussing taboo topics; maintain status inequality; and provide tension release, hostility, and anger toward any group that is seen as marginal, inferior, or threatening. A single joke can serve several of these functions.

Jokes about the "Jewish American Princess" (so-called "JAPS") date back to at least the 1920s. Almost all of the jokes fall into two categories: Jewish women care only about the man's money, or they are sexually unresponsive. There may be several explanations for "JAP" jokes: By denigrating Jewish women, Jewish men hope to make them less attractive to potential suitors. And, by joking about their women, Jewish men ingratiate themselves with non-Jews.[18] It might also be the case that Jewish men are using Jewish women to parody anti-Semitic stereotypes. If, for example, men cast barbs at Jewish women's presumed greed, it must show that Jews are not clannish:

> Humor also reinforces group solidarity by creating consensus: If you can make people laugh with you, you have won them over, however briefly, to your side. You have created an atmosphere of consensus, a moment of agreement when everyone is in sync. Humor functions as a sort of social cement, especially in tense or competitive work situations. . . . Laughing together creates and reinforces a sense of solidarity and intimacy within groups.[19]

This may explain why sexual jokes are considered icebreakers and liveners at many male-dominated conferences and presentations.[20] Since women are often not seen as serious rivals for jobs, high salaries, and promotions, sexist jokes may be one of the few safe topics that build male camaraderie and ease tensions between competing (male) groups.

Humor also maintains status inequality. Whether it is done intentionally or unintentionally, men sometimes make sexist remarks to reinforce masculine values—especially in traditionally male-dominated occupations that are being "invaded" by women:

> One of my drafting instructors made a joke about the other woman in my class who was having a problem with her desk. Hers was the type of desk where the legs had to be pushed out the whole way, otherwise it would wobble. Well, she noticed that it was unsteady one day and so she asked the teacher to take a look at it. He pushed the legs apart, turned to one of the guys sitting in class and said, "This desk is just like a woman; it's no good until you spread its legs." (Engineering student)

Although the functions of humor and jokes are relatively universal, there are several notable differences between men's and women's humor.

Differences in men's and women's humor.   Over the years, men's jokes about women have ranged from good-natured banter to crude and sadistic comments. A cursory examination of comics and cartoons in newspapers and such magazines as *The New Yorker* and *Playboy* reveals a changing orientation toward women. In the 1950s and 1960s, women were depicted in stereotypical roles as dumb but manipulative housewives (*Dagwood*), sexpots (*L'il Abner*), or well-meaning but meddling widows (*Mary Worth*) who help men resolve their personal problems. By the mid-1970s and the 1980s, women's sexuality and independence became threatening. Cartoons attacked lesbianism, worried about men's "emasculation," and portrayed women as victims of rape, incest, and sadism. Alice Courtney and Thomas Whipple found that both men and women find it funnier when women rather than men are ridiculed, that women are more likely than men to enjoy women's self-disparagement, and that men enjoy sexist humor that does not threaten male status.[21]

From the 1950s to the early 1980s, female comedians used self-deprecating humor or directed their stereotypical jokes at women, not at men.[22] Lucille Ball (*I Love Lucy*) played the role of the scatter-brained housewife who was always getting into trouble because she wanted to be in show business but was "saved" by her husband when her antics failed; Carol Burnett often caricatured housewives, secretaries, or wives; Phyllis Diller made a career of joking about her supposed homeliness; Joan Rivers worried about being sexually unappealing or ridiculed female stars who were sometimes overweight; Jean Stapleton played the loving but dumb Edith Bunker in *All in the Family;* and Goldie Hawn became famous through her stereotypically dumb-blonde roles in several television shows and movies.

In the mid- to late-1980s, female comedians started portraying women in more aggressive roles. One of the most popular television sit-coms is *Roseanne.*

> Wisecracks about men are a trademark of [Roseanne Arnold's] stand-up gigs, and they remain part of the loving barbs she trades with Dan, her show hubby played by John Goodman. After learning their teen-age daughter has lost her virginity, Dan says, "It almost makes me want to go back and apologize to your father for having had sex with you." Retorts Roseanne: "Oh, that's all right Dan. It's enough that you apologized to me."[23]

For the most part, however, irreverent women in such popular television programs as *Cheers, Roseanne, Murphy Brown,* and *Northern Exposure* make fun of incompetent male bosses and arrogant men rather than of husbands or lovers.[24] Such popular comic strips as *Sally Forth, Cathy, Hagar,* and *Geech* typically ridicule sex stereotypes, but the female characters are loving, tolerant, and nurturing.

Our interviews suggest, finally, that the manner of telling sexist jokes, rather than the content, has undergone subtle changes. Both men and women we interviewed felt that the number of sexist jokes they hear has been increasing. Instead of just plunging into a joke, however, most men acknowledge their awareness of a possibly unenthusiastic reception with such introductions as "Some of you libbers may not think this is funny, but . . ." Thus, women are *told* that they will be ridiculed.

Women's complicity in sexist humor.   In some cases, women refuse to reinforce sexist humor—they frown or walk away. At a sixtieth birthday party for his wife, Senator Alan Simpson remarked, "I never imagined I'd be sleeping with a 60-year-old woman." Barbara Bush replied with an icy smile, "That wasn't very funny!"[25]

Barbara Bush's response is not the norm. *Cosmopolitan* magazine has advised women to giggle at men's jokes even when they are stupid or insulting. Many women laugh at sexist jokes:

> Last week I walked into a conversation of a mixed crowd, where a man told a joke: "How do you fix a dishwasher?" "Slap her." I was appalled, and surprised that some of the women were laughing along with the men. (Male graduate student in sociology)

Even though they reinforce women's devaluation, some women laugh at sexist jokes because they want to be "one of the guys."

Psychological Intimidation

There are many types of serious harassment—ranging from the explosive physical violence discussed in Chapter 4 to subtle psychological intimidation. The most common forms of psychological intimidation we found were sexual innuendo, seduction, lesbian stigma, gender fixation, and emotional preying.

Sexual innuendo. Of the more than 400 men and women we interviewed, most reported at least one recent instance of having been harassed (or having harassed) through intimations about physical intimacy. Women faculty in a variety of disciplines report that male students regularly use sexual teasing and double entendre messages instead of getting to the problem at hand (such as a late paper or a missed exam). Secretaries, faculty, and women in the private sector said that their names are used in tones that suggest unwanted intimacy. A director of a college information office said that pregnant women are often targets of sexual innuendoes. They routinely encounter offensive statements about the baby's paternity, jokes about the ability of pregnant women to have sexual intercourse, or comments about their bodies. A mid-level manager in a utilities company said that while she was pregnant, one of her male supervisors would often smirk and say, "My, you're getting bigger and bigger" while he stared at her breasts.

Seduction. A devious form of psychological intimidation is that of setting the stage for seduction. In the case of faculty, for example, male instructors lay the groundwork for future sexual overtures through selective attention and reward:

> Friendliness, extra help, flexibility in grading and extended deadlines were seen by respondents as means by which [male] instructors tried to accumulate credit for potential sexual exchanges. . . . [Some male instructors] falsely praised [women] students' work to render them more vulnerable to future sexual advances.[26]

Because some companies and universities discourage blatant sexual harassment, women are more likely to find themselves inundated with kindness and attention—not out of respect or affection but to facilitate future seduction.

The lesbian stigma. In a recent cover story, *Newsweek* magazine showed two women in an affectionate embrace and described lesbians as "stepping front and center."[27] Several recent magazines and talk shows have suggested that it is suddenly chic to be lesbian. In reality, homosexual behavior is still feared and tabooed by most people in the United States. Inferences of being a lesbian can decrease women's credibility and professional acceptance. Because women are already in powerless positions, they are especially vulnerable to accusations of homosexual activity: "There is still a great deal of discrimination against women in academe, and it gives men a double reason to want to keep them out of departments if there are questions about whether a woman is a lesbian."[28]

Elaine Blinde and Diane Taub feel that one of the most vulnerable targets of lesbian accusations is the female athlete.[29] She is especially susceptible to harassment because the growth of women's sports is often perceived as a threat to male sports. Intercollegiate athletes engage in a variety of stigma management techniques in response to such labeling. Some simply withhold information about their athletic status in conversations with outsiders. Others disassociate themselves from masculine images of lesbianism and consciously conform to appropriate gender roles in a variety of ways: They accentuate their femininity by wearing dresses and earrings or by letting their hair grow; they make a point of being seen with men or establish a reputation as promiscuous with men; or they are careful not to be constantly seen in public with a group of women.

Gender fixation.   Many men are still uncomfortable with women as colleagues. To avoid charges of discrimination, they sometimes overreact and treat women more toughly than men. One faculty member said she had recently been on a search committee where the two women candidates were treated differently from the four male candidates: The women were asked many factual questions about the university and were often interrupted during their responses. Male candidates, on the other hand, were allowed to ramble, to talk about nonacademic issues, or to digress. They were encouraged to ask—rather than to answer—questions and were rarely, if ever, interrupted. Because women are more likely to be grilled, they are more likely to make mistakes, to become tense or worn down earlier in the day, and to be perceived as not being "collegial." (A male, by the way, was hired.)

Women in corporate sales and marketing departments are similarly kept in their "place" through condescending behavior that focuses on gender rather than on professional roles. One mid-level manager in marketing said she was at an important meeting where she and a comparable-level male manager disagreed on a critical issue. As the disagreement grew, her male counterpart exploded, "Look here, little girl . . ." and plunged into a patronizing attack. She was so taken aback, she responded in a "typically female" way—she withdrew from the debate. After the meeting, one of her peers put his arm around her shoulders and said, "Don't worry, hon, [X] will cool off." In the first instance, the woman was clearly put in her "place" as a woman and a child. In the second instance, and however well intentioned, the behavior focused on the woman's sex rather than her professional role. (How often does a man comfort another man with a little hug and refer to him as "hon"?).

A woman faculty member in a business school provided the following example of her male colleagues' fixation on her sex:

> I was in the hall reading the riot act to one of my students—a tall, big, basketball star—who had missed several exams. My chairman was walking by, came

over, put his arm around my waist, smiled, and said to the student, "Isn't she cute? Don't you just L-O-V-E her?" They both laughed. It took a while to reestablish my professional credibility with this student.

Emotional preying.   Many women are recent entrants to the work force. Their inexperience, low power, or problems experienced in dealing with two full-time jobs—one at home and one at work—may make them especially accessible to harassers who prey on vulnerable women:

> After the divorce, my relationship with my ex-husband got even worse. Most of the people in the office knew what was going on. . . . One day, one of the engineers asked me out to lunch to discuss a project we were working on. I was flattered because engineers usually look down on community planners. Pretty soon we were talking about my personal problems. [Sam] was very understanding, supportive . . . very sweet, and I really let my hair down. Within a few months, we were having an affair. When I started getting serious, he became really angry. He said he was happily married and had gone to bed with me to help me through some tough times! Like hell! I'm not the one who scheduled bogus golf games Saturday mornings. . . . We barely talk to each other now. . . . (Planner in a highway administrative department)

Besides taking advantage of the situation, the harasser-as-scavenger may create emotional needs and then swoop in to fulfill these needs. One of the most subtle ways to do this is through a role that Billie Dziech and Linda Weiner describe as "confidante":

> He may invite her confidences, but he also offers his own. In an attempt to impress or win sympathy from the student, he may relate or invent stories about his private and professional life. . . . The student often feels that he values and trusts her, so she becomes an involuntary confidante. . . . The relationship is moved into an intimate domain from which she may find it difficult to extricate herself.[30]

Although Dziech and Weiner's observations are based on an analysis of higher education, the confidante-harasser also exists in the business, industry, and government sectors.

SUBJECTIVE OBJECTIFICATION

Subjective objectification refers to a form of subtle sex discrimination by which women are (1) treated as children or property, (2) viewed as sex objects, or (3) perceived as "Smurfettes."

Women as Children or Property

Women are often not seen as able and intelligent people but as possessions or conduits for male accomplishments. A number of authors have documented women's treatment as male *property*.[31] Historically, some women's work was plundered by men who walked off with the prizes or usurped them after marriage:

> The McCormick reaper, patented by Cyrus, was actually invented by his wife, a seamstress. . . . Rosalind Franklin's X-ray spectrograph evidence of the double helix structure of DNA was pilfered by Crick and Watson, who went on to publish the proof of its structure and become Nobel laureates. Jocelyn Bell Burnell's discovery of pulsars was attributed to her senior co-workers, who carried off the Nobel prize. . . . A composer before her marriage, Alma Mahler did orchestration for her husband, but he forbade her to write music independently after their marriage. Zelda Fitzgerald was warned by F. Scott not to refer to their common experiences in her writing because the material belonged to him as resources for his own fiction.[32]

In terms of professional development, women are still expected to sacrifice their own interests for those of their husbands or boyfriends or to accept having their contributions ignored. In the arts and literature, "women may not only be renamed as non-artists; their contributions of art may be absorbed into a man's and recategorized as his."[33] Even today, courts are slow in protecting women from sexual assault by husbands and rapists, from discriminatory social security benefits, and from unequal insurance coverage.

Women are often seen and treated like children. As we discussed earlier, women are often referred to as "baby," "little girl," or other similar terms that are used to address children. Like children, women are not expected to be able to handle responsibility or money or take part in important discussions and decisions. They are often interrupted or excluded from important discussions:

> When it comes to issues like politics and things like that, I am never asked my opinion, or if I am, it's not taken seriously. I voted for Clinton, and of course, nobody ever thought I voted for him for any issues that I might have agreed with. Rather, I voted for him because he is good looking. Why on earth would a woman vote for a president based on his looks, and a man would vote based on political reasons? I find it very irritating. (38-year-old woman in advertising)

Women are often punished like children—their "allowances" may be taken away, they may be forbidden to associate with their friends, their physical mobility may be limited, they may be given curfews, or they may be threatened with punishment similar to that of children. In 1990, for example, nearly a quarter of the 600 seniors graduating from Wellesley College, a women's college, signed a petition criticizing the selection of First Lady Barbara Bush as a commencement speaker. They felt she did not "embody the Wellesley experience" because her prominence was a result of her husband's accomplishments rather then her own. One reaction of a woman who was associate professor of medicine at Johns Hopkins School of Medicine and former acting president of Wellesley was especially interesting: "I'd like to spank some of those young women."[34]

Consider the following experience reported by a female faculty member in a political science department at a large university:

> One of the senior male faculty was very unhappy about the woman faculty member we had just hired. She challenged him during departmental meetings and disagreed with him in public. As we talked, he got more and more angry about her behavior. Finally, he exploded, "What that young lady needs is a good spanking!"

What is interesting about both these cases is that administrators and faculty do not threaten seemingly rude men with *spanking*. Instead, we usually say things like, "I respect your opinion even though I don't agree with it."

Victor D'Lugin notes that women are often perceived as children rather than adults in the law. Trial practice manuals often have statements like "Women, like children, are prone to exaggeration; they generally have poor memories." Women, like children, are seen as less serious, competent, and able to report accurately on what has occurred than men. This lack of credibility has widespread negative effects: In damage claims, women are awarded lower cash assessments than men; the likelihood of successful litigation decreases drastically with age for a female plaintiff but increases for a male plaintiff; and juries perceive female attorneys as less intelligent, capable, and expert than male attorneys.[35]

A number of the women we interviewed said that their bosses treated them like children or dim-witted adults by speaking very slowly, giving the instructions more than once, asking "Did you understand that?" after giving directions, or asking the women to repeat what they said.

Women as Sex Objects

Besides being nonpersons, women are often treated as sex objects. Among other characteristics, being a sex object includes being devalued as an individual, seen as a decoration, or depersonalized as a sexual acquisition:[36]

> Frequently, treating women as sexual objects is very blatant: The president [of Company X] has openly admitted that he does not think highly of the women who work for him. He hires only pretty women. Women are seen as objects and are never taken seriously. One time, the president asked one of my female coworkers to go to his office for a business meeting. As she made her presentations, the company president kept making comments about her figure and at one time asked her, "Since you are wearing a leather skirt, where is your whip?" The woman left the office in tears. . . . (Manager in a small, black-owned retail store)

In many other situations, women do not know that they are being degraded. A male director of personnel told us that one of the recent interviewees for a job was a young woman who had been awarded her department's prestigious Accounting Award at graduation. When she was invited back for a second interview, a job offer seemed imminent. It wasn't. The personnel director told us that "she was an attractive, well-endowed young lady. After the first job in-terview, she was called back a second time because some of the men who had interviewed her told the rest of the guys to be sure to be there to see 'the biggest tits in Washington.'" The fact that she was one of the top students in her graduating class was totally irrelevant!

Even when women have jobs or expertise in nontraditional female oc-cupations, their friends or boyfriends expect them to be ornaments. A tennis coach at a girls' high school said that her boyfriend, who picked her up after work, would complain continuously, "I don't understand why you always wear sweat suits to work. Don't you have any skirts?" Pointing out that sweat suits were her work uniform did not decrease his complaints. Another coach said that she can sustain friendly relationships with men only if she doesn't beat them:

> As long as we play *other* teams in racquetball, the guys don't mind my being the only woman on the team and beating the other men. When I beat my team-mates on a one-to-one basis, however, they don't talk to me for days. Sometimes I lose purposely because I don't want to ruin our club's morale; it's not okay to beat your own teammates when you're the only woman in the club.

A few years ago, the father of tennis champion Steffi Graf turned down *Playboy*'s offer to photograph his daughter nude, but allowed *Vogue* magazine to feature her in several photographs—in sultry poses—with lots of cleavage and showing "lots of leg." According to *Newsweek* magazine, Mr. Graf wanted to show that Steffi is "more woman than tennis machine."

Some women recognize that they are being treated like sex objects and try to regain control of the situation:

> I used to be the assistant comptroller at a shoe company and the plant superin-tendent was always coming on to me. He would always call me "dear" and I'd say, "Do I look like Bambi? Do I have antlers? I have a name." His favorite thing was to stand in front of my desk and scratch his crotch. Like this is supposed to be something interesting to watch. I got flea powder one day and said, "If you got a problem, go use this."

Many women either do not realize they are being treated as sex objects, do not object because they are afraid to lose their jobs, or go along with it be-cause the sexism is customary and "all in good fun:"

> There was a girl who worked at the car dealership who was very well endowed and the men were always making crude comments about her. In fact, they re-ferred to her as "boobs." Because I'm not big chested, I would get remarks like "Well, Dee, I guess you don't have any problems with chest colds." Or they would say "Well, you don't have much chest, but you've got great legs." At Christmas the boss would give people in the office presents. All the men would be in a room and the women would have to go in, one at a time, and sit on the boss's lap to receive "Santa's" gift. Then they would have to model it. It might be a jacket or a sweater. (Woman selling cars at a large dealership)

Women may also be demeaned because they are *not* sex objects. For example, a railroad engineer, who described herself as a "big-boned woman," said that "Xeroxed pictures of St. Bernards were posted on bulletin boards with my name on them."

In a study of fraternities at Florida State University, Patricia Martin and Robert Hummer found that some fraternities intentionally used women as sexual bait to attract new members. For example, photographs of shapely, attractive coeds were included in fraternity brochures, and videotapes were shown to potential pledges. The women pictured were often dressed in bikinis and were hugging fraternity brothers. One university official said that such materials gave the message that "We have the best looking women. Join us and you can have them too."[37]

Women as Smurfettes

In the popular television show, *The Smurfs,* the only woman in the community of tiny, blue male creatures is a girl—a smurfette. In a critical analysis of children's programs on television, journalist Katha Pollitt referred to the "Smurfette principle" as a situation in which "a group of male buddies will be accented by a lone female, stereotypically defined."[38] On television, girls are usually invisible, simply tag along after boys, or are cast in stereotypical roles: the Muppets of *Sesame Street* are almost all male; the hosts of *Reading Rainbow, Mr. Rogers' Neighborhood, Captain Kangaroo,* and *Barney & Friends* are all males; Kanga, the only female in *Winnie-the-Pooh,* is a mother; and April, of the popular *Teen-Age Mutant Ninja Turtles,* is a girl Friday to the male superheroes. Pollitt concludes: "The message is clear. Boys are the norm, girls the variation; boys are central, girls peripheral; boys are individuals, girls types. Boys define the group, its story and its code of values. Girls exist only in relation to boys."[39]

Besides being treated as nonadults and sex objects, adult women are typically evaluated in terms of their sex rather than their accomplishments. Much of what women do is undervalued because many men see the work as reflecting innate gender characteristics. What women do inside and outside the home is often labeled as "women's work" and thus as not terribly important:

1.   The lifting of heavy objects occasionally by men is evaluated higher than women's repeated lifting of lighter loads for more exhausting periods.
2.   Men are responsible for property, and women for persons. The latter are evaluated as less important and less skilled than the former.
3.   Because decision making is seen as more important than doing the homework that leads to decisions, men in white-collar jobs get rewards and secretaries don't.
4.   Because evaluation systems "reward brass and ignore tact," men's verbal aggressiveness is rewarded and women's interpersonal skills are ignored.
5.   Men are rewarded and subsidized for on-the-job training, while women are expected to have the necessary training (e.g., "anyone can type").

6. Men and women both work in unpleasant and dangerous jobs. Because, however, men's dangers are more dramatic (for example, fumes and the heat of steel mills), they are noticed more than women's equally hazardous but less dramatic problems (for example, continuous clatter of office machines, unhealthy ventilation, radiation).[40]

RADIANT DEVALUATION

Although women are less likely to be openly maligned or insulted than in the past, they are devalued more subtly but just as effectively. Often, the devaluation is done in glowing terms:

> Newly commissioned Ensign Kristine Holderied and her family met with President Reagan at the White House yesterday as he congratulated her for being the first woman to graduate at the top of a military academy class. . . . Holderied, 21, spent several minutes with the president before he escorted her to a briefing session being conducted for female editors in the Old Executive Office Building. . . . *After meeting Reagan, the U.S. Naval Academy graduate said the president "said it was fantastic, that it shows what a woman can do."*[41] [emphasis added]

A psychologist, one of the most popular instructors in her college, said she would get good teaching evaluations from her male chair but that the positive review would be couched in sex-stereotypical rather than professional terms—she was described as being "mama-ish" and as having a "charming" approach to teaching. Being "mama-ish" and "charming" are *not* the criteria used by tenure and promotion committees.

A number of the women we interviewed complained that their husbands or partners ignore their work: "He comes home with videotapes of his meetings, and he'll say, 'Come sit down and watch this,' but he doesn't take much interest in my work;" "I started a historical society and I would get excited about findings for the museum. My husband would say things like 'Everybody knows that,' or 'This is nothing.'"

In the medical sector, men are sometimes encouraged to pursue nursing and women may be encouraged to enter medical schools. In both situations, however, men's activities are often valued more highly. Several male nurses we interviewed said that male physicians are more likely to accept and act upon the advice of male nurses and to ignore the input of female nurses. Similarly, female medical students were angry because men are taken more seriously:

> Just a few days ago, a patient needed to have a cardiac catherization procedure and I was the first in the group to volunteer. I felt confident that I could insert the catheter without any problems. The Chief of Residents half smiled at me and said, "Bill is coming forward." After the procedure I approached Dr. [X] and asked him why he chose Bill when clearly I was first to volunteer. He replied, "Bill is familiar with this patient, I think he is more comfortable in doing this procedure than you, and the patient is also more at ease with Bill. Don't worry, there will be other opportunities." Of course I was furious but I

held my piece. The truth of the matter is Bill was just as nervous doing that procedure as I may have been but he is a man and sometimes even male patients discriminate against female physicians. (Black, first-year medical intern)

Many women said that physicians sometimes instructed male students to double-check women's work, but not vice versa.

Besides exclusion, women's achievements may be belittled by "damning with faint praise." In a study of 243 letters of recommendation for a junior-level faculty position in sociology, Jeanne Guillemin and her colleagues concluded that "blatant references to physical appearance" have disappeared and descriptions of women candidates in wife and mother roles are "probably much less common." However, "the representation of woman as future colleagues falters instead on the more abstract criteria of career performance and potential." That is, there is little discussion of the woman's past or potential contributions in such important areas as research, scholarly productivity, and teaching effectiveness.[42]

Women and women's work are often devalued not because women's jobs are different from those of men, but because the work is done by women. In the areas of speech and communication, for example, some studies have suggested that women may be taken less seriously than men because women express themselves in less powerful ways. They use more tag questions ("It's a good movie, isn't it?"), unfinished sentences, and disclaimers ("I could be wrong, but . . ."); they ask questions rather than make statements and generally "support" rather than guide conversations.[43] A study of the usage of tag questions and disclaimers showed that men, but not women, are able to use tag questions and disclaimers "with virtual impunity"; they are *not* seen as less credible, weak, or nonassertive.[44]

LIBERATED SEXISM

Liberated sexism refers to the process that, at face value, appears to be treating women and men equally but that, in practice, increases men's freedom while placing greater burdens on women. Two examples of liberated sexism are overloads and women's entry into nontraditional jobs.

Overloads

Since the 1970s, many women found themselves with two jobs—one inside and one outside the home. Ironically, women working these "double days" are often defined as "liberated women." But, liberated from what?

Working wives still do most of the housework. Time-budget surveys from Canada, Denmark, Holland, Norway, the United Kingdom, and the United States show that women spend an average of 214 minutes per day on domestic work, compared to 27 minutes per day for men.[45] In the United States, women have decreased their housework from about 27 to almost 20 hours per week since the mid-1960s. Men's housework has increased, respectively, from about 5 hours to 10 hours per week, but most of the increase has been in such male-dominated tasks as minor repairs and yardwork. Overall, women are still doing 80 percent of the female-dominated jobs, such as cooking, cleaning, and laundry, as well as 37 percent of the male-dominated jobs. Although women decreased much of their housework because they took on paying jobs and had fewer children, this decrease has not been affected significantly by men's greater contribution. Men's participation in female-dominated tasks has increased by only 2 hours a week since 1965. Overall, employed housewives do nearly twice as much housework as men.[46]

A working wife's housework time has decreased by about 10 hours a week, not because the husband helps out but because the housework doesn't get done. The woman uses shortcuts (frozen dinners, reliance on fast-food stores) or hires help to do work she used to do herself (child care, laundry). Men's domestic activities increased between 10 and 60 minutes a week—and usually only in households with preschool children. Even when the husband/father occasionally volunteers (or is asked) to help, organizing his help may be as time consuming as the woman's doing it herself:

> Yes, dad will take Mary to the dentist. But it was mom who (1) remembered that Mary needed to go to the dentist, (2) made the appointment, (3) wrote the note to get Mary excused from school and reminded her to take it to school, (4) saw that Mary brushed her teeth and wore one of her least disreputable pair of jeans, (5) reminded dad to take Mary the morning of the appointment, (6) paid the bill when it came in the mail, and posted the next six month appointment on the family calendar afterwards.[47]

The woman is seen as "liberated" because she works outside the home. In reality, her work has freed her spouse from having total economic responsibility for the household while only modestly increased sharing of housework and child-care tasks.

Entry into Nontraditional Jobs

A highly publicized specter of equality has focused on the entry of men and women into nontraditional jobs. Many fields still resist women's entry, however. One of these is music, where only 6 percent of composers are women:

> A few years ago Renate Birnstein sent a manuscript to a well-known music editor. It was immediately returned with a terse note that the firm took no "ladies' music, because it was rarely of general interest." Ms. Birnstein, a pupil of [a well-known composer], sent the manuscript back, this time with a masculine pseudonym at the top: it was accepted by the same editor.[48]

In most cases, women have more difficulty being accepted into traditionally male jobs (as carpenters, engineers, mechanics, firefighters) than do men into traditionally female jobs (as nurses, flight attendants, elementary school teachers). As a male nurse put it: "I'm singled out by the male doctors as the most competent nurse on the floor. I'm always told what's happening with the patients even though I'm not the nurse assigned to the patient." In contrast, women nurses often note that doctors treat them like domestic help rather than like professionals.

A second difference is that men can use "female" jobs as stepping-stones to management slots. Although women enter nontraditional jobs, they rarely receive the training necessary for job transfers to upper-level positions. They often encounter much hostility and pressure from male bosses to quit. In one case, the only woman garbage truck driver in suburban Maryland filed a formal complaint after enduring continuous harassment for almost a year. She said, for example, that her supervisor always hung the keys to her truck above the men's urinals. When she protested, she was fired, but won back pay and the right to return to her job. After the settlement, she commented that "This is 1991, and I see things happening that make me think it's 1941. People have no idea how much discrimination goes on."[49]

BENEVOLENT EXPLOITATION

Women are often exploited. Benevolent exploitation refers to taking advantage of people for selfish reasons. Since the exploitation is done by those we respect or care about, or is carried off gracefully, it often goes unnoticed. The most common types of benevolent exploitation include dumping, sponsorship abuses, showcasing, and technological and advertising abuses.

Dumping

One of the most common forms of exploitation is dumping—getting someone else (i.e., a woman) to do a job you don't want to do and then taking credit for the results:

> Whenever my supervisor gets a boring, tedious job he doesn't want to do, he assigns it to me. He praises my work and promises it will pay off in his next evaluation. Then, he writes the cover letter and takes full credit for the project. . . . I've never been given any credit for any of the projects—and some were praised very highly by our executives. But, I suppose it's paid off because my boss has never given me negative evaluations. (Female engineer in aerospace industry)

> When I worked at the shoe company, all the big cheeses had gone away to this shoe fair and I had gotten this catalog in the mail from this place where they sold all kinds of hiking boots. And I thought, "Hmm, we don't sell hiking boots to them." I called them and found out who the purchasing agent was and as soon as I found out who the purchasing agent was and said "Can I send you a sample?" They sent back an order for $100,000 worth of shoes! Well, I never once got anything out of it. I was never even told "Oh, well, that was really great." It turns out that the salesman in that area wound up getting the commission because he threw a fit and said that was his area even though he had never even bothered to go there. If I had been a guy, it would have been different, you know, "Oh this is great; we'll make you a salesman." But it's like, "Ahh, that's cute, good girl" and they pat you on the head. (Manager at a manufacturing company)

Women also get dumped on by coworkers who take advantage of the situation because they know that powerful people (who are typically men) will support them. As one of the nurses we interviewed said:

> One of the male nurses will do all the "glory" work, but he feels above doing the other "busy" work. He won't do paperwork or clean up his station, the mundane stuff that needs to be done each day. He simply refuses to do it! Supervisors let him get away with it because they feel it's not worth the time and effort to make him do it. Besides, they don't want him to quit because certain people think he is wonderful, especially one of the male physicians who has an international reputation.

A more creative form of dumping is to segregate top workers by sex and depend on the women to get the work done while the men merely critique the work and implement the results in highly visible and prestigious ways. An aide in a highly placed political office said that one of the reasons her boss was successful politically was because he recognized that most of his female aides were harder working, more committed, and more responsible than the male aides. He gives the women fancy titles and gets 60 to 70 hours of work out of them at much lower salaries than those of men. When the projects are finished, he gives a lunch for all his aides and praises the women's work. Even as the dessert is served, new projects for the women are announced. The male aides, in contrast, publicize the projects and get widespread recognition.

Sponsorship Abuses

A very effective form of benevolent exploitation is to teach women to be dutiful and loyal to men in leadership roles because such sponsorship will "eventually pay off." Many women spend lifetimes being research assistants, invisible coauthors, and even authors—believing that their sponsor will one day recognize the contributions publicly. During their highly publicized divorce proceedings several years ago, Mrs. Spock claimed that she should have been a coauthor of Dr. Spock's best-selling books on baby care.

In the past decade, many men's work, previously published under their own names, is now being published under the names of both the husband and the wife. For example, Ariel Durant began to publish with her husband, Will Durant, in their famous series, *The Story of Civilization,* only in 1961, after he had published six volumes under his own name. Social scientist Gabriel Kolko acknowledged his wife, Joyce, in *Wealth and Power in America* (1962) as follows: "This book is in every sense a joint enterprise and the first in a series of critical studies on which we're presently engaged." Yet Joyce Kolko appeared as the coauthor of a subsequent book only in 1972.[50]

Sponsorship abuses include the lack of mentoring. Mentors perform a number of important functions that include counseling, building confidence in the mentee, and suggesting job opportunities. If, however, there is a shortage of minority mentors in positions of power, African-American, Latino/a, and Asian students and workers will be at a disadvantage. A white mentor may not identify with the mentee because their attitudes are different, may be insensitive to some cultural problems because of language difficulties, and may not even initiate mentoring relationships.[51] As we showed earlier, since most women are in less powerful positions than men, are deluged with gender-related assignments, and have few role models at the higher ranks, women mentees often have fewer mentors.

Showcasing

"Showcasing" refers to placing women in visible and seemingly powerful positions in which their talents can be pulled out, whenever necessary, for the public's consumption and the institution's credibility. One form of showcasing is to make sure that the institution's token women are present (though not necessarily participating) in the institution's meetings with outsiders. In higher education, a woman faculty member is often expected to serve on student recruitment committees, faculty search committees (in case affirmative action officers are around), and a variety of external "women's-type" activities such as panels, commissions, and advisory boards. There is no compensation for these additional duties. Women are not rewarded later in personnel reviews because this work has low status. If an occasional committee is an important one, the women chosen are typically nonfeminists who won't embarrass the organization by taking women's issues too seriously. Instead, they may be "Queen Bees,"* naive veterans, women who are either not powerful or are insensitive to sex discrimination. Another form of showcasing is giving women directorships in dead-end jobs that are considered a "natural" for women:

> There's probably less discrimination in personnel offices because the job needs a person with traditionally female skills—being nice to people, having verbal abilities, and not being a threat to anyone because a director of personnel is a dead-end job. (Director of personnel in higher education)

Technologically Based Abuses

Americans place a high value on progress, product improvements, and technological advances. In the case of new technologies, employers often convince women that their newly developed skills are inadequate and should not be rewarded:

> While office technology creates opportunities for higher pay for some of us, for many others it is used as an excuse for keeping salary levels down. An employer may ignore the new skills you have learned in order to operate your ma-

---

*"Queen Bees" refers to women who are convinced that they have been successful solely because of their own efforts and abilities rather than recognizing that their success could not have become a reality without the sacrifices, pioneering efforts, and achievement of their female predecessors and coworkers. Because of their adamant "I'm-terrific-because-I-pulled-myself-up-by-*my*-bootstraps" beliefs, Queen Bees typically either ignore or resist helping women become upwardly mobile. Thus, Queen Bees openly support men who reject sex equality and provide men (and other Queen Bees) with public rationalizations for keeping women in subordinate positions (in other words, as female drones).

chine and argue it's the machine itself that does all the work so that you are worthless.[52]

"Progress" has been a higher priority than the job hazards resulting from new technologies and automation. In most cases, the people using the new technologies are office workers—almost all of them women. The most commonly used new office equipment is the video-display terminal (VDT). There is evidence that long-term exposure to VDTs may be dangerous: Operators experience eyestrain, neck and back pain, and headaches. The radiation emitted by the terminals is believed by some researchers to cause stress, cataracts, miscarriages, and birth defects.[53] Yet, management has done little to improve work conditions even when many of the remedies are not costly. As one respondent put it, "Why save labor when it's cheap?"

Advertising Abuses

One of the most widespread forms of exploitation is to use female bodies and nudity to sell everything from toothpaste to tractors. We dealt with some blatant forms of sexism in advertising in Chapter 2. Much sexism in advertising may not be seen by most people as exploitative, because it seems normal or because women are expected to be "decorative." The implicit message to men and women is that the primary role of women is to provide pleasure or sex:

> Often the advertisements imply that the product's main purpose is to improve the user's appeal to men, as the panty-hose advertisement which claims "gentlemen prefer Hanes." The underlying advertising message for a product advertised in this manner is that the ultimate benefit of product usage is to give men pleasure.[54]

The health and fitness craze has provided marketers unparalleled opportunities. William Rudman and Akiko Hagiwara examined photographs from advertisements in five magazines focusing on health and fitness and exercise products (*National Fitness Trade Journal, Mens* [sic] *Journal, Club Business International, Natural Body Fitness,* and *Shape*). A high percentage of the advertisements portrayed women with sexual expressions (such as a pouting mouth), in heavy makeup or jewelry, or emphasized the dismemberment of women's body parts (such as cutting off a woman's head, legs, and arms and showing only the torso). In some cases, a logo was printed across the woman's breasts. Rudman and Hagiwara concluded that "What is being sold, through use of the female body, is an image of sexual attractiveness. . . . Women are used as a sexual prop to sell an image or look rather than health and wellness."[55]

The consistent and continuous message that advertisements send is that women's roles are primarily limited to being a sex object. Women may dominate advertising space, but they are often demeaned.

CONSIDERATE DOMINATION

Men often occupy preeminent positions and control important decision-making functions. The dominance is accepted because it has been internalized or institutionalized and is often portrayed as amicable.

Internalized

Language teaches and reinforces sex-role expectations and relationships between women and men. Children learn at a very young age, through interaction with parents and other adults, that males are dominant. In a study of sex differences in parent-child conversations, Esther Greif found that fathers demonstrate their high status and control through interruptions and simultaneous speech, especially with daughters. (Simultaneous speech refers to the process in which two or more people start talking at once. The less powerful person withdraws, allowing the more powerful person to continue.) Wives often reinforce their husbands' dominance: "Fathers are more likely to interrupt and engage in simultaneous speech with their preschool children, and . . . both mothers and fathers are more likely to interrupt and speak simultaneously with daughters than with sons.[56]

The message is learned well and dominates many male-female interactions even when the adult woman has a higher status than the man. In a study of social work graduate students, Virginia Brooks found that although male students interrupted both male and female professors more often than did female students, they interrupted female professors significantly more often than male professors.[57]

Besides interruptions, men demonstrate their dominance in interpersonal relations in other ways that show they control the situation. Even when a respected woman is speaking, men in less prestigious positions will often yawn, engage in side conversations, look at their watches, leave the room to make phone calls, read their mail, pass notes, or turn away from the speaker.

In *You Just Don't Understand,* Deborah Tannen gives numerous examples of how men dominate communication. Even though Tannen is an acknowledged expert on gender communication, she often finds that men challenge or ignore her expertise:

> My experience is that if I mention the kind of work I do to women, they usually ask me about it. . . . But when I announce my line of work to men, many give me a lecture on language—for example, about how people, especially teenagers, misuse language nowadays. Others challenge me, for example, questioning me about my research methods. Many others change the subject to something they know more about.[58]

How do women respond when men are "educating" them? Most are considerate—they smile, become silent, listen attentively, or nod (even though they may feel like nodding off). To avoid male domination, women sometimes try to exclude men. At a conference on female biology, female primatologists closed the meeting to male researchers. The justification by the female organizers of the conference was that "male posturing and filibustering slow conferences down. [Without men] at the end of the first day, we were where we'd be after three days of other conferences. At the end of two and one half days we were miles ahead."[59]

Institutionalized

Men's dominance is built into our language, laws, and customs in formal ways as well. The "hyphenization" phenomenon—such as woman-doctor, woman-executive, woman-athlete, woman-driver—suggests women's "occupational deviance":

> Since high status occupations and prized competencies tend to be stereotypically "male," the hyphenated designations of women imply a further "put-down." Because she is female, a woman is assumed not to have overall competence for the prized roles that a man would have. Hence, she should be described . . . only relative to the occupation's other female occupants, rather than in terms of universalistic (i.e., sex-neutral) criteria.[60]

Thus, when women move into professional or other roles reserved for men, their anomalous position is marked by qualifiers (such as female surgeon).

As we noted previously, the media are male dominated. The media routinely ignore women or present them as second-class citizens. A survey of the front page of 20 national and local newspapers found that although women make up 52 percent of the population, they show up just 13 percent of the time in the prime news spots. Even the stories about breast implants quoted men more often than women. Two thirds of the bylines on front pages were male, and three quarters of the opinions on op-ed pages were by men. Fewer than a third of the photographs on front pages featured women. Since the old "women's sections" are now more unisex and focus on both men and women, news about and by women has lost space even in these life-style sections.[61]

Television news is not much better. In a study of the content of evening news programs on CBS, NBC, and ABC, Lana Rakow and Kimberlie Kranich found that women as on-camera sources of information were used in less than 15 percent of the cases. When women did speak, they were usually passive reactors to public events (as housewife or wife of the man in the news) rather than participants or experts. Even in critical analyses of issues that affect more women than men, women may not appear on the screen. For example, a lengthy story on CBS on welfare reform did not use any women or feminist sources.[62]

Amicable

Much domination is accepted by women because they share intimate relationships with men who have convinced women that domination is "for your own good." A female faculty member in an all-male department was refused a leave of absence to finish her dissertation because "you need all the teaching experience you can get" and "the department needs you." She continued to get outstanding student evaluations, served on committees tirelessly, did not finish her dissertation, and was not reappointed two years later.

COLLEGIAL EXCLUSION

> It is sometimes impossible for any woman, no matter how high her qualifications, to be hired at certain schools. A Harvard department head stated that he has men on the staff who will vote against a woman for a job just because she is a woman. They just don't want women around.[63]

Men are currently less likely to make such blatantly sexist statements. Instead, they make them in more subtle ways—such as through physical, social, and professional exclusion.

Physical Exclusion

Physical exclusion takes many forms—being ignored, isolated, excluded from decision-making processes, overlooked in textbooks and reading materials, or squeezed into small physical spaces.

Being ignored. Many women feel invisible. Women students often feel left out of the curriculum and classroom discussions. According to a high school student, for example, women's contributions were routinely ignored in her classes:

> In history we never talked about what women did; in geography it was always what was important to men. The same in our English class; we hardly ever studied women authors. I won't even talk about math and science . . . I always felt that I didn't belong. Sometimes the boys would make jokes about girls doing science experiments. They always thought they were going to do it better and it made me really nervous. Sometimes I didn't even try to do an experiment because I knew they would laugh if I got it wrong. Now I just deaden myself against it, so I don't hear it any more. But I feel really alienated. My experience now is one of total silence.[64]

College women report similar exclusion and, ultimately, withdraw from class participation:

> I don't speak in class anymore. All this professor ever talked about was men, what they do, what they say, always just what's important to men. He, he, he is all I ever heard in class. He wasn't speaking my language. And whenever I tried to speak about what was important to me, whenever I tried to ask questions about how women fit into his scheme all I got was a negative response. I always felt I was speaking from inside brackets, like walls I couldn't be heard past. I got tired of not being heard so I stopped speaking altogether.[65]

Women students have often accused faculty and administrators of ignoring them outside the classroom as well. A senior at Yale University complained, for example, that women's sports get minimal attention: "You hardly ever see a story about women's sports in the student newspaper. At the Varsity Night dinner, the president was talking about men's teams. He didn't even mention that the women's cross-country team won a championship."[66]

Isolation.   A more subtle form of physical exclusion is isolation. Isolation during important meetings, get-togethers, lunches, and conferences makes women feel like outsiders:

> I've attended several dean's conferences where about six out of the seventy participants are women. Women are usually ignored—during panels and informal discussions—because men think they have nothing to learn from women. (Woman vice-president at a university)

The American Chemical Society's women chemists committee publishes a list, known by some as the "Dirty Dozen," which identifies major chemistry departments, some with dozens of faculty members, that still have *no* women in tenure-track positions.[67] The few women in nontenure-track positions often feel isolated and vulnerable.

Exclusion from decision making.   Women may be ignored during critical decision making even though they provide the background research:

> Several times, my male colleagues used records of my patients to do research. It's never occurred to them to ask me to participate on these projects or to ask my opinion about diagnoses. I know I'm doing a good job, but I feel very isolated professionally. (Female physician at a major medical school)

Another form of physical exclusion is to keep women out of male clubs and training programs. In a study of women employed in traditionally male craft jobs, one of the women's most common reports was that men excluded them from critical on-the-job training.[68] Some of the most prestigious institutions are also among the most adamant in excluding women. Skull and Bones, a secret, all-male society at Yale University, changed the club's locks and shut down for a year when the seniors voted unanimously to bring in women. The alumni board of the 159-year-old society—whose members include President Bush, several U.S. senators, and other luminaries—wanted the men to meet separately for the society's most important ritual, when new members share their emotional and life histories.[69]

In these and other cases, women are complaining or suing not because they want male companionship, but because it is illegal for organizations that get federal funds to discriminate on the basis of sex. Women feel they should have the option of attending gatherings at institutions that are supported by *both* men's and women's taxes.

Qualified, intelligent women are more likely than less-qualified men to be appointed to trivial committees for long terms. A common reason for not granting women tenure, promotion, or salary increases, however, is that they have not participated in "important" committees:

> Last year, I found out, by accident, that my salary was about $5,000 lower than that of my male colleagues with comparable experience, seniority, clerkships, where we got our law degrees, and publications. When I asked the dean why my salary was so much lower, he said it was because I had never chaired any committees. Well, he's *never* appointed women faculty to chair committees, even after we often volunteered to do so. (Female law school faculty member)

Although there have been some improvements, many college textbooks still exclude women almost entirely. In a study of the 27 top-selling textbooks for introductory psychology and all 12 textbooks for human development courses, Sharyl Peterson and Traci Kroner concluded that the work, theory, and behavior of men continue to significantly exceed those of women. Men are more likely to author such texts, to review them, and to have their work cited in them. Women who have contributed to the field of psychology are remarkably absent from the historical discussions. Despite the fact that 56 percent of psychologists and 78 percent of developmental psychologists who receive Ph.D.s are women, textbooks give the impression that the majority of psychologists are men. Women are much more likely to be used to illustrate various pathologies and to be shown as clients in therapy, whereas males are typically portrayed as healthy and competent. Results of studies that are comprised only of males (and usually only of white, middle-class college students) are generalized to all people.[70]

Squeezed into small spaces.   An intriguing example of physical exclusion comes from the literature on the usage of physical space. According to Nancy Henley, women's environment is largely man-made, man-controlled, and designed to make men (not women) comfortable and secure.[71] Women are expected to take up as little physical space as possible (for example, secretarial pools), to have limited spatial mobility, and to create living spaces that nurture men and children but ignore women (for example, dens, family rooms, "master" bedrooms, small kitchens, children's playrooms). Also, women's time is often constricted and not valued. It is assumed that most women's time is unimportant and can be extended at the last minute (for example, waiting for hours at a pediatrician's office, putting in a "few hours" after work without compensation).

Regardless of job responsibilities, many men typically assume that women's time and space are less important than their own:

> I was an account executive and my ex-husband was in sales. He made less than I did but always acted as if being a wife was more important than my job. This went on for years and I accepted it. The straw that broke the camel's back was the time that he called me at work one morning and said he had invited thirty-

five people to a sit-down dinner that evening. When I said that I had to work, he got annoyed: "Well, just take the day off; this is important to me." (Manager in banking industry)

Many women change their schedules at the last minute to accommodate men, anticipate men's and children's needs, and sacrifice their own time and space to those they serve.

Social/Professional Exclusion

Even when men and women share the same physical space, women are often excluded both socially and professionally. Whether in business, industry, or higher education, many women still report that they are battling an "old boy's network." A woman editor at *The New York Times* said that managerial meetings on the news floor sometimes give her "anxiety attacks":

We are drowned out, not listened to, we are dismissed, passed over. It makes me crazy. The men running the *Times* now truly do not believe themselves capable of sexist feelings. They have serious wives. They help with the dishes. But they are still looking for, and are only comfortable with, people in their own image—in other words, other white men. They have a joking camaraderie together that walls us out.[72]

In a similar vein, a college-educated woman who is the manager of the mortgage department at a bank said that her supervisor routinely ignores her expertise: "I know all of the regulations forward and backward, but because I am a woman, my boss won't ever ask me for answers. He usually goes to one of the few males in the office and ends up with the wrong answers."

According to a female law professor, women may suffer if they're not interested in playing men's games or don't know the rules:

The informal process starts from the day one walks in the door. If a faculty member doesn't enjoy the little jokes told about women in the faculty lounge, if she is not interested in the latest football rating, if she doesn't drink beer with the boys, if she doesn't join the Friday-afternoon poker games in the faculty lounge, she is not collegial. If a younger faculty member, facing some difficulty with teaching or research, opens up to an older professor for advice and guidance, the admitted "mistakes," reservations, or uncertainties may be brought up when she is later considered for tenure.[73]

Also, women are ignored or sanctioned if they violate stereotypical expectations about "proper attire":

Men—in comparable positions—can wear anything they want and people listen. But when I stand up to speak, people's attention is focused more on my outfit or figure rather than my verbal contributions. I must be color-coordinated or they won't listen. (Registered nurse at a teaching hospital)

Women in nontraditional positions are especially susceptible to exclusion. A member of the Maryland legislature said that her colleagues do not take women seriously because women are assumed to be "too principled and not political enough." On the other hand, women are ignored if they are tough, aggressive, and political because such behavior is "unfeminine." In a survey of female members of the American Astronomical Society, 31 percent said they were accused of being "difficult," "vocal," or "having a strong personality" when they expressed an opinion about subjects they were knowledgeable about.[74] The only woman on the board of trustees of an electric cooperative in a New England community wrote the following about her board's trip to inspect a hydroelectric site:

> When a team of engineers presented a study [on electricity produced by methane], they avoided eye contact with me and spoke directly to the men on the board. It was so obvious that they were presenting their findings "over my head," that I decided to take action in order to demonstrate I had an understanding of the project. I asked a technical question regarding "pelletizing" the dry end product for fuel. It made some difference, but I can see that I have to be ever alert to dealing with subtle discrimination constantly and that I am not being paranoid.

When social and professional activities overlap, women are often excluded. Women faculty are usually invited to functions where participants are asked to bring food. When just "the guys" are socializing, however, women are often not invited. One of our respondents, an engineer, said that she was excited when her male colleagues were setting up basketball teams during lunch. Because she's very athletic, she asked if she could join. They said, seriously, "Oh, sure, you can be the cheerleader."

On a more macabre note, even when women are seemingly accepted as equals during their lifetime, they are relegated to the ranks of "just women" after their death. When NBC's Jessica Savitch died during an automobile accident in 1983, a number of newspapers eulogized and highlighted her personal characteristics rather than her professional accomplishments. An editorial in the *Baltimore Sun* focused on her marriages, miscarriage, and looks: "She was so exquisitely beautiful that she could have been Miss America . . . despite demonstrable talent in her work, there were still whispers that she was 'a bit of fluff,' 'NBC's Playboy bunny.'"[75] When male anchors die, on the other hand, we rarely hear about their affairs, toupees, impotence, biceps, illegitimate children, or other nonprofessional activities and characteristics.

WOMEN'S COMPLICITY IN SUBTLE SEX DISCRIMINATION

However unintentional, liberated sexism also comes from women, including some feminists who accept the double standard. After the 1984 election, Geraldine Ferraro did a 30-second television commercial for Diet Pepsi in which she emphasized her role as mother ("We can be whatever we want to be, and being a mother is one of the choices I'm most proud of"). Both feminists and nonfeminists accused Ferraro of "selling out," being a political huckster, prostituting herself, and forsaking women's issues. Yet, when Lee Iacocca and Mikhail Baryshnikov did similar commercials, no one questioned their character or attacked their professional credibility.

During the last decade, there has been less criticism of women who choose to be full-time homemakers. Similarly, we now speak about a plurality of feminisms instead of a single, unified, and correct feminist perspective. Too often, however, women reaffirm the belief that men are better than women. In our interviews, several secretaries said that they resent watering plants, making coffee, and taking personal phone calls for women bosses but not men bosses. They expect women bosses to be more friendly, more accepting of tardiness, and to show a greater personal interest in the employees. These and other double standards free men from work and responsibility, reinforce sex stereotypes, and dilute women's authority.

Many mothers try to curb their daughters' but not their sons' sexual activities. If there is a premarital pregnancy, in most cases it is the girl, not the boy, who is blamed. Although some of the criticism of "deadbeat dads" has increased, it is still the girl or the woman who is expected to assume social and economic responsibility for the baby. In many households, children's chores are still assigned in terms of gender rather than on ability or interest or on a rotating basis.

Female talk-show hosts are among the worst offenders in promoting subtle sexism. On the one hand, they feature guests who belittle men's obsession with attractive women. Overweight women are told to "love yourselves for what you are inside" and to "accept yourself because you're beautiful." However, the next dozen shows often tell women how to lose weight, where to get makeovers, how to find Mr. Right, and applaud women who gush on and on about their face-lifts, liposuctions, and breast implants.

Many professionals are also either ignorant or accepting of sex discrimination. There are successful women who feel that "if you're willing to work, and if you are talented, you will be rewarded, whatever your sex is." Some are "Queen Bees," but others honestly believe that women just aren't as talented as men. One of our respondents—who is 67 years old and who received a master's degree in science in chemistry many years ago—stated: "I blame women for a lot of the discrimination. Women want equal rights but don't want to earn it." A division head at the National Science Foundation said that she sometimes receives grant proposals from female organizers who have no women on the platform because they want "only the best" (i.e., men).[76]

The subtle sex discrimination processes discussed in this chapter are not exhaustive. There are a variety of other processes that are often sophisticated and rarely suspected because they are not immediately visible and because men and women have been socialized to practice and accept subtle sex discrimination.

The next chapter will examine covert discriminatory mechanisms that are even more difficult to uncover and document.

NOTES

1. "Stanford Medical Dean Backs Female Surgeon's Charges of Sexism," *Baltimore Sun,* June 4, 1991, p. 16A.
2. Adria Libolt, "Bridging the Gender Gap," *Corrections Today,* Vol. 53, December 1991, p. 138.
3. Susan Fraker, "Why Top Jobs Elude Female Executives," *Fortune,* April 16, 1984, p. 46.
4. Carol Berkin, "'Dangerous Courtesies' Assault Women's History," *The Chronicle of Higher Education,* December 11, 1991, p. A44.
5. *The AAUW Report: How Schools Shortchange Girls: A Study of Major Findings on Girls and Education,* Washington, DC: American Association of University Women Educational Foundation, 1992, p. 63
6. Sarah B. Hechtman and Robert Rosenthall, "Teacher Gender and Non-verbal Behavior in the Teaching of Gender-Stereotyped Materials," *Journal of Applied Social Psychology,* 21, no. 6 (1991), pp. 446–459.
7. Anne Statham, Laurel Richardson, and Judith A. Cook. *Gender and University Teaching: A Negotiated Difference* (Albany, NY: State University of New York Press, 1991).
8. Desdemona Cardoza, "College Attendance and Persistence Among Hispanic Women: An Examination of Some Contributing Factors," *Sex Roles,* 24, nos. 3/4 (1991), pp. 133–147.
9. Ivan Amato, "Chemistry: Profile of a Field—Women Have Extra Hoops to Jump Through," *Science,* Vol. 255, March 13, 1992, pp. 1372–1373.
10. Joanna Russ, *How to Suppress Woman's Writing* (Austin, Texas: University of Texas Press, 1983), p. 13.
11. Paul Selvin, "Mathematics: Profile of a Field; Heroism Is Still the Norm," *Science,* Vol. 255, March 13, 1992, p. 1382.
12. Study by Janet Bickel, cited in Robin Herman, "Sex Stereotypes in Medicine," *Washington Post, Health Supplement,* February 16, 1993, p. 7.
13. Sarah Glazer, "Are Medical Schools Sexist?" *Washington Post, Health Supplement,* February 18, 1992, pp. 10–12.
14. Douglas Lederman, "Colgate U. Becomes a Battleground over Equity in College Athletics," *The Chronicle of Higher Education,* February 17, 1993, pp. A27–A28.
15. See, for example, Rees Hughes, "The Non-Traditional Student in Higher Education: A Synthesis of the Literature," *NASPA Journal* (1981), pp. 51–64; Melanie Rawlins, "Life Made Easier for the Over-Thirty Undergrads," *Journal of College Student Personnel* (1980), pp. 65–73; Katie Smallwood, "What Do Adult College Students Really Need?" *Journal of College Student Personnel* (1980), pp. 65–73; and Loribeth Weinstein, *Field Evaluation Report, Recruitment and Admission: Opening the Door for Re-entry Women* (Washington, DC: Project on the Status and Education of Women, 1980).
16. Yolanda T. Moses, *Black Women in Academe: Issues and Strategies,* Project on the Status and Education of Women (Washington, DC: Association of American Colleges, 1989) p. 19.

17. Janice Larch and Regina Ryan, *Strategies for Women at Work* (New York: Avon Books, 1984), p. 14.

18. Debra Kent, "'Jewish American Princess': How Teenage Girls Perceive the JAP Stereotype," *Women's Studies in Indiana Newsletter,* Indiana University Bloomington, 18, no. 3 (February/March 1993) 1, 3.

19. Regina Barreca, *They Used to Call Me Snow White . . . but I Drifted: Women's Strategic Use of Humor* (New York: Penguin Books, 1991), p. 142.

20. See Cynthia Cockburn, *In the Way of Women: Men's Resistance to Sex Equality in Organizations* (Ithaca, NY: Cornell University School of Industrial and Labor Relations, 1991).

21. Alice E. Courtney and Thomas W. Whipple, *Sex Stereotyping in Advertising* (Lexington, MA: Lexington Books, 1983).

22. See Regina Barreca, *They Used to Call Me Snow White . . .*

23. *Baltimore Sun,* "The Last Laugh's on Men," September 30, 1992, p. 1F.

24. Ibid., p. 13.

25. Eleanor Clift, "Taking the Low Road," *Newsweek,* October 28, 1991, p. 30.

26. Donna J. Benson and Gregg E. Thomson, "Sexual Harassment on a University Campus: The Confluence of Authority Relations, Sexual Interest and Gender Stratification," *Social Problems,* 29, February 1982, p. 243.

27. *Newsweek,* "Lesbians: Coming Out Strong; What Are the Limits of Tolerance?" June 21, 1993.

28. Cited in Cheryl M. Fields, "Allegations of Lesbianism Being Used to Intimidate, Female Academics Say," *Chronicle of Higher Education,* October 26, 1983, pp. 1, 22–23. For a recent, but very similar discussion of homophobia about women athletes, see Debra L. Blum, "College Sports' L-Word," *The Chronicle of Higher Education,* March 9, 1994, pp. A35–A36.

29. Elaine M. Blinde and Diane E. Taub, "Women Athletes as Falsely Accused Deviants: Managing the Lesbian Stigma," *The Sociological Quarterly,* 33, no. 4 (1992), pp. 521–533.

30. Billie W. Dziech and Linda Weiner, *The Lecherous Professor: Sexual Harassment on Campus* (Boston: Beacon Press, 1984), pp. 122–123.

31. See, for example, Sheila M. Rothman, *Women's Proper Place* (New York: Basic Books, 1978); Mary P. Ryan, *Womanhood in America* (New York: Franklin Watts, 1983); and Amy Swerdlow and Hanna Lessinger, eds., *Class, Race, and Sex: The Dynamics of Control* (Boston: G. K. Hall & Company, 1983).

32. Harriet Zuckerman, Jonathan R. Cole, and John T. Bruer, eds., *The Outer Circle: Women in the Scientific Community* (New York: Norton, 1991).

33. Russ, *How to Suppress Women's Writing,* p. 50.

34. Susan Baer, "First Lady Flap: Wellesley Students Find Little Support for Petition Protesting Barbara Bush," *Baltimore Sun,* April 27, 1990, p. 1F.

35. Victor F. D'Lugin, "On Credibility: Differential Treatment of Women and Men in the Law," in *Women in Politics: Outsiders or Insiders? A Collection of Readings,* ed., Lois Lovelace Duke (Englewood Cliffs, NJ: Prentice Hall, 1993), pp. 185–197.

36. See Edwin M. Schur, *Labeling Women Deviant: Gender, Stigma, and Social Control* (New York: Random House, 1984), pp. 33ff., for general and spe-

cific discussions of objectification from which some of the characteristic were drawn.

37. Patricia Yancey Martin and Robert A. Hummer, "Fraternities and Rape on Campus," in *Violence Against Women*, eds., Pauline B. Bart and Eileen Geil Moran (Newbury Park, CA: Sage Publications, 1993), pp. 114–131.

38. Katha Pollitt, "The Smurfette Principle," *The New York Times Magazine*, April 7, 1991, p. 22.

39. Ibid., p. 22.

40. These characteristics of "hidden employment biases" summarize and extend Clarice Stasz, *The American Nightmare* (New York: Schocken Books, 1983), pp. 189–190.

41. "Ensign Meets President," *Baltimore Sun*, May 25, 1984, p. E–3.

42. Jeanne Guillemin, Lynda L. Holmstrom, and Michele Garvin, "Judging Competence: Letters of Recommendation for Men and Women Faculties," *School Review* (February 1979), p. 169.

43. See, for example, Pamela M. Fishman, "Interaction: The Work Women Do," *Social Problems*, 25 (April 1978), pp. 397–406; Robin Lakoff, *Language and Woman's Place* (New York: Harper & Row, 1975); Judy Cornelia Pearson, Lynn H. Turner, and William Todd-Mancillas, *Gender & Communication*, second ed. (Dubuque, IA: Wm. C. Brown Publishers, 1991); and Laurie P. Arliss, *Gender Communication* (Englewood Cliffs, NJ: Prentice Hall, 1991).

44. Patricia H. Bradley, "The Folk Linguistics of Women's Speech: An Empirical Examination," *Communication Monographs* 48, March 1982, pp. 73–90.

45. J. Gershuny and J. P. Robinson, "Historical Changes in the Household Division of Labor," *Demography*, 25, no. 4 (November 1988): pp. 537–552.

46. J. P. Robinson, "Who's Doing the Housework?" *American Demographics*, 10, no. 12, December 1988, pp. 24–28, 63. See also, Beth Anne Shelton, *Women, Men, and Time* (New York: Greenwood Press, 1992).

47. Jean Curtis, cited in J. Gap, D. St. John-Parson, and J. O'Barr, "The Dual Careers of Faculty and Family: Can Both Prosper?" (paper presented at the American Association for Higher Education meetings, Washington, DC, 1982).

48. "Air Combat Would Be Easier," *The Economist*, 324, September 19, 1992, p. 108.

49. Stephen Buckley, "Truck Driver Settles Bias Case in Md.," *Washington Post*, April 24, 1991, p. A17. See also, Shari Rudavsky, "Recalling Tales of Sex Discrimination," *Washington Post*, July 1, 1992, p. A21.

50. Harriet Zuckerman, Jonathan R. Cole, and John T. Bruer, eds., *The Outer Circle: Women in the Scientific Community* (New York: Norton, 1991).

51. Stephen B. Knouse, "The Mentoring Process for Hispanics," in *Hispanics in the Workplace*, eds., Stephen B. Knouse, Paul Rosenfeld, and Amy L. Culbertson (Newbury Park, CA: Sage Publications, 1992), pp. 137–150.

52. Ellen Cassedy and Karen Nussbaum, *9 to 5: The Working Woman's Guide to Office Survival* (New York: Penguin Books, 1983), pp. 93–94.

53. Ibid.

54. Courtney and Whipple, *Sex Stereotyping*, pp. 103–104.

55. William J. Rudman and Akiko F. Hagiwara, "Sexual Exploitation in Advertising Health and Wellness Products," *Women & Health,* 18, no. 4 (1992), pp. 77–89. Citation on p. 87.

56. Esther B. Greif, "Sex Differences in Parent-Child Conversations," *Women's Studies International Quarterly,* 3 (1980), p. 257.

57. Virginia R. Brooks, "Sex Differences in Student Dominance Behavior in Female and Male Professors' Classrooms," *Sex Roles,* 8 (1982), p. 688.

58. Deborah Tannen, *You Just Don't Understand: Women and Men in Conversation* (New York: Ballantine Books, 1990), p. 126.

59. Jennie Dusheck, "Female Primatologists Confer—Without Men," *Science,* 249, September 28, 1990, p. 1494.

60. Schur, *Labeling Women Deviant,* p. 25.

61. Reported in Ellen Goodman, "A Woman's Place Is in the Paper," *Baltimore Sun,* April 7, 1992, p. 15A.

62. Lana F. Rakow and Kimberlie Kranich, "Woman as Sign in Television News," *Journal of Communication,* 41, no. 1, Winter 1991, pp. 8–23.

63. Cited in Janice Pottker, "Overt and Covert Forms of Discrimination Against Academic Women," in *Sex Bias in the Schools: The Research Evidence,* eds., Janice Pottker and Andrew Fishel (Cranbury, NJ: Associated University Presses, 1977), p. 386.

64. Magda Lewis, "Interrupting Patriarchy: Politics, Resistance, and Transformation in the Feminist Classroom," *Harvard Educational Review,* 60, no. 4, November 1990, p. 472.

65. Ibid., p. 472.

66. Michele N-K Collison, "20 Years Later, Women on Formerly All-Male Campuses Fight to Change Their Institutions' 'Old Boy' Images," *The Chronicle of Higher Education,* December 12, 1990, p. 24.

67. Ivan Amato, "Chemistry: Profile of a Field—Women Have Extra Hoops to Jump Through," *Science,* 255, March 13, 1992, pp. 1372–1373.

68. Brigid O'Farrell and Sharon L. Harlan, "Craftworkers and Clerks: The Effect of Male Co-Worker Hostility on Women's Satisfaction with Non-Traditional Jobs," *Social Problems,* 29, February 1982, pp. 252–265.

69. Denise K. Magner, "Alumni Shut Down Secret Society at Yale U. over Attempt to Admit Women." *The Chronicle of Higher Education,* April 24, 1991, p. A2. Jerry Adler with Mary Talbot and Clara Bingham, "God, Men and Bonding at Yale," *Newsweek,* April 29, 1991, p. 66.

70. Sharyl Bender Peterson and Traci Kroner, "Gender Biases in Textbooks for Introductory Psychology and Human Development," *Psychology of Women Quarterly,* 16 (1992), pp. 17–36.

71. Henley, 1977. See also, Gerda R. Wekerle, Rebecca Peterson, and David Moreley, eds., *New Space for Women* (Boulder, CO: Active Press, 1980).

72. Quoted in Nan Robertson, *The Girls in the Balcony: Women, Men and the New York Times* (New York: Random House, 1992), p. 235.

73. Marina Angel, "Women in Legal Education: What It's Like to Be Part of a Perpetual First Wave or the Case of the Disappearing Women," *Temple Law Review,* 61 (1988), p. 831.

74. Kim A. McDonald, "Many Female Astronomers Say They Face Sex Harassment and Bias," *Chronicle of Higher Education,* February 13, 1991, pp. A11, A15.

75. "A Fallen Star," *Baltimore Sun,* October 28, 1983, p. D3.

76. Boyce Rensberger, "Women's Place: on the Podium," *Washington Post,* August 26, 1992, p. 21A.

CHAPTER SIX
HOW COVERT SEX DISCRIMINATION WORKS

Covert sex discrimination refers to the unequal and harmful treatment of women that is hidden, clandestine, and maliciously motivated. We call this type of discrimination "covert" because it typically is crafted or implemented behind the scenes or with rationalizations that try to make it appear to be nondiscriminatory. Covert discrimination has generally received less attention than the other types we have examined. It is usually difficult to prove because records are not kept or are inaccessible, the victim may not even be aware of being a target, and witnesses are too afraid or self-serving to come forward.

Six types of covert sex discrimination are discussed in this chapter—tokenism, containment, manipulation, sabotage, revenge, and co-optation. Tokenism and containment typically prevent large numbers of women from entering high-paying, high-status, powerful positions. Manipulation, sabotage, and revenge are likely to discourage moving up the ladder. In the corporate world, for example, tokenism and containment ensure that a limited number of women will be hired as supervisors or managers; manipulation, revenge, and sabotage will prevent their advancing into higher positions as vice-presidents, presidents, or board members. Similarly, in higher education, token women might be hired, especially in male-dominated departments, at the lower levels—that is, as lecturers, instructors, and assistant professors. Whether they are tokens or not, many will be contained at lower-level positions with little chance of promotion. Tokenism and containment are entry-level employment barriers, whereas manipulation, revenge, and sabotage limit vertical mobility. Because it enlists and rewards women's support for maintaining sex inequality, co-optation provides a double dosage of discrimination: Women who are co-opted often play an active role in reinforcing tokenism, containment, manipulation, revenge, and sabotage.

TOKENISM

Tokenism refers to the unwritten and usually unspoken policy or practice of hiring, promoting, or otherwise including a minuscule number of people from such underrepresented groups as women, minorities, the physically challenged, and the elderly. Through tokenism, organizations maintain the semblance of equality because no group is totally excluded. Tokenism has the superficial look of fairness that conceals modern sexism in practice.

General Characteristics

Across almost all occupational areas and often regardless of age, experience, religion, color, education, intelligence, and ability, female tokens are typically marginal members of the work group; they are highly visible but are excluded from upward mobility. They are trophies—placed on a public shelf and dusted off when "company" comes.

There is a close relationship between tokenism and powerlessness. Adrienne Rich described female tokenism as a "false power which masculine society offers to a few women who 'think like men.'"[1] According to Judith Long Laws, "tokenism is likely to be found wherever a dominant group is under pressure to share privilege, power, or other desirable commodities with a group which is excluded."[2] Tokenism is usually a conscious, calculated effort to avoid charges of discrimination and possible investigations that might uncover widespread exclusionary policies and practices.

How Tokenism Works

There are three types of commonly-practiced tokenism that limit women's equal participation in the labor force—numerical tokenism, pragmatic tokenism, and symbolic tokenism.

Numerical tokenism.   Numerical tokenism, a widespread form of exclusion, uses quotas to maintain a predominantly male work force:

> As soon as they come into my office, a lot of recruiters tell me exactly how many women they plan to hire and in which departments. They say things like, "This year we need two women in accounting, one in marketing, and one in data processing." Some [of the recruiters] have fairly detailed data showing exactly how many women they should be hiring for their company. (What if the most qualified candidates are all women?) Most recruiters automatically assume that women are not the most qualified—they got high grades because they slept around, they're not serious about long-term job commitments, they don't understand the business world and so on. . . . They interview the [women] students we schedule, but rarely hire more than the one or two they're told to hire. (College job placement director)

Because male quotas are high—95 to 99 percent—it is not difficult to fill the low percentage of slots allocated to token women.

Numerical tokens report two types of problems. First, they are often in lower-ranking positions that require a great deal of work but have little career mobility and get minimal attention from supervisors:

> International studies is a low priority. At many universities, people in my position report to the provost rather than to the admissions office. I have little mobility because I'm not a supervisor but a one-person office with no secretary. I might spend a whole day with a student, but I'm not taken seriously at staff meetings because we have small international enrollments—even though my services are indispensable. (Director, International Student Office)

Numerical tokens are often ignored, overworked, or both. One of our respondents—a black, female medical student—felt that she was often discounted during important training opportunities:

> We were in a surgical procedure and I was told to hand the instruments as others helped in cutting and suturing the patient. There were surgical nurses there to hand over the instruments, so how did I end up doing the job?

At the other extreme, numerical tokens may be overwhelmed with attention and unwanted responsibilities:

> Because of the paucity of Black professors at my university, I am placed in the dilemma of being all things to all Black students. There are only two other females (in a university of 16,000 students), one in the school of medicine and the other in agriculture, and both . . . have little contact with Black students."[3]

Because Latina faculty are underrepresented even more severely than African Americans and Asian Americans, they are even more vulnerable to tokenism. Since they are often called on to represent two historically disenfranchised groups—women and people of color—on committees and various forums, they are especially prone to stress, burnout, and failure.

Even women in high business positions are not immune to the devastating effects of overattentive tokenism:

> Shannon, an advertising industry executive, described the problems of being the only woman on the board. "Whenever one of the members would address the board, they'd say 'Gentlemen and Shannon.' It made me feel singled out, different. Also, whenever they wanted a 'woman's point of view' for a commercial, they'd all turn and look at me like I was a spokesperson for womankind."[4]

The second problem is that tokens are often stereotyped. Such stereotypes create numerous dilemmas that "regular people" never encounter. When one of the men misses a meeting or fails to contribute, no one notices because men are present and contributed. When a group's lone woman is absent or silent, everyone notices.[5] Because tokens feel intimidated by their visibility, they might not take advantage of valuable resources:

There were occasions when I was having problems and wasn't really under-standing [the material], and just didn't feel comfortable enough around the professor to go in there and ask questions. I guess I was afraid they would think I was dumb . . . because I was a woman and I was trying to prove that I *wasn't* dumb. . . . Unfortunately, that hurt, because in that last year I just fell behind in a lot of stuff because I was not willing to ask questions. I didn't want to draw at-tention. (Mechanical engineering student)[6]

Tokens often recognize that they are different but must pretend that the differences do not exist to preserve a cooperative work environment. Al-though they are the most noticeable performers, they are often in the organi-zational backstages. They rarely relax because they are not really equal to their peers. They often feel lonely and alone.[7]

Pragmatic tokenism.   Pragmatic tokenism hires and retains women only when it is cost-effective to do so. As long as there is a large pool of talented women who are happy to get any job, have high productivity rates, do not protest about serving as window dressing, and do not demand genuine progress, tokenism runs smoothly. If tokens push for real improvement, they may be fired. Turnover is inexpensive because there is usually a plentiful sup-ply of replacements, even at higher levels: "There are already more candi-dates for management than business could ever use. And the benefits of a cheap labor force far outweigh the dubious value of having a larger pool of managerial talent."[8] This revolving-door brand of tokenism is profitable for companies because it ensures a continuous flow of hard-working and compe-tent employees at low costs.

Symbolic tokenism.   In contrast to pragmatic tokenism, symbolic to-kenism is less transparent because the tokens appear to be treated just like anyone else—their salaries are competitive, and some receive training for higher-level jobs or hold responsible positions. Despite such embellishments, however, these women are also tokens. They are placed in specially reserved, visible niches to symbolize the institution's commitment to equal opportunity. Because they are always on display, symbolic tokens enjoy some of the accou-terments that accompany all attractive showcases, such as fancy titles, raises, and expense accounts. Since they are being paid for their visibility and not their credibility, however, they are usually marginal members of the organiza-tion—isolated, excluded from powerful peer networks, and placed in "sex-stereotypical role traps that limit effectiveness."[9] Some of our respondents said that they were promoted to "assistant vice-president," "assistant to the vice-president," or similar impressive positions, but they had little significant input. In fact, their decision-making power may decrease after a promotion:

I had worked all the way up to loan officer . . . and a part of that is that you have a responsibility in approving loans or whatever when people come to apply. And, all of a sudden, when I took this job, a man had the job before and he made vice-president and I became assistant vice-president. All of a sudden he still had the approval responsibility for the job; I didn't have it anymore. I could type up the applications, I could file the applications, I could do all of those little things that really was the secretarial work for the position and it was almost like it was down-graded. And when I asked about the loan approval process and things like that, well all of these things had been turned over to a loan committee. I could bring them the coffee and set up for the meeting and do all of those things. But I had the title. Can you believe it?

Playing Tokenism Games with Nontokens

Even when women are not tokens, accusations of tokenism are effective strategies for keeping women in their "place." Such allegations create suspicion; raise doubts about women's intelligence, abilities, and achievements; and decrease competition because women might not enter or might withdraw from the economic race. For example, women who are told that they are being hired to "meet a quota" will sometimes refuse the interview or the job offer:

> I have a 3.9 [on a 4.0 scale] and I'm in the top 5 percent of my graduating class. When I went to the interviews at school, the recruiters from two of the biggest firms said they were interested in me because they had to hire women. . . . The more I thought about it later, the angrier I got. Doesn't my 3.9 mean anything? I'm not working for a company which tells me, to my face, that my years of hard work don't mean anything. (Undergraduate accounting major)

Bright and hardworking women may be especially offended by tokenism and may turn down attractive offers. They are probably wise not to enter a company or agency that openly treats women as tokens. Yet, such refusals reinforce and encourage companies to use tokenism as a successful ploy in discouraging women's entry into jobs.

In other cases, women—and especially minority women—may experience what Yolanda Moses describes as the "shifting sands syndrome." That is, even when minorities are hired, the "rules of the game" may shift:

> Minority administrators who appear on paper to have the necessary qualifications are told, "Yes, you are technically qualified, but the person we hired had additional experience in this specialized area that we need." Generally, the specific experience hasn't been mentioned as desirable and doesn't appear to be all that relevant. Many of us thus come to feel that we are not trusted to be leaders.[10]

CONTAINMENT

"Containment" refers to the unwritten and usually unspoken practice of restricting women's entry into designated jobs and positions so as not to threaten or displace the composition of dominant group members. While tokenism establishes the limits on how many women will be allowed *entry* into (especially nonfemale) jobs, containment ensures that they will not move up after being hired into an entry-level position. Containment is primarily a matter of limited mobility. Although tokenism and containment are discussed separately here for analytical purposes, the two processes are often interdependent.

Establishing Male-Female Domains

Women's and men's behavior is limited or "contained," from the time they are born. Both sexes learn that girls and boys (and, later, men and women) speak, think, act, dress, smell, feel, play, work, pray, fight, drink, eat, smoke, sit, stand, bend, walk, drive, shop, sleep, make love, write, urinate, belch, and argue *differently*. In most activities men are typically expected to be independent, in control, knowledgeable, and in command; women are expected to be dependent, submissive, uninformed, and controlled.

Recruiters and employers often try to channel prospective employees into positions that are informally designated as "women's jobs" or "men's jobs:"

> When I applied for employment at the railroad, I applied for a brakeman position based upon my experience of tuning motors at the mine. I was a skilled equipment operator. However, the recruiter told me that my experience wasn't good enough and offered to hire me as a car cleaner. I quickly objected. I realized he was preordaining what would be "most appropriate" for me to do. We eventually came to an agreement. I left his office a brakeman, or I should say a brakewoman, trainee. It turned out that some of the new guys they hired at the same time had less truly relevant experience than I did. (Railroad worker)

Several of our respondents reported that when they were hired at assembly plants, they were steered into "less grueling work" that was also much lower paying. One of the women we interviewed said, "I simply ignored the lecture and took the better paying, more difficult job [at an auto parts assembly plant]. I was up to the challenge and I performed my job just fine." Another respondent observed that strenuous physical work is often devalued in female-dominated jobs:

> My stepfather helped me the last time I moved, but he asked if I was getting any other men to help. I told him that I could lift the heavy stuff with him, but he said that he needed another man. He doesn't think about how I have to lift 200-pound patients that are literally "dead weight." I guess he sees that kind of lifting as OK because nursing is women's work.

Maintaining Male-Female Turf

Upon entering adulthood, some people have the opportunity and resources to dig their way out of the avalanche of sexist rhetoric and behavior in which they grew up. Many do not—in large part, because containment procedures, especially in employment, maintain male-female domains through such activities as mentoring, stalling, demotions or promotions, exclusion from decision-making functions, and gatekeeping.

Mentoring.   Women do not achieve as much as they might in education and employment because they lack mentorship: "I have a goal of being a dean, maybe even a college president someday. But how do I go about doing that? I don't know how to get that without mentors."[11]

Because mentorship processes differ by sex, they can feed containment. In the mid-1990s, Dr. Margaret Jensvold at the National Institutes of Mental Health (NIMH) sued her supervisor for not being a mentor. Dr. Jensvold had impeccable credentials: she graduated from the Johns Hopkins School of Medicine, had been named by the Association for Academic Psychiatry as one of the six most promising psychiatric residents in the country, and won a prestigious fellowship to the NIMH. Dr. Jensvold said that "I went to all the right schools, did all the right research, won all the right awards and it didn't help." She alleged that her mentor at NIMH failed to guide her research, kept her in the dark about important meetings and conferences, did not watch out for her professional interests, and favored her male colleagues. When she took her mentor and NIMH to court, she won a $1 symbolic award. The federal judge who heard the case will decide if she is eligible for back pay and possible reinstatement.[12] The case is important because it may be a precedent in suing (male) supervisors who are not providing reasonable mentoring.

Male mentors often use female mentees to do their time-consuming "dirty work"—such as data collection and entry, handling correspondence, and even writing first drafts of articles—and do not reward the mentee's productivity. The women are contained in such positions as research assistant or clerk. Male mentors may also promote containment by encouraging mentees to pursue sex-stereotypical specializations:

> It is true that women traditionally have not become surgeons and have instead pursued specialties such as pediatrics or psychiatry; however, a number of the respondents argued that this was not a "free will choice" but rather was the "line of least resistance . . ." Several [medical student] women noted that they had been "turfed" to specialties, such as pediatrics, because women were seen by the decision makers as "better in some situations than others."[13]

Other payoffs are more direct. In business and industry, female mentees who turn out well-written reports, write successful grant proposals, and generate innovative marketing strategies enhance the mentor's reputation for being intelligent and productive. In academia, hard-working women can double or triple the mentor's publication rate. Because the mentee is "only an assistant," however, she often has no access to immediate or long-term professional benefits.

Some of our female interviewees reported that women mentors may discourage upward mobility. In business and industry, female supervisors sometimes give lukewarm recommendations for job transfers or promotions that would compete with their own positions. In academia, several women felt that their female mentors did not acknowledge their research contributions, expected more work from them than from male graduate assistants, and placed a high priority on the faculty member's research while ignoring the student's progress on her master's thesis or doctoral dissertation. Since, to our knowledge, there has been no systematic research on this topic, it is not clear how widespread such abuses are and whether they are engaged in by Queen Bees (as we discussed in Chapter 5) or by well-meaning women who are imitating male mentors.

Stalling.   Another effective containment procedure is stalling. When women try to move beyond their token positions (especially in male-dominated areas), supervisors and peers discourage such ambitions through a variety of delaying techniques:

> I worked in the shipping and receiving department but wanted to drive the trucks for more money. My supervisor claimed that he couldn't spare me, that the trucks were difficult to drive (even though I had driven eighteen wheelers in the past) and that driving a truck would cause trouble with the rest of the women in the department. (Female employee in a parcel service company)

Women's applications for promotion are sometimes "misplaced" or sent to the wrong department. After completing the necessary training or educational requirements, some women are told that there is a hiring freeze even though men are hired. Or, women may give up after waiting, sometimes for several months, because "the committee hasn't met," a key person is "out of town" or "we can't make a decision until the department has been reorganized."

Promotions and demotions.   Promotions can be used to maintain established sex-segregated jobs or ranks. A female chancellor at a large university noted that the departments that deal with money and budgets (comptrollers, fund-raising, grants) are usually led by men; women are promoted as "assistant to" but not "director of" such departments. In legal firms, similarly, women attorneys are often promoted, regardless of specialization, to female-dominated areas:

> My specialty is labor law. The only promotion offers I've gotten were in domestic and family law. The promotions would have meant more money initially, but not in the long run. Divorces, child custody, and all of that are important, but our company sees it as a service, a throwaway. (Female attorney in a large legal firm)

One of the most controversial issues today is the role of women in the military. When the draft ended in the early 1970s, the military recruited women to meet soldier shortages. The typical route to high ranks in the military is through combat. Because women are not allowed to serve in combat, promotion opportunities are limited to command of support units and other peripheral positions.

The Panama invasion, and especially the Persian Gulf War in 1991, generated intense debate about women in combat. Although none participated in direct armed combat, women served in all military assignments. Some women served as helicopter pilots, ground radar specialists, and truck drivers, or in close proximity to the enemy. Some women were injured or killed, and one was captured and tortured. In 1993, Defense Secretary Les Aspin announced that he would support an expanded combat role for women. Opponents argued that this would "degrade military readiness and further demoralize a military already disheartened by down sizing, budget cuts, the Navy's Tailhook scandal and the prospect that homosexuals may be allowed to serve openly."[14] Proponents pointed out that most Americans support an expanded combat role for women, that women made important contributions during the Persian Gulf War, that combat assignments would encourage talented women to seek careers in the military, and that such reforms might decrease sexual harassment and challenge the notion that women are second-class citizens. Women serve in military positions in at least ten countries and fill combat roles in half of those countries (Canada, Britain, Denmark, Norway, and the Netherlands).

The media sometimes publicize the cases of women who win lawsuits in hiring and promotion litigation. In reality, positive outcomes are not the norm. In a study of academic discrimination cases between 1970 and 1984, George LaNoue and Barbara Lee found that only one in every five plaintiffs prevailed.[15] This is still the case today. Even when the woman wins, she may have sacrificed a decade of her energy and time on litigation and may jeopardize her professional development (see the box entitled "Pursuing Sex Discrimination").

PURSUING SEX DISCRIMINATION

Dr. Jean Y. Jew, an American of Chinese descent and a medical-school professor at the University of Iowa, was awarded tenure in the anatomy department in 1979. She sued the university in 1985, charging that faculty members in her department, especially one colleague, had spread false rumors that she had had a sexual relationship with the former department head and had received favorable treatment from him. Dr. Jew charged that the university had failed to respond promptly to her complaints even after a faculty committee in 1984 found that she had been sabotaged and harassed, that the rumors had created a hostile work environment, and that the rumors resulted in being denied promotion to full professor. In 1991, a federal judge ruled in Dr. Jew's favor and ordered the University of Iowa to promote her to full professor and to pay her nearly $100,000 in back pay and benefits and $895,000 in legal fees. The judge also stated that the university must "take all reasonable steps to ensure a hostility-free work environment." Although Dr. Jew finally won the case, she says that for several years she has had no graduate students working with her and that some of her colleagues have been reluctant to collaborate with her.[16] Even though some lawsuits might discourage future sex discrimination, women who persevere in litigation suffer enormous personal, professional, and financial costs.

Most of us rarely hear about the discrimination cases that do not reach the Supreme Court. Many newspapers feature a police blotter that summarizes such street crimes as burglaries, robberies, and assaults. There is no similar compendium of gender discrimination cases, however. In 1992, ten women police officers in a Maryland suburb filed complaints with the Equal Employment Opportunity Commission (EEOC) that there was a pervasive locker-room attitude that subjected female officers to sexist statements and caused them to be overlooked in promotions and assignments:

- a female officer was told not to apply for a position because she had children; the vacancy was filled by a male officer with children;

- male officers were given individual coaching by their superiors to help them prepare for promotion exams; female officers were denied such assistance;

- some of the women officers had more than 15 years on the force and received excellent ratings, but they were unable to find out what they had to do to get promoted.[17]

Such complaints are representative of thousands of cases filed with discrimination agencies, but most Americans rarely hear about them.

A final method for maintaining boundaries between men's and women's jobs is to hire women at relatively high levels and later move them into lower-paying or less responsible positions:

> When I was hired, I needed job training to meet the specialized computer needs of the department. Several months went by—no training. I learned some things on my own through trial-and-error, but the progress was slow and I made mistakes. Every time I reminded my boss about the training, he'd say, "In a couple of weeks," but nothing happened. Eight months into the job I was told that my position was being terminated but that I could move into similar positions in other departments. The other positions turned out to be word-processing jobs—at lower levels and lower salaries. After I left, I heard that [Company X] hired a guy in my job and started training him the first day. (Data processor at a large department store)

An initially promising job can deteriorate, covertly and almost imperceptibly, into a demotion.

Gatekeeping. Screening by gatekeepers creates and maintains containment. Gatekeepers are people (usually male) who privately examine an applicant's credentials and routinely decide who is qualified for employment consideration. They may act independently (as a personnel director) or within a larger group (such as a union, referral agency, or search committee).

It is no accident that many men rise rapidly to technical and supervisory positions while women make up the bulk of the lower-paid employees. In the electronics industry, for example, an estimated 80 to 90 percent of the production workers are women, and about half are newly arrived Asian women immigrants. Gender and ethnic stereotypes, among other factors, are used by gatekeepers to target particular groups of people to poorly paid work. Women—and especially Asian-American women—are seen as "unusually dexterous" and as "suited for tedious work since they are so patient and docile."[18]

Gatekeepers use stereotypes to exclude women from higher-level jobs. While women comprise two thirds of all teachers, there are few women in public school administration. In a study of public school superintendents, Susan Chase and Colleen Bell interviewed 50 male and female gatekeepers— 44 school board members and 6 consultants across the country. They found that women applicants were not selected because of stereotypical attitudes about men and women:

> Comparing her with her opposition [the other final candidate for the job, who was a man], there was a little concern whether she'd be able to stand up to, you know [laugh] the teachers and the union, and I mean, really run the place, be recognized . . . In a very religious small town like this, the man is the breadwinner and the woman stays home.[19]

Containment procedures are usually both interlocking and cumulative. In higher education, a faculty search committee may be the gatekeeper. The committee members often reject applicants who are not like them, using a variety of formal (Ph.D. degree, publications, teaching experience) and informal (sex, physical appearance, personality) criteria. Either the committee, the dean, or both can use stalling techniques to discourage qualified candidates. Even if a woman is hired, her salary may be low or her exclusion from important decision-making bodies (such as personnel and budget) may negatively affect both her own chances for promotion ("She has never served on important committees") and those of other women (by not being an associate or full professor, she cannot participate in groups that determine the criteria for promotions). Without tenure and a higher rank, her influence may be minimal on committees that deal with budgets, hiring personnel, and formulating academic policies.

Whether it is a university search committee or a job interviewer in business or industry, gatekeepers are typically men who are often uncomfortable in dealing with women. According to a consultant for several Fortune 500 companies, the biggest hurdle women face is fitting in with male managers: "At senior management levels, competence is assumed. . . . What you're looking for is someone who fits, someone who gets along, someone you trust. . . . How does a group of men feel that a woman is going to fit in? I think it's very hard."[20] Anne Harlan and Carol Weiss found that such discomfort often results in male managers' excluding women from informal mentoring situations:

> Sometimes I see store managers who invite the guys for coffee in the morning because they feel comfortable and they can talk sports with the guys or whatever it might be. But they leave out their women department managers. And when you do that, the guys are getting more information than the girls [sic] are . . . because while you're sitting there having coffee, you might be talking about the Red Sox, but most of the time you're talking about what we're going to do with the department here or whatever we're going to do with this or business in general.[21]

Tokenism and containment limit women's entry; manipulation, sabotage, and revenge discourage their occupational progression and actively encourage job exits.

MANIPULATION

Questioning or casting aspersions on a woman's qualifications or ability behind the scenes will threaten, weaken, or subvert a woman's power or credibility. If, especially, the woman is seen as a "troublemaker," male superiors "may insinuate that the misbehaving woman is basically incompetent, which may lead other women to fear being associated with her cause:"[22]

> I've been working for this operation for six years. Our supervisor makes a point of reminding me and the other women of our routes and transfers almost every week even though the written schedules are posted on the bulletin board. He treats us as though we can't remember what we're supposed to be doing. (MTA bus driver)

Another manipulative strategy is to give women undesirable jobs under the guise of equal treatment:

> Some of us [women] have more seniority than men but our schedules are changed more often, we get the undesirable routes, and the buses we're assigned are in the worst possible working order. When we go to the union meetings to complain, there is always a male driver who complains that women are "too soft for the job" and reminds us that we can't expect any "special treatment." (MTA bus driver)

Such hazing is not uncommon in some jobs; it is a way of testing new employees regardless of sex. Women undergo such treatment for a much longer period than men, however. This testing is a justification for assigning women—under the equal opportunity cloak—to unpopular, dirty, and sometimes dangerous jobs.

Some manipulators intentionally create conflict among women because it is profitable. A former NBC news correspondent describes how the media benefited from the recent so-called "mommy wars":

> One talk-show producer I met with spoke of "capitalizing on the current war between mothers who work and mothers who stay home." I told her I didn't think there was a case, that it was something created by the media to wrap commercials around. She thought for a minute, brightened, and said, "Well, we'll do a segment on the way the media is creating this war!" The point being, you can always sell tickets to a female cat fight.[23]

Women may be especially susceptible to manipulation by respected and powerful men. Recently, a senior officer on the faculty of the Naval War College in Rhode Island was forced to resign after soliciting female Navy employees to pose nude for photographs—presumably for training posters on "ship safety, security, fitness, nutrition, proper procedures, communications as well as remembering loved ones at home." According to the official-sounding letter, "a cleaning sequence could move from routine deck scrubbing to a wet T-shirt then even more revealing poses." The posters were to be used aboard combat surface ships, submarines, or merchant vessels involved in the Persian Gulf War. It is tempting to dismiss women who participated in this project as getting what they deserve because they were naive. However, the letter looked official, came from a high-ranking officer, and was circulated among Navy employees who might have been afraid to refuse to participate or were caught up in the surge of patriotism that swept over the United States during the Persian Gulf War.

SABOTAGE

Through intentional sabotage, male employers and employees consciously undermine or undercut a woman's position. Although sabotage can be contrived and carried out by individuals, it often involves covert agreements between two or more people. Sabotage is difficult to prove but easy to deny. It usually comes down to "my word against yours" because saboteurs do not leave paper trails.

Traditionally Female Jobs

In many traditionally female jobs, male sabotage may be normative because men in parallel or adjacent jobs often have higher status or supervisory positions. There is a substantial literature on male supervisors' sexual harassment of women subordinates because some men expect women to service their "needs" at all occupational levels.

In adjacent job positions, men may use sabotage to disrupt or decrease a woman's performance:

> I was hassled by the bartender and the male kitchen staff. When you're a waitress, you have to keep in the good books of the guys backing you up. If the bartender takes a dislike to you, he can slow down on your orders to the point where you get no tips at all. The kitchen staff can sabotage you in other ways. The food can be cold, it can arrive late, and orders can be all mixed up.[24]

Traditionally Male Jobs

In traditionally male-dominated jobs, sabotage strategies may be sophisticated. Men may react to women negatively because they are "invading" such male territory as assembly lines or corporate headquarters. Such fears are justified. Both during World War II and more recently, women have shown that they can learn "men's jobs" quickly and do them well.

To preserve long-accepted strongholds, men use a variety of sabotage techniques to discourage women's success:

- I've been in this job nine years and I still have problems with the guys. About a year ago, whenever I returned from my route, I'd find a bunch of mail that I hadn't picked up. The district manager said I wasn't doing my job and gave me an undesirable [high-crime] route. I found out later that the district manager gave my route to a new guy who was a friend of the family. (Black female mail carrier)

- My coworkers would watch me talking to customers. When I went in to get the paperwork, they'd ridicule me to the customers. "She hasn't been here that long," "Women don't know much about cars." Then, they'd go over the same questions with the customers and get the sale. (Automobile salesperson)

- Every time there's a promotion [for corporal], I put my name in. I always get rejected even though I have seniority, have put in the same number of years on the street as the guys, and have the same firing range results as the men. When there's a temporary opening, a sergeant from another precinct is pulled into the temporary spot even when I request the assignment. . . . I think my supervisor is trying to mess up my work record purposely—I'm the last one to find out about special events and new cases, and I have been late for important meetings because I was told about them five or ten minutes before they start. (Female police sergeant)

- Ever since I became a meter reader, the guys have always teased me that I'd be attacked by dogs, raped, kidnapped, or not return. . . . That's scary, but I tried to ignore it. . . . What gets me is that sometimes I get to the customer's house and none of the keys I picked up fit. I have to go back to the company to get the right keys. I don't know who's doing it, but someone doesn't want me in this job. (Black seven-year meter reader for a gas and electric company)

In contrast to women in female-dominated jobs, women in male-dominated jobs find that they are "set up" to fail but are not told, openly, that this is because of their sex. In the case of women of color the sabotage may be because of both sex and race.

Professional and Managerial Jobs

Sophisticated sabotage strategies often occur in professional, technical, and administrative jobs where sex is totally irrelevant to job performance. Because these occupations do not require physical strength but professional or academic credentials and longer and more specialized training, there is presumably a greater objective reliance on sex-neutral qualifications. That is, being a chemistry professor requires neither such "female" traits as a "cute" figure and pleasant personality (often required in female-dominated jobs) nor the muscles to lift heavy equipment (sometimes required in other male-dominated jobs). One would expect, then, that professional and managerial jobs would be the least discriminatory.

Quite to the contrary, high-status job categories have been the most discriminatory because women entrants are often threatening to males dominating them. The sabotage techniques are so well orchestrated that women may recognize the sabotage only after it is too late:

One mid-level manager at a nationally known company said she had gotten excellent ratings from her supervisors throughout her first year of employment. In the meantime, the company psychologist had called her in about once a month and inquired "how things were going." She was pleased by the company's interest in its employees. At the end of the year, one of her male peers (whose evaluations were known to be very mediocre) got the promotion and she didn't. When she pursued the reasons for her non-promotion, she was finally told, by one of the company's vice presidents, that "anyone who has to see the company psychologist once a month is clearly not management material." She had no way of proving she had been sabotaged. (Authors' files)

Another successful ploy is to discredit competent women. Beth Haslett and her associates note that when men become professionally threatened by a competent woman, they may treat her in a way that casts her into the stereotypical role of girlfriend, wife, mother, daughter, or outcast. This diminishes the woman's credibility. For example, Shelly, a sophisticated and popular manager, was rumored to be one of six candidates for the job of regional vice-president in her company. Suddenly, one of the other candidates, Dan, started asking her extensive questions about her two children. How was their health? Were they doing well in school? Was it hard to work late and leave them home alone?:

[Shelly] became very suspicious of this sudden solicitude, when a few of her colleagues started voicing the same concerns about whether she was neglecting her children. She realized that Dan's goal was to have her perceived as a mother who worked when her "real" job was at home rather than as a professional who was also a mother. A popular topic of discussion among her staff became whether it would be fair to her children if she took the vice-president's job.[25]

In other examples, a female insurance agent is directed by the manager to nonelitist client accounts (in contrast to her male counterparts) and then not promoted because her clients take out only "policies for the poor"; an urban renewal administrative assistant who is more qualified than her supervisor and is open about wanting his job finds the information in her folders scrambled over a period of months and is told that her "administrative chaos" will lead to a demotion; and a faculty member in an all-male political science department is thanked for her committee and advising work but dismissed because of insufficient publications, while her male counterpart, who has several publications because he has been protected from committee or advising work, is promoted.

Women Sabotaging Women

A few years ago, one of the most popular films was *Working Girl*, in which the heroine (played by Melanie Griffith), a bright and ambitious secretary, sabotages her (female) boss, manipulates male supervisors, and climbs to the top of the corporate ladder. There are several reasons why the film was so popular—especially among women: the heroine was a "winner" rather than a victim; she outsmarted her Queen Bee boss; and she fulfilled many women's fantasies of getting even for being ignored or put down at work by men.

In *Sisterhood Betrayed,* Jill Barber and Rita Watson explore some of the ways in which women sabotage one another. Many women don't see how men encourage women to compete with one another, pressuring them to sabotage other women:

> Take, for example, the director of a unit at a major teaching center. His secret for keeping women from assuming power? He gives two women the same position. He decides on a budget, pays the two low salaries, gives them the same title, then lets them fight it out. His position is secure, and the two women work twice as hard. The male orchestrates the competitive behavior by pitting the women against each other.[26]

Women are easy targets, not just because of the drive to succeed, but also because U.S. culture pits women against each other. We teach women to safeguard relationships, to be nurturant, and to help others feel good about themselves. This learn-to-please behavior sets up competitions between women for the praise of others, especially men. Even in the workplace, women may sabotage other women to be liked or promoted by men.

Although it is true that women sometimes sabotage and betray other women, it is not the norm. There are hundreds of networking newsletters and organizations that promote women's self-confidence, exchange information, and encourage women to achieve their career objectives. Academic electronic mail services have bulletin boards that focus on women's issues: They are typically overwhelmed with exchanges on finding jobs, locating teaching and research resources, or dealing with sexual harassment.

REVENGE

Some forms of male revenge lash out at women who are making inroads into male industries. Some men take revenge by creating a hostile work environment. A woman who became a successful sales associate for a prestigious Wall Street firm discovered that internal memos announcing the arrival of new female employees were sometimes accompanied with nude pinups.[27] Other vengeful actions are physically threatening. Judith McIlwee and J. Gregg Robinson provide an instructive and frightening example of men's "getting even" with successful women. Denise, a mechanical engineer at a large aerospace firm, had just bought a new car. On her way to lunch one day, she stopped by an adjacent building to drop off some paperwork:

> I had been in and out of the building for a few days, working on a different type of aircraft . . . I was away from my car for ten or fifteen minutes. When I came back, a guy who worked out there in the shop had run a hydraulic hangar door into the side of my car, doing about $900 worth of damage. I hadn't even made the first payment! I had never spoken to him—never seen him . . . [but I found out later that] he had been watching me walk in and out of the shop, and then

watched me pull up in my shiny new sports car . . . I kept getting calls from the guys in the shop that this fellow was going around bragging about what he'd done to the bitch engineer's car, and what he was going to do to the bitch when she came back. He had a real problem with a woman in power.[28]

Revenge, especially when it is done "creatively," is effective in limiting women's upward mobility. Revenge punishes vocal women who complain about sex inequality, and it discourages open criticism from observers. A study of women in the newsroom showed that women who sued their employers found themselves writing more obituaries, working more graveyard shifts, and often passed over in promotions. Even when out-of-court settlements have included promises to remedy discriminatory practices, management has sometimes pursued devious activities—such as moving women laterally but describing the moves as promotions in internal newsletters or giving inflated experience ratings to new male employees so that their starting salaries are higher than those of women with equal experience.[29]

Women who sympathize or appear to sympathize with the complainant(s) may also become targets of revenge:

After [Company X] settled out-of-court, there was a great deal of resentment. Even the women who benefited from the settlement were hostile toward the women who had filed the class-action suit. To ease some of the tension, I got permission and some money to organize a workshop to discuss future opportunities. I was very careful. . . . I hired some men as speakers, provided a light lunch, and sent out attractive, carefully worded but upbeat invitations. The turnout was modest, but not a single man showed up—not even the guys in management who had approved the workshop and paid for it! About three months later, my position was abolished. They changed the title and hired a man. (Assistant director of personnel and labor relations in manufacturing)

Besides being punished for her seemingly sympathetic stance toward the women who sued the company, in this case the respondent may also have been sabotaged. By supporting the workshop on paper, management had proof that the company was not bitter about the settlement and was showing an interest in improving the work climate for women. Yet, the "troublemaker" was fired. After she lost the job, some of her coworkers said, privately, that the workshop had been described as "creating even more conflict," "divisive," and "antimanagement." As in other forms of covert discrimination, there was no hard evidence to prove this common knowledge.

White men who strongly endorse women's (and minority) rights may be seen as "biting the hand that feeds them" or "betraying the system" and may be punished accordingly. They may be stigmatized falsely as "knee-jerk liberals" who support women and minorities no matter how qualified they are. Some reprisals are economic: Salaries may be frozen, prestigious jobs taken away, and fringe benefits decreased.[30] Other reprisals are noneconomic: A social network may be closed, vicious gossiping may increase, and work sabotage may become common.

Most men are very aware of such reprisals and avoid incurring the wrath of their male peers. They are especially careful about their relationships with feminists:

> Of the [43] male faculty, I'm pretty good friends with two of the men. We read each other's work, go out to lunch once in a while, drop by each other's office and call each other almost on a daily basis. But if they're going to lunch with a couple of the other guys and I bump into them, they *never* ask me to join them. They're cool and businesslike and act as though they barely know me. Even worse, when they're in my office, they criticize sexist remarks that they laughed at during a committee meeting two hours earlier.[Pause] Maybe you should be doing research on "unpaid whores." (Woman faculty member in a computer science department)

A number of the women we spoke to reported being treated very differently by their male friends in public and private situations. Some women accept such contradictory behavior because, ironically, they don't want the men to be hurt by reprisals. According to a woman hospital administrator:

> One of the doctors is also a family friend. His wife is a nurse. When we get together socially, we spend hours discussing the crap that nurses get from doctors. He's more radical than his wife and keeps encouraging me to fight for nurses' rights at the hospital. Not too long ago, I sent around a proposal to modernize the nurses' stations and to increase the salaries of the nurses who teach specialized courses at the hospital. I heard that [Doctor X] jumped all over the proposal and made some snide remarks about hospital administrators.
> (Have you ever talked to him about the ridicule?)
> Oh, no. I was very hurt. . . . My feelings toward him have changed. . . . But why bring it up? He's not going to change their attitudes anyway. Why should I ask him to jeopardize the respect he gets from the other doctors?

Promoting women's equality or associating with women who are fighting for women's rights may result in social and economic reprisals for both men and women. Revenge is an effective method of maintaining the status quo.

CO-OPTATION

Co-optation refers to the process of bringing selected women into the system and then using them to control the entry and promotion of other women. Co-optation can be a source of upward mobility. Because mobility is often severely limited (there are always more applicants than available positions), the co-opted typically attribute their progress to their own intelligence, success, and hard work. They identify themselves with the "deserving elite": "The token woman is encouraged to see herself as different from most other women; as exceptionally talented and deserving; and to separate herself from the wider female condition; and she is perceived by 'ordinary' women as separate also. . . ."[31]

By improving the position of a few women, co-optation usually reinforces the subordinate position of the majority of women. Scattering a few women throughout seemingly powerful positions gives the appearance that the institution recognizes talent and is "sex blind" and egalitarian; it also implies that there are few women in top levels because most women are unqualified or not competitive enough.

If, moreover, the co-opted are also gatekeepers, the responsibility for sex equality shifts from the dominant group to the co-opted. Thus, the dominant group can be "innocent bystanders" while the (few) women maintain group solidarity against "outsiders" (that is, other women).[32]

Finally, co-optation provides false role models to other women. Women who are newcomers to the job market are unaware of covert sex discrimination or those who are in isolated positions may assume, mistakenly, that the co-opted really did "make it" on their abilities, are powerful, and are worthy of imitation, respect, and admiration.

THE INSIGNIFICANCE OF MERIT

Merit is commonly used to rationalize the unequal distribution of rewards and resources. Merit is determined through both formal and informal procedures that are typically undefined, uncodified, and vary across individual situations, agencies, organizations, and even states.

Formal Procedures

The civil service was established in the 1920s to replace upper-class favoritism and patronage by politicians with more "objective" selection procedures based on merit. Although neither the civil service nor other groups have ever defined or established criteria to measure merit in a systematic or comprehensive way, there are a variety of formal methods for determining merit, such as seniority, credentials, IQ tests, exams, grade-point averages, and numerous licensing procedures.

Regardless of the method used, the results of trying to determine merit have not been scientific, objective, or fair, for several reasons. First, what is meant by merit? Does it mean those individuals who are deserving of rewards because they are hard-working, intelligent, self-sacrificing, competent, or talented? One of these characteristics? Two? All? Second, in the U.S. workplace, there is often no relationship between merit, ability, and rewards:

> Material rewards *do* seem to be necessary, not to attract people to do "important" jobs, but to get them to do dull and uninteresting ones that make very little use of their abilities. Not that all the so-called important jobs always require much ability, either. A great many highly paid executive and professional jobs are not particularly difficult, and the conditions of work connected with them often demand little effort or product.[33]

Third, although merit remains undefined, the measures used to gauge merit—such as IQ tests—are seriously flawed and may be measuring social class and socioeconomic background rather than ability or intelligence. Finally, even when formal measuring instruments are developed, they are often not applied uniformly because of waivers (for example, veterans preference) or political considerations.

Informal Procedures

Merit decisions based on informal procedures tend to be even more subjective, personal, and capricious. Informal procedures include word-of-mouth recommendations, referral through friendship or work networks, reference letters, class-based affiliations (such as belonging to the same social clubs), alumni donations, nepotism, and tradition.

Informal merit procedures are based on selecting people with whom the (usually white male) incumbents can identify and feel comfortable inside and outside the work environment—in other words, "someone like me." Consequently, women will be perceived as outsiders, intruders, and interlopers. As one woman pointed out, "Conversations at the urinal still seem to be the dominant factor in advancement."[34] Because informal merit criteria and selection are unwritten, however, they are effective mechanisms of covert discrimination. Both formal and informal merit criteria and selection procedures ignore a great deal of talent, creativity, and promise:

> The stupidity problem—the plain fact that so many of our leading men are, at best, only marginally more competent than the average person, and, at worst, downright incompetent—is the direct result of our misplaced faith in tests, in the "proving ground of education," and in other formal and informal methods of picking out the "best men."[35]

We typically assume that merit is an important and fair method of differentiating between the "winners" and the "losers": The most powerful, the rich, and those in leadership positions—95 percent of whom are white men—*must* be meritorious or else they would not be rich, powerful, and in leadership positions. We continue to place our faith in merit as an important ideological guidepost even though merit remains undefined and unmeasured. Finally, we often assume that merit is working even though we continuously see evidence to the contrary. Most of us fail to consider the possibility that "merit procedures" are frequently used as weapons to reduce competition and resources rather than to reward hard work and talent regardless of sex.

By categorically excluding most women (as well as minorities, the elderly, and other groups), our "merit" systems have largely ignored the abilities and intelligence of some of the "best and the brightest." The consequences of ignoring women through overt, subtle, and covert discrimination are discussed in the next two chapters.

NOTES

1. Adrienne Rich, "Privilege, Power, and Tokenism," *Ms.,* September 1979, pp. 42–44.

2. Judith Long Laws, "The Psychology of Tokenism: An Analysis," *Sex Roles* 1, January 1975, p. 51.

3. Yolanda T. Moses, *Black Women in Academe: Issues and Strategies,* Project on the Status and Education of Women (Washington, DC: Association of American Colleges, 1989), p. 16. See also, Yolanda T. Moses, "The Road-blocks Confronting Minority Administrators," *The Chronicle of Higher Education,* January 13, 1993, p. B2.

4. Jill Barber and Rita E. Watson, *Sisterhood Betrayed: Women in the Workplace and the All About Eve Complex* (New York: St. Martin's Press, 1991), p. 56.

5. Beth J. Haslett, Florence L. Geis, and Mae R. Carter, *The Organizational Woman: Power and Paradox* (Norwood, NJ: Ablex Publishing Corporation, 1992), p. 75.

6. Judith S. McIlwee and J. Gregg Robinson, *Women in Engineering: Gender, Power, and Workplace Culture* (Ithaca, NY: State University of New York Press, 1992), p. 59.

7. See Rosabeth Moss Kanter, *Men and Women of the Corporation* (New York: Basic Books, Inc., 1977).

8. Janice LaRouche and Regina Ryan, *Strategies for Women at Work* (New York: Avon Books, 1984), p. 113.

9. Kanter, *Men and Women of the Corporation,* pp. 248–249.

10. Yolanda T. Moses, "The Roadblocks Confronting Minority Administrators," *The Chronicle of Higher Education,* January 13, 1993, p. B2.

11. Liz McMillen, "Despite New Laws and Colleges' Policies, Women Say Sexism Still Lingers on Campus," *The Chronicle of Higher Education,* February 6, 1985, p. 28.

12. Richard O'Mara, "Mentor Suit Against NIMH Leaves No Clear Winner," *Baltimore Sun,* May 13, 1994, p. B1.

13. Diana Kendall and Joe R. Feagin, "Blatant and Subtle Patterns of Discrimination: Minority Women in Medical Schools," *Journal of Intergroup Relations* 9 (Summer 1983), pp. 16–17.

14. Bruce B. Auster, "The Navy Sets a Different Course," *U.S. News & World Report,* May 3, 1993, pp. 49–50. See also, Bernard Adelsberger, "Move Expected to Add Talent to Aviator Ranks" and William Matthews, "Aspin Completes Change He Started as Congressman," *Army Times,* May 10, 1993, pp. 1, 6, 22.

15. George R. LaNoue and Barbara A. Lee, *Academics in Court: The Consequences of Faculty Discrimination Litigation* (Ann Arbor: University of Michigan Press, 1987).

16. Debra E. Blum, "Medical Professor, U. of Iowa Face Aftermath of Bitter Sexual-Harassment Case," *The Chronicle of Higher Education,* March 13, 1991, pp. A15–A16.

17. Patricia Davis, "Complaints of Sexism Detailed," *Washington Post,* August 3, 1992, pp. B1, B5.

18. Naomi Katz and David S. Kemnitzer, "Fast Forward: the Internationalization of Silicon Valley," in *Women, Men, and the International Division of Labor,* eds., June Nash and Maria Patricia Fernandez-Kelly (Albany: State University of New York Press, 1983), p. 334.

19. Susan E. Chase and Colleen S. Bell, "Ideology, Discourse, and Gender: How Gatekeepers Talk About Women School Superintendents," *Social Problems* 37:2, May 1990, p. 169.

20. Susan Fraker, "Why Top Jobs Elude Female Executives," *Fortune,* April 16, 1984, p. 46.

21. Anne Harlan and Carol Weiss, "Moving Up: Women in Managerial Careers" (Wellesley, MA: Wellesley College Center for Research on Women, 1981), p. 53.

22. Virginia E. Pendergrass, Ellen Kimmel, Joan Joestring, Joyce Peterson, and Edilee Bush, "Sex Discrimination in Counseling," *American Psychologist* 31, January 1976, p. 38.

23. Robin Young, "The Selling of Motherhood," *Newsweek,* October 1, 1990, p. 12.

24. Constance Backhouse and Leah Cohen, *Sexual Harassment on the Job* (Englewood Cliffs, NJ: Prentice-Hall, 1981), p. 9.

25. Haslett, Geis, and Carter, *The Organizational Woman,* p. 190.

26. Jill Barber and Rita E. Watson. *Sisterhood Betrayed: Women in the Workplace and the All About Eve Complex,* p. 47.

27. Anetta Miller, Martha Brant, and Jolie Solomon, "Taking on the Great White Way," *Newsweek,* July 19, 1993, p. 35.

28. McIlwee and Robinson, *Women in Engineering,* pp. 103–104.

29. Terri Schultz-Brooks, "Getting There: Women in the Newsroom," *Columbia Journalism Review* (March-April 1984), pp. 27, 29.

30. Ibid., pp. 28–29.

31. Rich, "Privilege, Power, and Tokenism," p. 44.

32. Laws, "The Psychology of Tokenism," p. 59.

33. William Ryan, *Equality* (New York: Vintage Books, 1981), p. 84.

34. Cited in Miller et al., "Taking on the Great White Way," p. 35.

35. Ryan, *Equality,* p. 82.

CHAPTER SEVEN
WOMEN OF COLOR: FIGHTING SEXISM AND RACISM

Patricia Williams, an African American law professor, has written an account of Austin Miller, her great-great-grandfather, a 35-year-old white Tennessee lawyer who bought Williams's 11-year-old black great-great-grandmother Sophie and her parents. Miller, a distinguished Tennessee lawyer and (later) judge, soon forced the 12-year-old Sophie to become the mother of Williams's great-grandmother Mary. Like many African Americans, Williams carries the heavy burden of having white ancestors who are not only part of their family heritage but also rapists and child molesters.[1]

During the nineteenth century, the growing number of outspoken feminists included black women as well as white women. Many of these early black feminists developed their ideas about the liberation of women while working in the abolitionist movement to free African Americans from the shackles of slavery. One influential black abolitionist was former slave Isabella Van Wagener, better known as Sojourner Truth. In the mid-1800s, she became an influential lecturer against slavery and an early advocate of women's rights. At the second women's rights convention in Akron in the 1850s, Sojourner Truth, uninvited and the lone black woman, responded to a white man who spoke against women's equality and for female dependence on men by saying that much change was in the wind, and then added: "And ain't I a woman? Look at me! . . . I have plowed, and planted, and gathered into barns, and no man could head me—and ain't I a woman? I could work as much as any man (when I could get it), and bear de lash as well—and ain't I a woman? I have borne five children and I seen 'em mos all sold off into slavery, and when I cried out with a mother's grief, none but Jesus hear—and ain't I a woman."[2]

White feminists such as Elizabeth Cady Stanton were emboldened in their attacks on sexual oppression by their involvement in the abolitionist movement. By the 1860s, gender discrimination had become a major concern, and vigorous arguments raged between male and female abolitionists, with most male abolitionists arguing that "this is the black man's hour." To this argument, Stanton replied that women, black and white, could not wait: "But I believe this is the hour for everybody to do the best thing for reconstruction. A vote based on intelligence and education for black and white, man and woman—that is what we need. . . . Again, if the two millions of Southern black women are not to be secured in their rights of person, property, wages, and children, then their emancipation is but another form of slavery."[3] Stanton was one of the first whites to emphasize the importance of black *women* being secure in their rights of person and property.

In the twentieth century, racial discrimination and gender discrimination have continued to be linked. The proposed Equal Rights Amendment (ERA) for women, not yet a part of the U.S. Constitution, is patterned closely after a nineteenth-century amendment to the Constitution, the Fourteenth Amendment, which guarantees equal rights for blacks, particularly black men. Moreover, the 1964 Civil Rights Act, the most important of all antibias legislation passed since 1900, was initially phrased to prohibit employment discrimination on the basis only of race, religion, and national origin. A conservative member of the U.S. House, Howard Smith, introduced an amendment to include gender in the prohibition, hoping to kill the entire bill by including a provision many male supporters of the bill could not accept. However, after a vigorous struggle, including significant pressure from women's groups, Smith's amendment was passed.

This congressional history illustrates that the world faced by women of color is not just a man's world, but a *white man's world*. The world of employment is dominated by white, usually Anglo, male employers and managers. The world of higher education is usually dominated by white male administrators and teachers. The world of politics is still dominated by white male presidents, legislators, judges, and local officials. For example, the number of black elected officials in the United States increased between 1964 and the early 1990s, from about 100 to more than 7,400, and the proportion of women among them also grew from less than one in twelve in 1970 to more than a quarter by the early 1990s.[4] Yet, these officials still constitute a disproportionately small percent of all U.S. elected officials. Just because there are a few white women or women of color scattered about, often as organizational tokens, does not mean that the employment, educational, and political worlds are truly desegregated.

GENDERED RACISM

Social science theories of racial relations have for the most part ignored issues of gender roles and discrimination. However, several scholars, mostly women of color, have recently written about the situations of women within the racial stratification systems in the United States, Canada, and Europe.

Their analyses assess the ways in which male dominance interacts with racial stratification. Asking whether racism or patriarchy has been the primary source of oppression, psychologist Philomena Essed interviewed black women in the United States and the Netherlands and found *racism and sexism* constantly interacting in their lives.[5] Essed terms much oppression of black women a "gendered racism," where one type of oppression reinforces or interacts with the other. This gendered racism can be seen in a variety of settings, from the neighborhood, to the school, to the work place. In a recent study of the black middle class by Joe Feagin and Melvin Sikes, a black male executive in New England argued that black women have suffered from double jeopardy:

> I think a black woman would have it really tough to get through because they have two obstacles to overcome, being a woman, trying to prove that they can do as good as a man, and then trying to prove that they can do as [good as] any white person, a white man in particular. So, that's a lot for a woman to overcome. And I think that's more stressful than what a black male would have to do, because he's just fighting against racism, as a woman is fighting against racism and sexism.[6]

For black women, gendered racism means that those in power positions in institutions, usually white men, have two different ways to control or oppress them.

Gendered racism is deeply imbedded in the core culture of the United States. To take one important example, women of color suffer much from the dominant culture's image of female beauty (see Chapter 2). In advertising and the mass media, the white female, often thin or blond, is the standard. Black women models and actors have been relatively rare in the movies or advertising, and those who do appear are often light-skinned or white-looking. Other women of color are also victimized by this white European standard. They are even rarer in ads and the media. And they suffer in other ways as well. In the early 1990s, Japanese American skater Kristi Yamaguchi became the center of much public discussion after she won a gold medal at the 1991 Winter Olympics. Previous gold-medal winners, all European Americans, became household names as companies came to them for advertisements. Some corporate officials said that Yamaguchi's Japanese ancestry would stop her from getting as many lucrative endorsements as European-American skaters. Marketing people pointed to the strong anti-Japanese feeling among many non-Asian workers as a reason advertisers might not use someone who looked Japanese. Kristi Yamaguchi was forever stigmatized as a "skater with Japanese ancestry."[7]

Gendered racism involves a range of negative evaluations of women of color. Patricia Hill Collins has critically analyzed the negative images of black women held by many white Americans. In her important and pioneering book *Black Feminist Thought,* Collins dissected the antiblack stereotypes of the "docile mammy," the "domineering matriarch," the "promiscuous whore," and the "irresponsible welfare mother." These severely negative portrayals of black women are common among many whites; they reinforce and flow out of whites' discrimination against black women. Other women of color have faced similar stereotypes. Native American women have long been stereotyped as inferior "squaws" or seductive "princesses," and Latinas, particularly Mexican American women, have been portrayed as "lazy" or "flirting señoritas."[8] Looking at Latinas, Denise Segura has developed the concept of triple oppression, the mutually reinforcing and interactive set of race, class, and gender forces whose cumulative effects place women of color in reinforced subordinate social and economic positions in U.S. society.[9]

WORKING OUTSIDE THE HOME

For many years women of color have worked outside the home in much larger proportions than white women have. African American women have been holding down steady jobs outside the home for more than three centuries: first as slaves; then as poor farmers; then as maids, restaurant and laundry workers; and, most recently, as clerical and sales workers. African American women have long had to work for the survival of themselves and their families, and the proportion of black women in the labor force outside the home has long been higher than that for white women. In 1960, only 37 percent of white women were in the labor force, compared to 83 percent of black women. By the early 1990s, the white figure had grown to just over half, still much lower than the three quarters of black women working outside the home. Black women have long struggled in jobs outside the home, often serving as the chief breadwinners because of discrimination against black men, discrimination that results in low wages and unemployment. Nonetheless, most black women do not define themselves solely in terms of their work or their occupations, for they have long been used to balancing home, family, and work.[10]

Black women have been subordinated and exploited in their jobs outside the home. The freedom to develop personally is sharply limited in the cold reality of daily work. Anthropologist John Gwaltney interviewed an older black woman from Tennessee who told him her father used to say that the "only two people who were really free was the white man and the black woman." Yet this woman went on to say that her father was wrong. Life had taught her that neither black men nor black women were truly free. By the time of the interview she had worked for 64 years "busting the white man's suds and mopping the white man's floors and minding the white man's kids." From her point of view the only people who are free in this world are "the people that can tell other people what to do and how they have to do it." Exploited labor outside the home does not make one free, just a different type of servant.[11]

The Character of Outside Work

What type of work have women of color done outside the home? What sort of incomes do they have? Do they face high unemployment? During slavery,

African American women in the South had a labor force participation rate near 100 percent. Whether girls or women, they worked as slaves in the field and in factories and homes of the white male slaveholding class. Jacqueline Jones has written about the lives of black women during and after slavery in vivid terms. The harsh nature of their lives is evident. Black female slaves had no choice in regard to back-breaking labor during slavery. One woman noted, "If you had something to do, you did it or got whipped." Slaveowner brutality was not lessened for black women: "Beat women! Why sure he [master] beat women. Beat women jes lak men. Beat women naked an' wash 'em down in brine." One woman recalled that "the things that my sister May and I suffered were so terrible . . . It is best not to have such things in our memory."[12] After slavery, most black women remained in the fields of the South as farm workers, sharecroppers, and tenant farmers. Many also served as domestic workers, a group that grew in numbers as blacks left the fields for towns and cities from the 1910s to the 1960s.[13]

With the black migration to the North came better working conditions for many. During a 1920 interview conducted by the Chicago Commission on Race Relations, a young black woman working in a factory showed her hatred of domestic work: "I'll never work in noboby's kitchen but my own any more. No indeed! That's the one thing that makes me stick to this job."[14] Nonetheless, most of the work done by black women in the North took the form of domestic service, and conditions could be every bit as bad as in the South. One woman from Florida was reduced to near slavery in the 1920s by a white middle-class family in Chicago. She somehow managed to get away from the family but not before her employer "had kicked, beaten, and threatened her with a revolver if she attempted to leave."[15]

By the 1960s, nearly four in ten black women workers were still employed as maids and servants. Yet by the mid-1980s, the percentage had dropped to only 6 percent, as black women finally moved into new job categories, including those traditionally occupied by white women. One recent analysis of the dramatic changes in racial segregation within traditional female jobs concluded that the biggest decline in segregation among women took place in the 1960s: "Clearly, the events of the 1960's—whether economic growth, the civil rights movement, or something else entirely—shook the longstanding structure of segregation of black women in the labor market. Segregation continued to diminish rapidly through the 1970's. Very little change was apparent in the 1980's."[16] Bureau of Labor Statistics (BLS) data have shown occupational progress for black women, but still a less favorable job distribution than for white women. In 1990, there was still a larger proportion of black women than of white women in lower-paying, blue-collar jobs. And just under a fifth of black women were employed in managerial and professional jobs, compared with more than a quarter of white women. Note too that these government data can be misleading, for many women in professional-managerial occupations are in lower-paying jobs. This is particularly true for black women, who are often dieticians in school cafeterias, cafe and bar managers, and practical nurses. Although many are schoolteachers, few are lawyers, doctors, or corporate managers.

Elizabeth Higginbotham has pointed out that historically most black women professionals, such as teachers and nurses, have worked in more or less segregated settings. Even today, these professionals tend to be disproportionately "in agencies and hospitals located in Black communities and serving Blacks, Latinos and other people of color."[17] To a substantial degree, this segregation signals the racial limitations on employment opportunities that black professionals still face in the United States.

A large proportion of black women are employed in clerical and sales jobs, many in lower-paying positions such as typists and retail clerks. In addition, many black women have labored outside the white-collar category. Like black men, black women are more likely than their white counterparts to be in jobs in the service, operative, transportation, and handler-laborer categories, altogether about 40 percent in BLS data, as compared with 25 percent for white women.[18] In blue-collar job categories, black women serve disproportionately in jobs such as nurse's aides, cooks, janitors, and maids. As Cydney Shields, the author of a job guide for black women, recently put it, for a large number of black women the problem "isn't as much breaking through the glass ceiling as it is . . . getting off the sticky floor."[19]

Other women of color have long labored in low-wage positions in order to enable their families and communities to survive. Mexican American women, for example, have worked in agriculture, as domestic servants, and in low-wage manufacturing jobs. And, regardless of the job, Mexican American women often earn less than comparable Anglos and are often assigned more physically demanding tasks. Like African American women, Mexican American women today are located primarily in clerical and sales positions and in service (e.g., maids) and operative (e.g., low-wage manufacturing) jobs.[20] Some Latinas have played a central economic role in their communities. Most Cuban women who immigrated to the United States beginning in the late 1950s were not used to working outside the home, but such work was essential for family and group mobility. Today, Cuban American women, including those who are married and those with young children, are more likely than other Latinas to be in the paid labor force. This high level of labor-force participation is a major factor in the relative prosperity of Cuban American communities.[21]

From the beginning of immigration, Asian American women have also been critical to the economic development of their communities. One researcher has reported that "from the moment they arrived, Japanese American women labored alongside the men to secure their own and their families' livelihood."[22] This work was frequently unpaid family labor on farms and in a variety of other businesses. Some women worked as domestic servants for whites. Until the 1950s, blatant discrimination against Asian American women precluded most from moving into white-collar work. Although many have moved into white-collar work in recent decades, discrimination has persisted. Research studies from the 1970s to the present have found significant occupational segregation and promotion restrictions for Japanese American and other Asian American workers, both male and female, when compared with white workers. One research examination of private employers in San Francisco found Asian American workers to be underrepresented in such employment areas as manufacturing, construction, and wholesale trade. Asian Americans were also underrepresented in better-paying jobs (such as managerial jobs) and overrepresented in lower-paying work (such as clerical jobs).[23]

The Case of Domestic Workers

Many women of color, in the past and in the present, have labored in the homes of white men and women. Not only black women but also Mexican and other Latin American immigrants often work in low-wage domestic positions. These domestic household workers are sometimes said to be in an "obsolete" job category that is disappearing from U.S. society. Yet, the number of women in this category is still as large as it was a hundred years ago. Today, a disproportionate amount of this domestic work is being done by women of color.

Domestic work is usually seen as "women's work" and is thus low-wage work. Numerous employers ignore the law passed in 1974 that requires a minimum wage for these household workers; and many employers also ignore the legal requirement (since 1951) to pay social security taxes for domestics. As we noted in an earlier chapter, in 1993 the failure to pay social security for domestic employees, who were illegal immigrants from Peru, forced Zoe Baird, one of President Bill Clinton's nominees for U.S. attorney general, to withdraw her name from consideration.

Domestic workers are often exploited, and those who are illegal have little recourse. As a recent report in *Newsweek* put it, "They feel powerless to complain in the face of outrageous demands—even sexual advances from employers."[24] Still, they cope with exploitation and struggle hard to maintain their dignity. Some even fight exploitation. One woman from El Salvador worked as a domestic for one year for a white family "that made her sleep on the kitchen floor, piled chores on her, then fired her, still owing her much of the $100 a week they had agreed to pay." This case had a happier ending than most, however. The woman filed suit against her white employers and managed to win a $5,000 default judgment when they failed to show up in court.[25]

A significant aspect of domestic work by women of color is that it is often done for white female employers. White middle- and upper-income women, Rollins notes, use the physical labor of women of color to free themselves for more enjoyable activities and thus to "provide ideological justification for the hierarchical social structure which affords them privilege."[26] The domestics are exploited not only in material terms, in getting the most work for the lowest wage, but often in psychological terms as well. Rollins found that white women emphasize deference and treatment of domestics as "children" or "inferiors." From her own experience as a domestic and from interviews with domestics and employers, Rollins concludes that white women employers feed off "the low paid labor and the personhood of the domestic" in order to reduce their own repetitive domestic work and thus to make their own lives better.[27] The exploitation of domestic workers also points up the larger issue of male domination of economic systems. In the case of domestics, some white women employers are "go-betweens," with their husbands controlling the purse strings and deciding how much domestic work is actually worth.

Unemployment and Low Incomes

Women of color tend to have high rates of unemployment. The black female unemployment rate has usually been double that of the white female and male rates for many decades. For example, in 1972 just under 6 percent of white women were unemployed, compared to almost 12 percent for black women. Two decades later, according to 1993 Labor Department figures, 7 percent of white men and 5 percent of white women were unemployed, compared to 13 percent for black men and 11 percent for black women. In addition, the *underemployment rate,* which includes those workers with very low wages and those who work part time but want full-time work, together with those so discouraged they have given up looking for work, is very high for women of color—at least a fifth of all these workers.

According to researchers Cunningham and Zalokar, historically about half the wage differential between black women and white women has resulted from black women's being forced to work in just a few occupations.[28] Black women get a low return for their outside-the-home work efforts; they are at the bottom in terms of earnings. White men earn far more than black men or women. Recent BLS data showed that median weekly earnings for black women were just $323, compared to $374 for white women and $509 for white men.[29] Black families with husband and wife working earned about 80 to 90 percent of similar white families; but for the many black families with just one earner, the proportion was about 60 percent. In addition, more than half of all black families headed by a woman fall below the government poverty level, compared to less than a third of comparable whites. The situation is similar for many Latinas. For example, the incomes of Mexican American women have been much lower on the average than those of Anglo women. Besides low earnings, women of color often get minimal employment benefits, and the majority do not have access to pensions or group health coverage because of unemployment or the type of low-wage jobs that they or their husbands hold.

There has been much recent discussion in the literature of the conditions and situations of the so-called "black underclass," the poorest 5 to 10 percent of black Americans. Looking at the situations of poor black women, sociologist William Julius Wilson has examined the "underclass" idea in a widely discussed policy book, *The Truly Disadvantaged.* In this book Wilson explores the fallacies in recent popular and scholarly analyses. As he explains, there are no real data that indicate welfare destroys the work effort or creates dependency among poor black Americans. Wilson also argues that the growing proportion of out-of-wedlock births among black women in recent years has nothing to do with their moral values or with poor welfare management. Instead, the growing proportion has to do with the *declining* birth rate among married women. Wilson focuses on what he calls the problem of women finding "marriageable black men."[30] The relative scarcity of young black men with decent-paying jobs is closely related to the problem of out-of-wedlock births. When young men cannot get jobs, they cannot afford to get married. Their girlfriends, as a result, establish their own households and often raise their children with the help of female relatives, sometimes relying on public assistance. The failure of the capitalistic economy and the federal government to provide decent-paying jobs for everyone who wants to work is the primary explanation for the problems of poor women, not some white stereotypical problem of "lazy black men" or "welfare queens." There are some weaknesses in Wilson's analysis. He does not deal with the gender and racial discrimination black women face today in many U.S. workplaces; this gender-racial discrimination is a major reason why many black women cannot earn enough in wages to support their families. For them life remains a constant struggle to survive.[31]

Discrimination in the Workplace

As we have seen, there is a great range of work that is done by women of color. They work in low-wage blue-collar jobs as well as in management and professional positions. Yet in most job categories they face racial discrimination at the hands of whites and sex discrimination at the hands of (mostly white) men. If white women seeking promotions in white-collar settings often encounter a "glass ceiling" beyond which they cannot move, women of color face what has been called the "concrete wall." One management consultant has argued that "Women of color are ten years behind white women in terms of promotion and upward mobility."[32] In the mid-1990s, less than 1 percent of those in top management positions are black women. In Bell and Nkomo's recent in-depth study of white and black women's experiences in management, black women reported receiving less support for career advancement from their bosses and less acceptance by colleagues, and felt that they had less control and authority in their jobs, than did their white counterparts. African American women also perceived greater gender discrimination compared with white women and were less optimistic about their company's commitment to improve the situation for women.[33]

Black women, in both the blue-collar and white-collar categories, experience much sexual harassment. We have seen in earlier chapters how widespread this form of sex discrimination really is. Some studies suggest that black women are twice as likely to be victims of sexual harassment as are white women. We noted at the opening of this chapter that during slavery the raping of black slave women was once a common practice of powerful white men. From the 1600s to the mid-1800s, many thousands of black female slaves, from 10 to 60 years of age, were raped by white men, including slave-holders and overseers, who considered black women to be property. Even after emancipation, and until recent times, white men have raped black women with impunity.[34]

Court cases have documented the sexual harassment of black women in the contemporary United States. In a Michigan case, a recently separated black mother was hired as an assistant collections manager. She soon became a sexual target of her white male boss. On her first day she was propositioned by her boss, who asked if "she would make love to a white man." After refusing many suggestions that she have sexual intercourse with him, she was fired.[35] Similarly, in a 1989 case a black woman who worked as a teleprocessor for Los Angeles County described how her superiors racially and sexually harassed her.[36] And in another recent case, a black woman working in accounting at a Chicago firm reported that she was sexually harassed by white male employees. Sometimes when the men were playing cards at lunch, the black woman was referred to as a "slave" and told to serve them. Her white male boss made racist jokes about the legs and walk of black women.[37] This racist-sexist behavior is common in white-collar workplaces. Similar harassment is faced by women of color in blue-collar workplaces and as domestic servants.[38]

White men are often the perpetrators of sexual harassment against black female employees in many business arenas because they are more likely than minority men to have the power to retaliate against women who reject their advances. Yet there are cases where men of color have harassed women as well. In a 1992 Alabama case, a white woman won a court suit on sexual harassment.[39] The federal judge ruled that, while she was employed at a convenience store in Montgomery, she was sexually harassed by a black male employee so much that she eventually quit her job. Assessing the evidence, the judge found that three black female employees had suffered sexual harassment from the same male coworker.

The issue of sexual harassment in the black community came dramatically to national attention during and after the Anita Hill/Clarence Thomas hearings in 1991. Anita Hill, a conservative black law professor who had worked several years for President George Bush's Supreme Court nominee Clarence Thomas, also an African American, testified that Thomas had sexually harassed her numerous times. Hill testified about sexist joking and other sexual harassment at the hands of a black man, yet the hearing itself had overtones of racism. President Bush nominated Thomas, a black right-winger, as the "best qualified man" for the position, even though the American Bar Association rated Thomas as barely qualified. Bush chose the nominee to fit in with his own conservative political agenda, and he knew white Democrats in Congress would have difficulty in voting against Thomas because he was a black candidate. Bush cared not at all that Thomas was out of touch with most African Americans. Moreover, an all-white male Senate judiciary committee judged the testimony of Hill and Thomas. Entrenched white male power was quite evident in the makeup of that powerful committee and in the rejection (by the majority) of Hill's testimony about harassment.

The reactions of some black women, including MIT scholar Ella Bell, were strong and supportive of Hill: "I awoke from this dream crying, with an eerie sense of helplessness" and "Hatch [a key white Senator] was making me physically ill."[40] In an article on the Hill/Thomas hearings, Bell has pointed out that Anita Hill was in a situation where she was sure to lose. By criticizing a black man for sexual harassment, Hill broke a taboo against black women speaking out on what some black men do to women. Bell speaks of a "Black Men's Club," which includes some of the black male civil rights leaders who supported the Thomas nomination. Not attending to the sexism of black men and viewing the black liberation struggle as mainly for "black manhood," Bell argues, makes no sense, for it is as much a struggle for black womanhood as for black manhood.[41]

Like black women, Latinas and Asian American women are vulnerable to sexual harassment on the job. An Asian American employee at a U.S. military base reported sexual harassment, but suffered serious retaliation for her report. A U.S. Civil Rights Commission review noted that "because of the stereotypic expectation of compliance and docility, a formal complaint from an Asian American woman might have been considered as a personal affront or challenge. Her notification of the alleged retaliation to the base authorities was to no avail: it aggravated an already bad situation."[42]

OTHER GENDERED DISCRIMINATION

Women of color face discrimination in many places and institutions, not just in the arena of employment.

Higher Education

When women of color move into educational settings, they often face racial and gender barriers. The impact of white male cultural dominance can be seen in our educational institutions, which are in the business of molding new students to fit established ways of doing things. For example, in an analysis of women of color in medical schools, Diana Kendall has highlighted the cumulative impact of racial and gender discrimination on women in a number of oppressed groups. Many white men in medical school faculties and student bodies remain convinced that every medical school student should adapt to the white male mold. In Kendall's research, one Mexican American respondent defined the requirements of that mold:

> Not only do we have to fit the "Anglo mold," which sees medicine as curative rather than preventive, and which is impersonal and disease-oriented, we also have to fit the "male mold," which is aggressive, competitive, authoritative, a "take charge attitude," and a "little boys don't cry" bit. Furthermore, we have to try to think like they do culturally if we want good evaluations because you have to be aggressive in patient management, but not too aggressive; you have to ask questions and get involved with the patient, but not emotionally involved.[43]

The fence that many female students straddle can be seen in the grades and evaluations given to these students during their clinical years in medical school. An example of how the white male mold shapes student evaluations is seen in these statements of health care workers evaluating the same Puerto Rican female medical student. The first evaluation is from a white male medical professor teaching at a hospital:

> This student consistently had difficulty in relating to . . . house staff and some patients. Her behavior, at times, was inappropriate and it was our feeling that she failed to appreciate her limitations as a student. She seemed to resent and have difficulty coping with authoritarian [sic] figures. Her manner, at times, was quite overbearing, demanding, and quite frankly, inappropriate. Unfortunately, her personality problems tend to overshadow her work as a student. . . . Although intellectually we feel she could make a physician, unless she is able to correct her personality deficiencies, her future as a physician remains questionable.

In this view the woman of color must change herself to fit the unconscious, or half-conscious, white male mold. In sharp contrast to this physician's comments are those of other health care workers with whom this same student had worked in neighborhood clinics in the city:

> (1) She is clearly a bright, energetic and capable person and has demonstrated both independence and initiative in a situation where there is little supervision available. . . . Her relationship with other people was good, she was cooperative and flexible in situations requiring teamwork, and she accepted direction and criticism willingly. (2) She demonstrates a broad intelligence, a refreshing individuality, integrity, and most of all, courage in opposing pretense and rigidity.[44]

The doctor's evaluation compared this Puerto Rican woman to the white-male subcultural mold and concluded that she had "personality deficiencies." The health care workers compared her to the sort of doctor needed for a more diverse set of minority patients and concluded that she was excellent. This minority student's career was nearly terminated by her white male professors because of her inability and unwillingness to fit the prescribed mold.

Recently, a black female medical student in a large southern city noted what her life was like inside and outside her historically white medical school:

> When I first moved to New Orleans, I had my own preconceived ideas about white people, but I was encouraged by other blacks to give them a chance. . . . However, I have been mistaken for a maid or a nurse and told that I'm in medical school because of a quota system, despite my high college average and my MCAT scores. I've been cussed out and called a stupid black bitch by several white males in Metairie while walking, driving or shopping. While eating in a restaurant, a white woman asked me to come and clean her house on my day off.[45]

The Problem of Violence

Black women, like white women, are often the victims of gender-related violence, including wife beating and rape. As we noted earlier, sexual attacks on black women by white men are a major problem that has long been ignored. Historically, the rape of black women by white men has been far more commonplace than black men raping white women, the latter a common white-racist fantasy. Today, however, the main threat of sexual violence against black women comes from black men in their communities. In the United States, most rapes occur between members of the same racial group. Recently, a prominent black psychiatrist, Alvin F. Poussaint, has noted, "Unfortunately, some Black men tend to direct their destructive rage against Black women, employing violence, rape, battery and sexual harassment. Extremist rap musicians have even advocated sexual abuse and murder of 'the bitches.'"[46] FBI data indicate that black women are twice as likely to be rape victims as white women, yet the rape of black women is less often reported in the media. More and more black women have begun to ask, as a woman writing in *Essence,* a magazine for black women, put it: "So why are there no protest marches in our communities, no impassioned speeches, no chest-pounding rhetoric from 'leadership' about that? When folks speak of Black-on-Black crime, shake their heads in shock, despair and sorrow, rarely is rape the crime that comes most to mind."[47]

FEMINISM AND BLACK WOMEN

Black women have long used a feminist language, including poet Phyllis Wheatley in the late 1700s, abolitionists Sojourner Truth and Harriett Tubman in the 1800s, and educator Ida B. Wells in the early part of the twentieth century.[48] One of the first national black organizations fighting for civil rights was the National Association of Colored Women's Clubs, formed in the mid-1890s, a decade before the NAACP. As Sabrina Miller has noted, "Individual clubs were responsible for providing economic and educational assistance and shelter to unwed black mothers when white women's organization providing the same services would not extend their facilities to black women."[49] The women in these groups also worked to rid the nation of the scourge of lynching, the brutal killing of blacks by white mobs.

Patricia Hill Collins has shown how black women were also central, later on, in the 1960s' civil rights movement, although the leadership was still reserved for black men.[50] By the 1980s and 1990s, more black women were moving not only into leadership positions in civil rights organizations but also in other sectors of U.S. society. In the early 1990s, for example, the nation witnessed the first black woman astronaut (Mae Carol Jemison), the first black woman in the U.S. Senate (Carol Moseley Braun), and three black women authors (Terry McMillan, Toni Morrison, Alice Walker) on the *New York Times* best-seller lists. Soon thereafter, Toni Morrison won a Nobel Prize for literature.

One might expect that women of color, given this history and their longtime involvement in work outside the home, would be leaders in the national women's liberation movement. Yet they have not been active in that movement in large numbers. Naomi Sims has dramatized the caught-between dilemma of black women who try to move into mainstream jobs and culture. She asks whether black women should ally themselves with the oppressed group of black men or with the also oppressed group of white women: "Can we trust either, as a group? Are we ever able to get ahead because we are Black or women, or only despite those attributes?"[51] Black women have often been left out of the national discussions that affect their lives. As writer Sharon Griffin has put it, "When the issue is sexism, traditionally, white feminists often do the talking. When the issue is racism, traditionally, black men do the talking."[52]

How feminist are black women in their views of the world? One study of opinion-poll surveys examined the question of whether black women are more feminist than white women in their support of women in politics or of women working outside the home. This study found only small differences between the two, with substantial majorities of both black and white groups taking generally feminist positions on these issues. Other surveys of gender-role attitudes have found that black women are more likely than white women to identify with such traditionally "masculine" job qualities as being career oriented, independent, and self-assured. Interestingly, black women have also emphasized the so-called "feminine" qualities, such as the importance of the nurturing role of the mother in the families. Black women are thus *androgynous* in their views and values.[53] Attitudinal studies suggest that black women strongly hold to feminist attitudes about women in the work place, in careers, and in politics, yet they also are strongly supportive of their spouses, homes, and children. This unique combination of views may help explain some of the differences of opinion among black and white women about the women's liberation movement.

In the 1970s, Joyce Ladner wrote that the "problems to which members of Women's Liberation groups are addressing themselves are far less relevant to Black women."[54] Ladner argued that the enemies of black women are not black men, but rather the major enemy is the oppressive racial discrimination facing all black women, men, and children. Ladner argued that black men need support, not a movement of equalization between the sexes. Some black men have echoed the sentiment that "women's lib" is irrelevant to the condition of black women.

However, since the 1970s more and more women of color have argued for a reshaping of feminist discussions and organizations to include women of color. For example, since the early 1980s the scholar bell hooks (she spells her pen name in lowercase letters) has been one of the most prolific writers on behalf of black feminism. Her book *Ain't I a Woman* presented data that indicate black women have been speaking and writing on feminism for two centuries. And she rejects the idea that black women must give up the fight against sexism to fight racism. Even though the mainstream women's movement has excluded many issues of concern to women of color and is in a numbers of ways racist, hooks argues that such a condition should not lead black women to ignore feminist issues: "We, black women who advocate feminist ideology, are pioneers. We are clearing a path for ourselves and our sisters."[55] In her view, black women can bring an awareness to the women's liberation movement that it is not enough to teach women to defend themselves against rapists and that women must also work to create a society where men will not rape. Modern feminism is an illusion if it does not threaten the foundations of capitalist patriarchy in the United States.[56] Similarly, Beryl Fitzpatrick, a Chicago activist, has argued that "white women created the word feminist. It is for them." She said, "I think our goals are more expansive. Our struggle is inclusive of women across different classes."[57] From this viewpoint the need is for a broad-based community movement that can unite progressives of all races, sexes, and creeds in the struggle to eradicate racism, sexism, and worker-exploiting capitalism.[58]

Black feminist organizations have not received much media publicity but have expanded and prospered since the mid-1970s. In 1977, the Combahee River Collective, a black feminist group formed in Boston, issued a political manifesto that said, "We are actively committed to struggling against racial, sexual, heterosexual, and class oppression." Black feminists have helped to set up a Third World women's clinic in Berkeley, California, and a women's Self-Help Collective in Washington, D.C. They have played a major role in establishing battered women's centers in several cities. In 1980, they held the First National Conference on Third World Women and Violence in Washington, D.C. In addition, they have established journals and newsletters to link women of color together across the nation. The black feminist movement has great potential for alleviating the feeling among many black women that they are the "mules of the world," to use Zora Neale Hurston's phrase. Barbara Smith suggests that the black feminist movement "clarifies the nature of the Black women's experience, makes possible positive support from other Black women, and encourages political actions that will change the very system that has put us down."[59] The major objective of black and other minority feminist movements is fighting against racism *and* sexism in employment, business, education, housing, and the legal system.

The confrontation between Clarence Thomas and Anita Hill over sexual harassment stimulated more black women to organize against sexism, in spite of much criticism from many whites and in spite of opposition from some minority men who feel that they are "betraying their race." In Chicago, a group called African-American Women in Defense of Ourselves was organized, with related organizations in several cities from New Jersey to California. In Philadelphia, the Ain't I A Woman Network was created. These women were among the 1,600 women who signed an ad supporting Anita Hill that appeared in major newspapers across the nation.[60]

An increasing number of black women writers have spoken out against sexism. For example, writing in an edited collection with a number of black female scholars on the significance of the Thomas-Hill hearings, Nellie Y.

McKay, an American literature professor, noted that many black Americans resented Hill's airing the issues and saw her as a traitor to solidarity: "This loyalty espouses that the oppression that black men have suffered and continue to suffer at the hands of the white world entitles them to the unqualified support of black women, even to their self-denial. Interestingly, there are no circumstances that require such a sacrifice of black men." Yet McKay adds that in the aftermath of the hearings "thousands of outraged African-American women . . . closed ranks and spoke out in one voice against the seating of Clarence Thomas on the Supreme Court."[61]

Johnnetta Cole, a leading African American educator and the first woman president of Spelman College, is clear about her feminism: "Feminism is quite simply the antidote to sexism. . . . Sisters have no trouble calling racism by its name, and we can talk about the antidote to that. We can also call sexism by its nasty name but we seem to have so much trouble confronting the antidote. Yet that's all that feminism is."[62] Similarly, the black writer Elaine Brown, a former Black Panther activist, has noted the lesser role of women in black communities and organizations: "I tried to focus this book on . . . black women in particular. I had issues in terms of feminism and my attitudes about the men. . . . I know what it was to be so totally alienated as black women not only from the larger society, but even our own society. I didn't want to write a chronicle of the Black Panther Party. I wanted to write a chronicle of a black woman's life."[63]

Black women have not been the only non-Europeans pressing for their own view of liberation. Other women of color have also been active as feminists in the past and in the present. The Mexican-American writer Marta Cotera has put it strongly: "Feminism has come easily for Chicanas because of the woman's traditional role and strength as center or heart of the family." Many Mexican American women are feminists because of a tradition of activism; women have been active in armed political rebellions in Mexico and generally in the political life of Mexico. This is the background of the Chicanas' feminist assertiveness.[64]

Like black feminists, Latina feminists have confronted barriers in the mainstream women's movement. Many issues of great concern, including poverty and discrimination, have not been important to the middle-class white feminists. These Latinas have also experienced sexist behavior from some Latinos opposed to women moving out of the usual family roles. These men have accused Latina feminists of betraying broader Latino movements and Latino cultures and of identifying too much with white Anglo individualism. As a result, much of the work of Mexican American and other Latina feminists has had to be done in their own organizations outside the Latino political movements.[65] During the 1980s, to take only one example, Latina feminists in California created the Comision Femenil Mexicana Nacional to work on problems of single-parent families. During mid-1993, one of their housing projects, Casa Loma, was opened in Los Angeles. This was the first housing project built in the United States by a Latina organization for poor families headed by Latinas.[66]

"SLAVERY UNWILLING TO DIE?"

Women of color face many obstacles in making their way in historically white worlds, whether that world is a white home, higher education, or the corporate work place. Black women in particular have a long history of racial and sexual discrimination, with these two types of discrimination often blending together to increase the disadvantage.

As we have seen, high achievement does not lessen the double-jeopardy discrimination that women of color encounter. Cheryl Harris, an assistant professor of law, recently commented that black female lawyers confront "the same barriers as other black women in the workplace, struggling against perceptions of race, gender, and class."[67] In connection with a criminal case, she had confronted gendered racism that assumed she could not be a lawyer: "When I walked up with my white client, the clerk asked me for my bond slip. Obviously, I had to be the client and the white man the lawyer. The same thing happened in the courtroom when I went to sit at counsel's table."[68] The oppression of women of color at the hands of white men is grounded in the belief that such women do not belong in historically white places and spaces, including the professional world.

Perhaps the saddest part of the current picture of gendered racism is that it reflects a "slavery unwilling to die." The current situation reveals a continuity with the past. Harris, commenting on the sexual harassment faced today by black women such as Anita Hill, noted that the bodies of black women "were the first workplace, where they as slaves were supposed to be sexually available to any man and the vehicle through which slaves were produced."[69]

NOTES

1. Patricia J. Williams, *The Alchemy of Race and Rights,* (Cambridge: Harvard University Press, 1991), pp. 154–156.

2. bell hooks, *Ain't I a Woman* (Boston: South End Press, 1981), p. 160.

3. Theodore Stanton and Harriet Stanton Blatch, eds., *Elizabeth Cady Stanton* (New York: Arno Press, 1969), vol. 2, pp. 109–110.

4. Dele Olojede, "Progress for Black Women in Politics," *Newsday,* February 24, 1992, p. 6.

5. Philomena Essed, *Understanding Everyday Racism* (Newbury Park, CA: Sage, 1991), pp. 30–32.

6. For more on this issue, see Joe R. Feagin and Melvin P. Sikes, *Living with Racism: The Black Middle Class Experience* (Boston: Beacon Press, 1994).

7. John Jeansonne, "Though Tremendously Popular after the Olympics, on the Marketing Front There's No Gold for Kristi," *Newsday,* April 16, 1992, p. 160.

8. Patricia Hill Collins, *Black Feminist Thought: Knowledge, Consciousness, and the Politics of Empowerment* (Boston: Unwin Hyman, 1990), pp. 40–46.

9. Denise A. Segura, "Chicanas and Triple Oppression in the Labor Force," in *Chicana Voices: Intersections of Class, Race and Gender,* eds., Teresa Cordova et al. (Austin, TX: Center for Mexican American Studies, 1986), p. 48.

10. See Angela Davis, *Women, Race and Class* (New York: Random House, 1981), pp. 231–233.

11. John L. Gwaltney, *Drylongso* (New York: Random House Vintage Books, 1980), pp. 143–144.

12. Jacqueline Jones, *Labor of Love, Labor of Sorrow: Black Women, Work, and the Family, from Slavery to the Present* (New York: Vintage Books, 1985), pp. 9, 13, 18–19.

13. Cheryl T. Gilkes, "From Slavery to Social Welfare," in *Class, Race, and Sex: The Dynamics of Control,* ed., A. Swerdlow and H. Lessinger (Boston: G. K. Hall, 1983).

14. Ibid.

15. Ibid., p. 164.

16. Mary C. King, "Occupational Segregation by Race and Sex, 1940–88," *Monthly Labor Review,* 115 (April, 1992), pp. 30–33.

17. Elizabeth Higginbotham, "Work and Survival for Black Women," in *Class, Race, and Sex: The Dynamics of Control,* eds., A. Swerdlow and H. Lessinger (Boston: G. K. Hall, 1983), p. 13.

18. The Bureau of Labor Statistics data are cited in David H. Swinton, "The Economic Status of Americans: 'Permanent Poverty and Inequality," in *The State of Black America, 1991,* ed., Jane Dewart (New York: Urban League, 1991), p. 63. Some portions of the discussion of occupation and income here and in the few paragraphs draw on Joe R. Feagin and Clairece B. Feagin, *Racial and Ethnic Relations,* Fourth edition, (Englewood Cliffs, NJ: Prentice Hall, 1993).

19. Donna Britt, "A Guide for Sisters Hard at Work," *Washington Post,* April 27, 1993, p. D1.

20. U.S. Bureau of the Census, *The Hispanic Population in the United States: March 1990,* Washington, 1990, p. 8.

21. Lisandro Perez, "Immigrant Economic Adjustment and Family Organization: The Cuban Success Story Reexamined," *International Migration Review* 20, Spring 1986, pp. 4–20.

22. Evelyn Nakano Glenn, "The Dialectics of Wage Work: Japanese American Women and Domestic Service, 1905–1940," in *Unequal Sisters,* eds., Ellen C. DuBois and Vicki L. Ruiz (New York: Routledge, 1990), p. 345.

23. U.S. Commission on Civil Rights, *Success of Asian Americans: Fact or Fiction* (Washington, DC: U.S. Government Printing Office, 1980), pp. 14–15. More recent data confirm this pattern. See Feagin and Feagin, *Racial and Ethnic Relations,* pp. 351–355.

24. Melinda Beck, "Mary Poppins Speaks Out," *Newsweek,* February 22, 1993, p. 66.

25. Ibid.

26. Judith Rollins, "Employing a Domestic: A Case of Female Parasitism," paper presented at the annual meeting of the American Sociological Association, August 1984, p. 4.

27. Ibid., p. 14. See Judith Rollins, *Between Women* (Philadelphia: Temple University Press, 1985).

28. James S. Cunningham and Nadja Zalokar, "The Economic Progress of Black Women Since 1940: Wages and Occupations," unpublished paper, Washington, 1990.

29. Janita Poe, "Black Women Join to Chip Away at Their Unique Problems," *Chicago Tribune,* May 18, 1992, p. C1.

30. William Julius Wilson, *The Truly Disadvantaged: The Inner City, the Underclass, and Public Policy* (Chicago: University of Chicago Press, 1987).

31. This paragraph draws on Leslie Inniss and Joe R. Feagin, "The Black Underclass Ideology in Race Relations Analysis," *Social Justice* 16, Winter, 1989, pp. 12–34.

32. E. Ray and A. Davis, "Black Female Executives Speak Out on the Concrete Ceiling," *Female Executives,* 6 (1988), pp. 34–38; see also, Ella Louise Bell and Stella M. Nkomo, "The Glass Ceiling vs. the Concrete Wall: Career Perceptions of White and African American Women Managers," unpublished paper, October 1992.

33. Bell and Nkomo, "The Glass Ceiling vs. the Concrete Wall," pp. 16–25.

34. See Williams, *Alchemy.*

35. The case is cited in MacKinnon, *Sexual Harassment of Working Women,* pp. 30, 74.

36. *Bobbie Jean Green,* v. *Los Angeles County of Superintendent of Schools,* 883 F.2d 1472; 1989 U.S. App.

37. *Viviann Jones* v. *Chicago Research & Trading Group, Ltd.,* 1991 U.S. Dist., Lexis 5634.

38. See Rollins, "Employing a Domestic," p. 16.

39. *Cathleen Cronin* v. *United Service Stations,* 809 F. Supp. 922; 1992 U.S. Dist., Lexis 19521.

40. Ella L. Bell, "Myths, Stereotypes, and Realities of Black Women; A Personal Reflection," *Journal of Applied Behavioral Science,* 28, September 1992, pp. 364–365.

41. Ibid., p. 366. This discussion draws on Joe R. Feagin, "On Not Taking Gendered Racism Seriously," *Journal of Applied Behavioral Science* 28, September 1992, pp. 400–406.

42. U.S. Commission on Civil Rights, *Civil Rights Issues Facing Asian Americans in the 1990s,* Washington, 1992, pp. 131–136, 153–156.

43. Diana Kendall and Joe R. Feagin, "Blatant and Subtle Patterns of Discrimination: Minority Women in Medical Schools," *Journal of Intergroup Relations* 9 (Summer 1983), pp. 21–22.

44. These quotes are taken from materials prepared for a court case by the second author.

45. "Readers Talk About Race Relations," *Times-Picayune,* June 20, 1993, p. A12.

46. Alvin F. Poussaint, "Enough Already!; Stop the Male-Bashing and Infighting," *Ebony,* February 1993, p. 86.

47. Marcia Ann Gillespie, "In the Matter of Rape," *Essence,* January, 1992, p. 60.

48. Sharon F. Griffin, "Double Struggle: Racism and Sexism Can Be Dual Burdens for Many Black Women," *San Diego Union-Tribune,* April 16, 1993, p. E-1.

49. Sabrina Miller, "A Spirit of Change," *St. Petersburg Times,* February 16, 1993, p. 3A.

50. Collins, *Black Feminist Thought.*

51. Naomi Sims, *All About Success for the Black Woman* (Garden City, NY: Doubleday, 1982), p. 169.

52. Griffin, "Double Struggle," p. E-1.

53. Edward Ransford and Jon Miller, "Race, Sex and Feminist Outlooks," *American Sociological Review* 48, February 1983, pp. 51–52; Marjorie R. Hershey, "Racial Difference in Sex-Role Identities and Sex Stereotyping," *Social Science Quarterly* 58, March 1978, pp. 583–596.

54. Joyce Ladner, *Tomorrow's Tomorrow: The Black Woman* (New York: Doubleday Anchor Books, 1971), p. 277.

55. hooks, *Ain't I a Woman,* p. 196.

56. Ibid., p. 191.

57. Poe, "Black Women Join to Chip Away at Their Unique Problems," p. C1.

58. See bell hooks and Cornell West, *Breaking Bread* (Boston: South End Press, 1991), pp. 60–62.

59. Barbara Smith, *Home Girls* (New York: Kitchen Table—Women of Color Press, 1983), p. xxv.

60. Griffin, "Double Struggle," p. E-1.

61. Nellie Y. McKay, "Remembering Anita Hill and Clarence Thomas," in *Race-ing Justice, Engendering Power,* edited by Toni Morrison (New York: Pantheon, 1992), p. 283, 288–289.

62. Quoted in Jill Nelson, "Johnnetta B. Cole; Sister President," *Essence,* January 1993, p. 50. See also, Johnnetta B. Cole, *Reading Conversations: Straight Talk with America's Sister President* (New York: Doubleday, 1992).

63. Quoted in Renee Graham, "She Still Believes in Panthers," *Boston Globe,* February 22, 1993, p. 30.

64. Marta Cotera, "Feminism, the Chicana and Anglo Versions," in *Twice a Minority,* ed., Margarita B. Melville (St. Louis: C. V. Mosby, 1980), p. 231.

65. Ibid., pp. 213–233.

66. Charisse Jones, "Home at Last; Casa Loma—A Housing Complex Built by Latinas for Latinas—Will Open Its Doors This Week," *Los Angeles Times,* May 31, 1993, p. E1.

67. Quoted in "Black Women Find Law Rewarding; Despite Racism and Sexism, more African-American Women Are Entering the Legal Profession," *Orlando Sentinel Tribune,* March 28, 1993, p. E28.

68. Quoted in ibid.

69. Quoted in ibid.

CHAPTER EIGHT
SOME CONSEQUENCES
OF SEX INEQUALITY

Both men and women have benefited from women's increased participation in the labor force. Many women enjoy the adult interaction, challenge, economic rewards, and self-confidence that a job outside the home may bring. Men have more options and feel less anxious if the family's economic welfare is not solely their responsibility. They can take more risks, leave unsatisfactory positions, or look for better jobs if their wives' income provides "unemployment insurance." A working wife may be more sympathetic toward and supportive of a husband who is unhappy with his job if she also is dealing with problems at work. Her greater independence can enhance her autonomy and provide a more egalitarian adult relationship. Some of the women we interviewed said that after they started working outside the home they became less dependent on their husbands for stimulating conversations, started reading newspapers more regularly to keep up with friends at work, and were more understanding of their husbands' time away from home:

> Our relationship improved after I started working. We talked about more things, he opens up more about problems at work, and he treats me like an adult, not just a wife. . . . He's even asked for my opinion when he gets into a disagreement on politics with his buddies. (Real estate agent)
>
> My husband is in sales and he spends about 60 percent of his time on the road. We used to fight about it all the time—especially after the youngest started school. I resented being alone, going to parties alone or not going because I felt uncomfortable among all the couples. After I started working, I made new friends and got involved in new activities. [Laugh] My husband sometimes complains that I'm hard to keep up with, but I think he enjoys not getting pressure from me about traveling. (Salesperson in department store)

Some of the people we interviewed felt that children of working mothers become more self-sufficient, more participatory in family responsibilities, and more realistic about prospective adult work roles. Several studies have found that mothers' employment usually has *positive* effects on children. Both sons and daughters of employed mothers hold more egalitarian gender-role attitudes and view women (and their own mothers) as more competent.[1] Daughters of employed mothers are more likely to be independent and to see their mothers as role models.[2] Contrary to some myths, working mothers do not neglect their children. Typically, an employed mother's contact with her children is not unlike that of full-time homemakers. Employed married mothers spend about 45 minutes per day talking with their children and helping them with projects compared to 64 minutes by full-time homemakers.[3]

Even some of the sex inequality battles in the workplace have had positive effects. Many people have developed clearer expectations of their own goals, a more sophisticated perspective about institutional constraints, a greater sense of economic stability, and less fear about changing gender roles. Encountering gender inequality has prompted many men and women to reappraise exploitative sex inequality and to develop relationships that are based on social or intellectual rather than on primarily sexual interests.

Despite these positive effects, sex inequality has widespread negative consequences on individuals, organizations, and society as a whole. In the real world, these effects overlap and are cumulative. For analytical purposes they will be discussed separately.

NEGATIVE EFFECTS ON INDIVIDUALS

Gender inequality has detrimental physical, psychological, and economic consequences for both men and women. These negative effects cross age, race, religious, and occupational boundaries. They can have long-term impacts on family relationships, jobs, and careers.

Physical and Behavioral Problems

Some discriminatory and harassing behavior includes physical assault. Even when there is no immediate bodily injury, job discrimination and hostile workplaces produce real illnesses in victims. Common complaints include headaches, ulcers, insomnia, eating disorders, teeth grinding, anxiety attacks, chronic fatigue, nausea, weight loss or gain, as well as drug and/or alcohol abuse.[4] In some cases, there may be suicides.

Victims' behaviors may also change. Some may try to overcompensate by working harder or longer. For example, the only female physics major in Yale's senior class in 1990 said that she spent time overpreparing rather than participating in class activities:

> At times I was really frustrated because I wasn't really being listened to. My views were constantly dismissed in discussions. So I started doing problem sets four days early so they had no reason to question my ability.[5]

Others may withdraw from the discriminatory situation. Some college students respond to sexual harassment by changing courses, majors, or even institutions even though such actions may result in losing credits, incurring economic costs, and prolonging their time in college. Others are deprived of educational or career opportunities because they avoid taking classes or working with faculty members who might have substantial resources and institutional prestige and who might be influential in helping students get jobs or financial awards for graduate work.[6] As the box entitled "Some Consequences of Sexual Harassment" shows, victims experience numerous behavioral problems both within and outside of academic settings.

SOME CONSEQUENCES OF SEXUAL HARASSMENT

Victims of sexual harassment experience many behavioral and related emotional problems:
- General depression, as manifested by changes in eating and sleeping patterns, and aches and pains that prevent women from attending class or completing course or work assignments
- Dissatisfaction with work, college, major, or a particular course
- A sense of powerlessness, helplessness, and vulnerability
- A loss of self-confidence and self-esteem and a decline in academic or job performance
- Changes in attitudes or behaviors toward sexual relationships
- Irritability with family, friends, or coworkers
- A general sense of anger, fear, or anxiety
- An inability to concentrate, even on routine tasks
- Alcohol and drug dependency

Some victims may exhibit the characteristics of post-traumatic stress disorder, such as intense terror, hypervigilance, helplessness, increased arousal, eating disorders, avoidance of stimuli associated with the event, and a numbing of general responsiveness.[7]

Psychological and Emotional Problems

Unlike most men, most women are taught to be passive, to accept being ignored or ridiculed, and to take the blame when things go wrong. Thus, the routine effects of sex inequality are generally emotionally and psychologically more harmful to women than to men.

During our many years of teaching, we have seen numerous women students accept poor grades on exams and papers with such docile and self-deprecating statements as "I guess I just didn't work hard enough," "I'm probably just not college material," and "My parents said I wasn't ready for college." Many male students, on the other hand, argue immediately that their low performance is not *their* fault: "I don't think you understood what I was trying to say in this paper," "I've heard that you're a really tough grader," "You didn't lecture clearly." Unlike women, many men are more apt to blame the situation, someone else, or such social structures as the company or the bureaucracy. In this sense, women are often less resilient in dealing with situations that may be unjust or unfair.

A major reason many women are not hostile is that they have been conditioned culturally to play primarily supportive roles:

> Women tend to view their relationships with others as ends in themselves. . . . It has been customarily accepted that women in the working world are more aware of, and concerned about, the human interrelationships in a working group; possibly because of their "family orientation" and "caring" [socialization]. . . . Women are inclined to suppress their own achievement and leadership roles by slipping into supportive roles. . . .[8]

Playing primarily supportive roles creates self-image problems. Women often display such traits due to victimization as withdrawal, defensiveness, passivity, in-group hostility, and identification with the oppressors, as well as seriously impaired self-esteem.[9]

Men are also victimized. They may be discriminated against—typically by other men—because of race, religion, physical disabilities, or social class. Unlike women, however, most men are not categorically and automatically devalued because of their sex. Most men have the opportunity to market their talents or hide such "handicaps" as age, ethnicity, or sexual orientation. Others can often compensate for such "handicaps" as ethnicity, obesity, or being homely or short (as can be seen in numerous prime-time television programs that are hosted by less than physically perfect men).

Whether at home, at work, or at play, men are often expected to be tough, aggressive, and strong. Many of these expectations are detrimental to men's psyches and emotional growth.[10] Although they can be debilitating, most male stereotypes are unchanging and consistent. Women, on the other hand, must cope with changing and often contradictory roles. They are expected to run their households but are sometimes labeled "castrating bitches" when they run offices. They are rewarded for being attractive but may not be taken seriously if they are *both* attractive and intelligent. Women are socialized to be nurturant in social relationships but are criticized as not having leadership potential when they play nurturing roles at work.

Embarrassment and Anger

Many women report that they experience embarrassment, anger, and even rage when they are treated in condescending ways. A physician practicing medicine in Maine says that although there are now more women in medicine and no pinups among the anatomy slides in medical school, being the only woman in a department of 50 men is "strikingly similar to practicing medicine in 1971." Despite her anger and embarrassment, however, she and many other women retreat rather than strike out:

A few weeks ago one of my colleagues called me into his office; on his desk were two large, partially clad "breasts" (created out of flour, eggs, sugar, and butter) on a plate. How did he expect me to respond? I didn't say a word, but retreated to my office, mortified and angry. . . . At an office Christmas party I received a present: a photograph of a bare-breasted woman on a do-not-disturb sign, purportedly for my examining room door. Did I confront the colleague who presented it? No, I laughed along with the rest of the guests (Who wants to be a party pooper?) and later, once again embarrassed and angry, threw the card away.[11]

Confusion and Loss of Self-Esteem

Often, the victim of sex discrimination feels that it will stop—especially if she has talked to the perpetrator, her supervisors, or internal grievance officials. If the harassment or other forms of discrimination continue or escalate, the victim will likely experience helplessness, self-blame, and confusion.

Victims of sex discrimination say they experience a general discomfort that often results in a lack of self-esteem or self-respect. A female physician reports that, after 15 years of practice, her receptionists still tell callers that "Dr. [X] is a woman, but she really is a good doctor." Also, "Nurses challenge my orders more often than those of my male colleagues. In one way I am pleased by this—the nurses, mostly female, are often intimidated by the male physician staff, and I am happy not to be intimidating; on the other hand, I do feel that my competence is sometimes unfairly judged."[12]

Disillusionment and Depression

Many women say that when they report sexual harassment and other forms of discrimination, the responses by both individuals and organizations are frequently hurtful and disappointing. Organizations are slow to react and often blame the victim. The accused may falsify data or deny that they have received complaints by the victim. Or the organization may require that the victim, but not the accused, provide supportive data and internal information that is difficult to secure because it is said to be "confidential."

When women realize that their companies or other organizations will not support them in serious sex discrimination complaints, they often experience depression. A woman might blame herself (for example, "If I had not used perfume, my boss might have not made passes at me"). Even if a woman recognizes that she is not to blame for the harassment or discrimination, the work situation may still deteriorate. She may be demoted, avoided by her coworkers, or given the silent treatment by management.

Economic Problems

Behavioral and psychological problems created by fear or anxiety can be costly in economic terms. Victims may experience low wages and high medical bills. Some complainants are fired; others may quit out of fear or frustration. The costs of leaving jobs under duress can include a loss of confidence, income, seniority, a disrupted work history, problems with references, and a failure to qualify for unemployment.[13]

Women who quit jobs because of hostile work environments may be doubly disadvantaged in searching for a new job. Traumatized by past events, they may feel lowered self-esteem. If their lack of confidence comes through during the interview process, they may reenter the workplace at positions well below their capabilities.[14]

Another way in which gender inequality affects women is by discouraging women's pursuit of male-dominated careers:

> I've always been a top student and came to [University X] on a math scholarship. During my first semester, my calculus professor really came on to me. He made advances and started sending me unsigned love letters. I rejected both and my grades started dropping. I can't talk to the other faculty because one of my friends is getting even more attention from the chair of the department. The only thing I can probably do is change majors or change schools. (Woman student at a large state university)

Women in male-dominated disciplines have few options when they encounter sex discrimination. They feel great disillusionment with and betrayal by the noble ideals publicized by educational systems. They may be afraid to approach faculty because this might increase the discrimination, or they may stay away from critical courses to avoid sexual harassment. They may also switch majors to female-dominated disciplines where they believe gender inequality is less widespread. Men who enter traditionally female-dominated careers are usually not similarly discouraged by women in female-dominated occupations:

> I've had no problems at all. As a matter of fact, I'm surprised that I get so much help because most of the nurses realize that we [male nurses] will be promoted to administrative positions in no time at all. No one seems to be resentful. . . . I'm not sure I'd feel the same way. (Male nurse)

Men in traditionally female-dominated jobs usually receive help and support and only minimal, if any, hazing from female employees.[15] Most women who work in heavy industries (such as steel, or automobile manufacturing) have spent years in rigorous apprenticeship programs where they have acquired skills, performed dangerous work, and proved to male colleagues that they can handle the job. When there is a recession, seniority rules ("last hired, first fired") force many women who have been successful in well-paying jobs out of work or into low-paying female job ghettos. Unlike their male counterparts, "instead of bumping down the economic ladder a rung or two to semi-skilled industrial jobs, the women are usually forced to revert to low-wage, pink-collar, sales and service jobs."[16]

Sex inequality results in stress. A number of studies have documented correlations between high-pressure jobs and stress, hypertension, ulcers, and other physical maladies. Even well-paid and powerful executives may be suffering from less job-related stress than female clerical workers. Secretaries may experience more stress than their supervisors: Secretaries typically have jobs that are low in status but high in responsibility; they frequently have unsupportive or absent bosses; they act as scapegoats, shields, or emotional sponges for dissatisfied consumers; and they must live up to job expectations outside of the formal job description. In a study of 419 clerical workers at a major university, Martha Balshem found that receptionists working in clinics run by physicians experienced high stress because they absorbed much of the hostility aimed at physicians:

> Although the doctor's lateness is, of course, not her fault, her position as the doctor's subordinate makes her a convenient target for the frustration of the patients. Excusing herself would be, she feels, moronic; she absorbs the sense that it is her responsibility to maintain at least a semblance of order in the clinic, but it is a strain for her to do so. Most likely, the doctor will never feel any of this hostility from his patients; it is all absorbed by his secretary.[17]

Women in responsible positions are more likely than their male counterparts to encounter stress that is due to their gender rather than to their occupational responsibilities. Unlike men, many women find themselves playing roles that are both contradictory and mutually exclusive in the workplace—that of reconciler and leader.[18]

Women may also experience job-related stress resulting from sexual harassment:

> The tension, fear, and anger build up inside sexual harassment victims who have nowhere to turn for relief. Most victims experience psychological depression and despair. Many suffer physical ailments such as stomach aches, headaches, nausea, involuntary muscle spasms, insomnia, hypertension, and other medical illness caused by continual, unrelenting anxiety and frustration.[19]

Although a few men have reported sexual harassment from women, these cases are anomalous rather than typical. For the offenders, sexual harassment releases, rather than creates, stress and tension (for example, "I was just having a little fun"). Nevertheless, the media are quick to play up the alleged sexual harassment reported by a few men. In 1993, for example, ABC's *20/20* devoted almost the entire program to a man who had charged his female supervisor with sexual harassment. In 1994, many male commentators praised Michael Crichton's new novel, *Disclosure,* in which a male files sexual harassment charges against a female supervisor, weeks before the book was even published. Since Crichton wrote the screenplays for *Jurassic Park* and *Rising Sun,* his meteoric rise to fame and attention to *Disclosure* are not surprising. One journalist described *Disclosure* as not being great literature because "the characters are little more than cardboard cutouts" but praised it, nonetheless, as "an intelligent look at sexual harassment."[20] Even in the mid-1990s, the handful of men (only about 5 percent of the cases reported to EEOC) who might experience sexual harassment get *considerably more coverage* than the millions of women who have to deal with sexual harassment on a daily basis.

Sex inequality limits women's job progression—even at high occupational levels. Women scientists charge that they are routinely shut out of the real centers of power: powerful university committees and the small groups that organize elite conferences and similar meetings. The foundation boards or university committees that allocate funds and space confirm that the "glass ceiling" for women is very much intact.[21]

NEGATIVE EFFECTS ON ORGANIZATIONS

Sex inequality at organizational levels has produced negative effects, which include suppressed talent, reduced creativity, and a loss of profits. Any organization whose hiring procedures are based on excluding or not promoting women will automatically exclude a pool of individuals who may be very talented and creative and who can enrich the organization's goals of higher productivity, better service, and better quality control.

Lowered Productivity

A related negative effect of sex inequality on organizations is lowered productivity. If women feel that their work is discounted, not recognized, and not rewarded because of their sex, the overachievement that typifies many women can be replaced with disillusionment or a lower commitment to the job:

> I used to really hustle in my job. For years, I'd work nights and weekends preparing really classy presentations, did a lot of homework before I saw a customer, and sent personal thank-you notes for meeting with me even if I didn't make a sale. Year after year, my sales records were higher than anyone else's in our division. After I was passed over for a promotion the second time, I realized I was breaking my back for nothing. I keep slightly ahead of most of the other people, so they wouldn't have an excuse for firing me, but I'm not a company man anymore. [Company X] can shove it. (Pharmaceuticals salesperson)

Some of the lowered productivity stems from a conscious decision not to be abused or exploited because many women's performance is not rewarded. In many cases, however, reduced productivity is unconscious or unintentional. Because it often takes women much longer than men to be promoted and recognized in other ways, women's output may plateau as a result of long-term stress, fatigue, overwork, and no raises. A number of women we talked to said that rewards were so slow in coming it was difficult to be motivated to work toward the next rung on the ladder:

> I had to have 50 percent more publications, do twice the committee work, and teach at least twice as many of the large, introductory classes as the men in my department before I was promoted [to associate professor]. I'm tired. . . . I'm especially tired of jumping hoops that men don't have to jump . . . and I know

> I've been jumping hoops because I now serve on personnel committees and see the standards applied differently to men and women. . . . Even with the $4000–$5000 salary difference, I'm not sure it's worth the effort to go for full [professor]. (Faculty member at a large state university)

This woman, like many others, initially did twice as much work as most men did to get promoted, to be seen as credible, and to be taken seriously. Perhaps one of the greatest depressors of productivity is having to fight sex discrimination:

> I'm forty-five years old. I started with this company right after high school. For years, my boss was promoted and took me with him. Last year, he decided he wanted a younger secretary even though my work has always received very high ratings. I'm efficient and attractive (according to my friends). I initiated grievance procedures. Because of my company's policies, I'm in my present position until the [grievance] committee makes a decision. . . . I still do the work, but it's been minimal. . . . I've spent a lot of my time either gathering evidence, worrying, or being angry about all of this. (Executive secretary in utilities company)

In all of these cases, women's productivity decreased, and the organization lost valuable talent.

Reduced Creativity

Psychological and physical oppression produce timidity, insecurity, and a lack of self-confidence. These reactions discourage the creative thinking and risk taking that can produce innovation. Many scientific breakthroughs and artistic contributions have come from work environments that foster autonomy and tolerate personal and professional "deviance" (for example, universities and research-and-development divisions in industry).

Treating women as though their sex is more important than their abilities can be detrimental in discouraging creative participation in an organization. Women's psychological oppression can include "the feeling of being caged, being kept on a leash, being limited and stunted." Women may see themselves as "limited beings, incapable of many activities, particularly societally important activities involving power, decision-making, and leadership." What may result is "a woman's conviction that there are many things which she cannot and/or should not attempt to do, simply because she is incapable, by virtue of being a woman."[22]

Because of sex-segregated occupations, many women are not involved in jobs and activities that encourage creativity. They have not demanded creative job assignments or greater control over jobs that could increase creativity. Even when women take an initiative, sex stereotypes discourage potential contributions:

> I spend most of my time typing statements. . . . After about the third notice, I have to send out threatening letters. It occurred to me that we might collect

more if someone from the office called the guilty party before the threats went out . . . you know, to find out what the situation is and whether we could set up a partial payment program. When I suggested this to my boss, he blew up. He said I was paid to type, not think. (Secretary at a collection agency)

Discouraging women's participation in interesting jobs is dysfunctional for an organization because it stifles talent and beneficial changes for a company or agency. Locking women into noncreative jobs can be detrimental to an organization because it limits competition to a very small group of people. This lack of competition reinforces male dominance:

After bullying for so long, are males more apt to move over quietly and welcome females into the sandbox . . .? Hardly! Being a bully . . . has its rewards. The bully has the entire sandbox to himself, every now and then he can experience the exhilaration of pushing another person around, of showing off to all the bystanders just how strong and powerful he really is. For males, being a bully is fun.[23]

Loss of Profits

Some observers feel that male dominance has cost American business big profits. The Big Three auto makers in Detroit did not lose out to the Japanese only because of quality, but also because of an absence of women's ideas in their male-dominated engineering departments:

Detroit designed quality cars for 6' males weighing 200 pounds. The Japanese designed quality cars that fit 5'5" women who weigh less than 200 pounds— quality cars in which women can sit comfortably with back support and still reach the pedals. Today, the Japanese still provide a range of cars sized to a woman across a range of affordability.[24]

Since women buy more than half the cars in the United States, the auto industry has lost money because most of their car designs and sales pitches have been targeted at men.

There are similar losses in the public sector. Changes in the workplace because of sexual harassment (such as decreased morale, absenteeism, and loss of concentration) cost the federal employment system alone at least $100 million each year. When good employees leave because of discrimination, employers lose money in recruiting costs, training costs, and loss of productivity.

Besides creating negative publicity, antidiscrimination lawsuits squander vast amounts of time, talent, and money. In 1987, for example, K-Mart spent $3.2 million in a sexual harassment settlement. If corporate managements responded quickly to discrimination complaints and followed their own sexual harassment policies, companies could save money, maintain employee morale and productivity, and attract better workers.

NEGATIVE EFFECTS ON SOCIETY

Sex inequality has widespread adverse effects at the societal level. The negative impact can be seen in many areas, including double days, divorce, child support, and health. Divorce and child support inequities were discussed in Chapter 3. This section focuses on double days and health issues.

Double Days

As increasing numbers of women entered the labor force, there was an implicit expectation that gender roles and family structures would change to accommodate working women. However, instead of men sharing in domestic responsibilities, women have had to work "double days"—a full day in paid employment and a full day in unpaid domestic work:

> I teach classes until about 1:00 P.M. every day. I usually have several hours of committee meetings, administrative work, or student appointments until about 4:00 P.M. The kids get out of school at 3:15. Even if I have to miss important meetings, I make sure I pick them up by 4:15 to avoid paying for the next hour. [This respondent pays $5.00 an hour for each child for the after-school program.] After we get home, I supervise their homework and music lessons, make dinner and clean up, drive them to Brownie meetings, religious classes, or the library. There's also the Little League, ballet classes . . . I do part of the laundry while they're getting ready for bed. My husband comes home at about 8:00, eats dinner, reads the paper, watches the late news, and goes to bed. The house is fairly quiet at about 11:30 P.M. From then until about 3:00 A.M., I prepare for classes, grade exams, and try to do research. (Community college professor)

Many working wives have accepted the "fact" that combining paid and unpaid work is entirely their responsibility, even when their husbands are present. Many working women have never even entertained the notion that domestic chores should be a responsibility shared equally. Quite to the contrary, the woman's job commitment has been viewed as secondary to her domestic responsibilities.[25] In contrast to their spouses, most working women have considerably less time for leisure or for socializing with friends:

> My husband and some of our friends are constantly pressuring me to have some couples over for a party or a dinner. Since I have to do all the work—prepare the food, clean the house, buy the booze—partying is a chore. I spend weekends doing the laundry, mending, shopping, and servicing appliances that keep breaking down. . . . Even going out is tiring business because it means I have to do all the housework on Sunday. (Manager in a public relations firm)

Double days are especially difficult for women with children. One of the major sources of tension is that many fathers do not participate in the "second shift"—household work and child care—after returning from work. In an in-depth study of 52 couples, Arlie Hochschild and Anne Machung found that women work roughly 15 more hours each week than do men in housework and child care. Even when men share the work, women feel more responsible for the home:

More women than men kept track of doctor's appointments and arranged for kids' playmates to come over. More mothers than fathers worried about a child's Halloween costume or a birthday present for a school friend. They were more likely to think about their children while at work and to check in by phone with the baby sitter.[26]

Although mothers get somewhat more domestic help from their spouses than do childless wives, the difference is negligible. Recent studies of working mothers show that most fathers perform very few child-care and domestic tasks. In a national study, Glenna Spitze examined the association between the wife's employment and the couple's sharing in grocery shopping, child care, cooking, washing dishes, housecleaning, clothing care, and yard care. Wives who worked full time were still responsible for almost 70 percent of these tasks. She concluded that when women get married they are automatically "assigned" a disproportionate share of the household tasks. These tasks do not change very much even when the wife's earnings increase.[27]

There has been little convergence in men's and women's child-care activities. In those households with children, most women are usually responsible for all or most of their family's laundry (79 percent), meal preparation (78 percent), gift buying (78 percent), child care (72 percent), housecleaning (69 percent), dishwashing (68 percent), bill paying (65 percent), and home decorating (60 percent). The three jobs that most men typically do all or most of the time are keeping the car in good condition (81 percent), making minor home repairs (74 percent), and doing yard work (63 percent).[28] The number of young children at home and the average age of the couple typically have no effect on the relative proportion of housework each spouse does. In black households, however, the husband is likely to do more housework than is his white counterpart.[29]

Women who work double days are vulnerable to role overload. Typically, women are expected to handle children's illnesses (and thus miss work), family get-togethers and festivities (anniversaries, holiday dinners, and birthday celebrations), and to care for both their own and even their husbands' aging parents:

> My husband's mother has Alzheimer's disease. My husband has three sisters, but none work outside the home. My husband and his sisters decided my mother-in-law should move in with us because, with my working, we have a higher income than my in-laws. Our income isn't much higher than theirs, but it is slightly higher . . . I guess, too, that since I've always worked full-time and managed a home, everyone figures I can manage. Since I'm a nurse, I didn't feel I could refuse. (Authors' files)

Although the home-cleaning industry has mushroomed during the last ten years, many middle- and working-class women either cannot afford housecleaning services or are reluctant to let strangers into their homes. For example, an East European bank teller in her early forties never got around to hiring much-needed household help because she never had time to "straighten things and clean the house" before the cleaning person came! In many working-class families, the woman is "allowed" to work out-side the home only if she keeps the house spic and span and is an outstand-ing homemaker:

> We need my income to survive, so I work. But my husband gets a lot of ribbing by his pals if I'm not around to make hamburgers and serve the beer when they play cards or watch football games. On top of that, the house better look good because the house always looked good when his mother worked. And she worked in a factory all her life. My mother worked in a local sweatshop. To the day she died, everything was always clean—plants, tops of refrigerators, chair rims, windowsills, pantry shelves . . . My house isn't as clean as hers, but I some-times clean house until midnight or later. (Garment worker)

Although 14 percent of all Americans pay for help with household chores, working women are no more likely than are nonworking women to have cleaning help; it is usually a matter of who can afford it.[30]

Even though women's working is not the major cause of divorce, dou-ble-day stress can exacerbate existing problems:

> There's always been tension about things like my entertaining his friends (which I didn't like), my husband not spending enough time with the kids and decorating the house according to his taste and not mine. After I went to work, these problems got worse. I became more insistent about his helping around the house. He got angry because I had even less time and energy for entertain-ing . . . When I started buying things I wanted for the house that he didn't like out of my own paycheck, he really exploded. (Administrative assistant in a pub-lic relations agency)

Women's double days might explain why women are less likely to re-marry than men. For the most part, divorce seems to decrease, rather than increase, women's domestic responsibilities. Divorced women that we inter-viewed said that they no longer had to attend their ex-husband's work-related functions, spend time entertaining and socializing with in-laws, or engage in time-consuming activities that met the husband's needs (taking clothes to the laundry, preparing elaborate meals, shopping for his clothes). Divorced women reported having considerably more time to pursue their own inter-ests and spend more time with their own friends. Divorce increases women's responsibilities in those jobs traditionally performed around the house by men, for example, yard work, car maintenance, fixing small appliances, and home improvements. Many women said, however, that they learned these skills when it was necessary to "survive or fall apart," resolved part of the prob-lem by moving into smaller, maintenance-free housing, or "exchanged" ser-vices with friends:

> One of my neighbors helps me with minor car repairs, advises me on things like buying painting equipment, and helps me do things like clean out the gut-ters. In return, my daughter or I babysit for them once or twice a month. . . . So far, it's worked out pretty well for both sides. (Executive secretary in legal firm)

Health

A number of studies have found that, overall, married women are less healthy than married men.[31] One contributing factor may be women's multiple role responsibilities. Working women with low family incomes and young children tend to have much higher depression rates than do married men, housewives, or employed married women who do not have child-care or economic problems. In general, employed mothers (married or single) with children at home report being much more unhappy and unhealthy than are employed women who do not have children.[32] Emotional disorders, such as depression and severe anxiety, are more commonly found among women than among men. Women are more likely to turn conflict inward and punish themselves while men are more likely to turn conflict outward and engage in antisocial behavior.[33]

Unhealthy behavior due to gender stereotypes is not limited to adults, however. An estimated 7 to 11 percent of adolescent males take steroids. Steroids can increase the size and strength of muscles in a few months. About 25 percent of adolescent users take steroids to improve their appearance.[34] Although many are unfamiliar with the side effects—such as strokes, heart attacks, liver disorders, kidney diseases, and even the possibility of psychoses—others knowingly take the risk to improve their athletic performance or physical attractiveness.

Anorexia nervosa is an emotional disorder characterized by extreme weight loss, an intense fear of becoming obese, and a distorted body image. Bulimia is an eating disorder characterized by a cyclical behavior of eating binges followed by self-induced vomiting, fasting, excessive exercise, or the use of diuretics or laxatives. An estimated 1 in 200 teenagers 12 to 18 years of age are anorexia; 90 percent of those affected are female. Anorexia and bulimia together affect 10 to 15 percent of adolescent girls and young women. Estimates of the prevalence of bulimia among college women range as high as a fifth.[35] Both disorders have serious physical complications that can result in death.

There is no one cause of anorexia and bulimia, but the most common explanation is that those who suffer from these diseases are trying to live up to a cultural fixation that equates thinness with beauty and success. Anorexics and bulimics become obsessed with living up to an image of female beauty promoted by the media and fashion industry.[36]

SOCIAL POLICY AND SEX INEQUALITY

Some social policies have widespread negative effects on both women's and men's economic and family lives. Many men as well as women work in unsafe or toxic environments, for example, and do not have access to health-care services. For the most part, however, social policies have created and reinforced sex inequality. Some of the major policies harmful to women include child care and parental leave, workplace inequities, health and reproduction, and poverty.

Child Care and Parental Leave

Very few families in the United States can afford quality child-care services. Because mothers, not fathers, take the majority of time off from work for child care, female workers, as a group, fall permanently behind male workers. The situation is worse for mother-only households. Poor mothers spend more than a quarter of their weekly family income on child-care expenditures. Women with infants often have employment gaps because they can't find satisfactory child care, and these employment gaps can lead to low income.[37] Nearly a quarter of mothers between 21 and 29 years of age are out of the labor force because of child-care problems. Because many of these mothers also do not have high-school diplomas, they commonly face serious labor-market difficulties.

Although an estimated 10 million preschool children and another 2 to 5 million children between the ages of 6 and 13 need child care or day care, facilities are currently available for less than half of these children. Compared to other industrialized countries, the United States's record of child-care provisions has been abysmal (as we will discuss in Chapter 9). Congresswomen Pat Schroeder of Colorado once remarked, "Under our tax laws, a businesswoman can deduct a new Persian rug for her office but can't deduct most of her costs for child care."[38]

Parental-leave policies are also archaic. A good example is the federal Family and Medical Leave Act (FMLA), which was first introduced in Congress in 1984. It was approved in late 1991 by both the House of Representatives and the Senate despite the threats of a veto by President Bush and was signed into law by President Clinton in 1993. Over the years, the original bill was politicized and diluted through bipartisan compromise.[39] As a result, the law is more symbolic than useful for several reasons.

Although the FMLA requires employers to provide up to 12 weeks of *unpaid,* job-protected leave per year for the birth or adoption of a child or the serious illness of the employee or a member of the immediate family, few employees are able to take 12 weeks of unpaid leave per year, especially if they have expenses for the birth or adoption of a child or suffer from a serious illness that may be only partially covered by medical insurance. Because employers with more than 50 employees account for a minority of businesses, 60 percent of all employees, including millions of women working for small businesses, are not covered by the FMLA. Finally, even though employees are guaranteed job reinstatement, there is no assurance that they will be allowed to return to the same job that they left. For example, a secretary could be given an "equivalent" job with an extra 30-minute drive to an unfamiliar office, a new boss, and a less desirable location.

The Workplace

As we discussed in Chapter 4, the U.S. labor force is very segregated by sex and race. Even in 1990, for example, over 95 percent of all secretaries, registered nurses, and child-care workers were women. Over 50 percent of the male-female wage gap is directly due to sex discrimination; such variables as education, years in the labor force, and experience explain the rest of the earning gap.[40] According to one observer, "At current rates of change, it would take between 75 and 100 years to achieve complete occupational [sex] integration in the workforce."[41]

Some people feel that workplace discrimination is bound to continue in the future because there has been so little progress during the 1980s:

> If working women have "made it," then why are nearly 80 percent of working women still stuck in traditional "female" jobs–as secretaries, administrative "support" workers and salesclerks? And, conversely, why are less than 8 percent of all federal and state judges, less than 6 percent of all law partners, and less than one half of 1 percent of top corporate managers women? Why are there only three female state governors, two female U.S. senators, and two Fortune 500 chief executives? Why are only 19 of the 4,000 corporate officers and directors women—and why do more than half the boards of Fortune companies still lack even one female member?[42]

As we discussed in Chapters 1 and 2 (and will discuss in Chapter 9), sex discrimination and affirmative action legislation were diluted under the Reagan and Bush administrations. Even before these reactionary efforts began, most of the legislation safeguarding and promoting women's employment rights was ineffective because enforcement was largely only symbolic.[43]

Health and Reproduction

Although women are responsible for child care, they have relatively little influence over reproduction and child-care policies. Although birth control is a personal matter, it is "controlled by decisions of the state, the social organization of scientific and medical institutions, and the normative system of public values and attitudes."[44] Recently, antiabortion movements have been trying to limit access to abortion counseling and services. These groups are also fighting the expanded welfare services that would be necessary to care for the millions of unwanted or abused children resulting, in part, from unwanted pregnancies.

Abortions have been legal since 1973. In 1989, however, the Supreme Court (in *Webster* v. *Reproductive Health Services*) allowed states to impose such restrictions as limiting public funding for abortions and requiring that the father be notified before an abortion is performed. In 1990, the Supreme Court placed further restrictions on the reproductive rights of young women under the age of 18. In both *Hodgson* v. *Minnesota* and *Ohio* v. *Akron Center for Reproductive Health,* the Court upheld state requirements that minors must inform parents before having an abortion or, as an alternative to parental approval, receive permission from the judge.

In addition, some in the Right to Life (antiabortion) movement have successfully intimidated abortion providers by harassing patients, bombing clinics, threatening providers and their families, and even murdering physicians who give abortions. As a result of court and private actions, abortion services to poor, minority, and rural women have been severely curtailed. For example, 93 percent of all rural counties have no abortion providers.[45] As a result, many women have unwanted children that they cannot support.

Welfare and Poverty

Of the almost 34 million people living in poverty in the United States, *two thirds* are women. Single mothers and their children make up more than a third of the poor. In 1990, female-headed families constituted 75 percent of all poor black families and 46 percent of poor Latino families.[46] This trend—the high probability of women who head families being poor—has been termed the *feminization of poverty*. Two major reasons for the feminization of poverty are the discriminatory wages and the limited employment opportunities that women face. Another reason is that divorce increases poverty for mothers. Courts often do not force ex-husbands and absent fathers to support women and their children (see Chapter 3).

Poverty is today disproportionately a woman's problem. Federal and state job-training policies (where they exist) have locked many women into poverty by forcing them to take jobs that are insufficient for their families' needs, have trained women for poverty-level, traditionally female, low-paying jobs, and have made no provisions for child care.

Many middle-class women can be plunged into poverty as well. Middle-aged women who are divorced or deserted by their husbands may be cut off financially, have difficulty in securing employment, and find that homes, cars, stocks, bonds, and other assets are inaccessible because they are registered in the husband's name. Widows may have limited access to their late husbands' retirement or health benefits. Because women constitute the vast majority of part-time and temporary workers, they are usually not eligible for disability, health, or retirement programs.

This chapter has discussed some of the negative effects of gender inequality at individual, organizational, and societal levels. These negative effects have an immediate impact on women, but they also affect men and children. In the end, gender inequality affects all of us. The next chapter proposes some individual, group, and governmental remedies for these problems.

NOTES

1. Jane Riblett Wilkie, "Marriage, Family Life, and Women's Employment," in *Women Working*, 2nd ed., eds., Ann Helton Stromberg and Shirley Harkess (Mountain View, CA: Mayfield, 1987).
2. Lois W. Hoffman, "Effects of Maternal Employment in the Two-Parent Family," *American Psychologist* 44 (1989), pp. 282–292.
3. Margaret M. Sanik and Teresa Mauldin, "Single Versus Two Parent Families: A Comparison of Mothers' Time," *Family Relations* 35:1, January 1986, pp. 53–56.

4. Mary P. Koss, "Changed Lives: The Psychological Impact of Sexual Harassment," pp. 73–92, in Michele A. Paludi, ed.; *Ivory Power: Sexual Harassment on Campus* (Albany, NY: State University of New York Press, 1990).

5. Michele N-K Collison, "20 Years Later, Women on Formerly All-Male Campuses Fight to Change Their Institutions' 'Old Boy" Images," *The Chronicle of Higher Education,* December 12, 1990, p. A24.

6. See Billie Wright Dziech and Linda Weiner, The Lecherous Professor: Sexual Harassment on Campus (Boston: Beacon Press, 1984) and Stephanie Riger, "Gender Dilemmas in Sexual Harassment Policies and Procedures," *American Psychologist* 46, May 1991, pp. 497–505.

7. See Vita C. Rabinowitz, "Coping with Sexual Harassment," pp. 103–118 in Paludi, 1990; Koss, 1990; and Riger, 1991.

8. Christine D. Hay, "Women in Management: The Obstacles and Opportunities They Face," *The Personnel Administrator,* April 1980, p. 33.

9. See Edwin M. Schur, *Labeling Women Deviant: Gender, Stigma, and Social Control* (New York: Random House, 1984), p. 39.

10. See, for example, Robert A. Lewis, ed., *Men in Difficult Times* (Englewood Cliffs, NJ: Prentice-Hall, 1981) and Michael S. Kimmel and Michael A. Messner, eds., *Men's Lives* (New York: Macmillan Publishing Company, 1992), 2nd ed.

11. Roberta Berrien, "Outside In," JAMA 268:19 (November 18, 1992), p. 2616.

12. Ibid.

13. Koss, 1990.

14. Nancy Dodd McCann and Thomas A. McGinn, *Harassed: 100 Women Define Inappropriate Behavior in the Workplace* (Homewood, IL: Business One Irwin, 1992).

15. See, for example, "As Men Move in on Women's Jobs," *U.S. News & World Report,* August 16, 1981, pp. 55–57.

16. Carol Hymowitz, "Layoffs Force Blue-Collar Women Back into Low-Paying Job Ghetto," *Wall Street Journal,* March 6, 1985, p. 37.

17. Martha Balshem, "Job Stress and Health Among Women Clerical Workers: A Case Study (preliminary results)," paper presented at the American Anthropological Association meetings in Denver, CO, November, 1984, p. 5.

18. See, for example, Sally Helgesen, *The Female Advantage: Women's Ways of Leadership* (New York, Doubleday, 1990).

19. Constance Backhouse and Leah Cohen, *Sexual Harassment on the Job* (Englewood Cliffs, NJ: Prentice-Hall, 1981), p. 39.

20. David Nicholson, "Crichton's Reverse-Harassment Tale," *Washington Post,* January 11, 1994, p. B2.

21. Marcia Barinaga, "Profile of a Field: Neuroscience—The Pipeline Is Leaking," *Science* 255, March 13, 1992, p. 1367.

22. Carol A. Whitehurst, *Women in America: The Oppressed Majority* (Pacific Palisades, CA: Goodyear Publishing Company, 1977), p. 119.

23. James A. Doyle, *The Male Experience* (Dubuque, IA: Wm. C. Brown Company, 1983), p. 266.

24. McCann and McGinn, *Harassed,* p. 93.

25. See, for example, Hilary M. Lips, *Sex & Gender: An Introduction,* 2nd ed. (Mountain View, CA: Mayfield Publishing Company, 1993).

26. Arlie Hochschild with Anne Machung, *The Second Shift: Working Parents and the Revolution at Home* (New York: Penguin Books, 1989), p. 24.

27. Glenna Spitze, "The Division of Task Responsibility in U.S. Households: Longitudinal Adjustments to Change," *Social Forces* 64:3, (March 1986), pp. 689–701.

28. Linda DeStefano and Diane Colasanto, "Unlike 1975, Today Most Americans Think Men Have It Better," *The Gallup Poll Monthly,* February 1990, pp. 25–36.

29. Catherine E. Ross, "The Division of Labor at Home," *Social Forces* 65 (1987), pp. 816–833.

30. DeStefano and Colasanto, "Unlike 1975 . . .".

31. See, for example, Ofra Anson, "Marital Status and Women's Health Revisited: The Importance of a Proximate Adult," *Journal of Marriage and the Family,* 51 (1989), pp. 185–194 and Walter R. Gove, "Gender Differences in Mental and Physical Illness: The Effects of Fixed Roles and Nurturant Roles,"; *Social Science and Medicine,* 19 (1984), pp. 77–84.

32. Walter G. Gove and Carol Zeiss, "Multiple Roles and Happiness," pp. 125–137 in Faye J. Crosby, ed., *Spouse, Parent, Worker: On Gender and Multiple Roles* (New Haven: Yale University Press, 1987).

33. See, for example, James A. Doyle, *Sex and Gender: The Human Experience* (Dubuque, IA: Wm. C. Brown Publishers, 1985) and Myriam Miedzian, *Boys Will Be Boys: Breaking the Link Between Masculinity and Violence* (New York: Doubleday, 1991).

34. Oliver Fultz, "'Roid Rage," *American Health* (May 1991), pp. 60–64.

35. U.S. House of Representatives, Eating Disorders: The Impact on Children and Families. Hearings before the Select Committee on Children, Youth, and Families, 100th Cong., 1st sess. (Washington, DC: Government Printing Office, 1987).

36. See Peggy J. Cantrell and Jon B. Ellis, "Gender Role and Risk Patterns for Eating Disorders in Men and Women," *Journal of Clinical Psychology* 47:1, (January 1991), pp. 53–56 and Naomi Wolf, *The Beauty Myth: How Images of Beauty Are Used Against Women* (New York: William Morrow and Company, Inc., 1991.

37. Jonathan R. Veum and Philip M. Gleason, "Child Care: Arrangements and Costs," *Monthly Labor Review* (October 1991), pp. 10–17.

38. Nancy Gibbs, Julie Johnson, Melissa Ludtke, and Michael Riley, "Shameful Bequests to the Next Generation," *Time,* October 8, 1990, p. 42.

39. See Melissa K. Gilbert and Nijole V. Benokraitis, "The Family and Medical Leave Act of 1988: One Step Forward and Two Steps Back?" *Family Perspective* 23:1 (1989) for a discussion of the history, content, and politicization of the FMLA.

40. National Committee on Pay Equity, "The Wage Gap: Myths and Facts," pp. 129–135 in *Race, Class, and Gender in the United States: An Integrated Study,* 2nd ed., ed., Paula S. Rothenberg (New York: St. Martin's Press, 1992).

41. Deborah L. Rhode, "Gender Equality and Employment Policy," pp. 170–200 in Sara E. Rix, ed., *The American Woman, 1990–91: A Status Report* (New York: W. W. Norton & Company, 1990).

42. Susan Faludi, *Backlash: The Undeclared War Against American Women* (New York: Crown Publishers, Inc., 1991), p. xiii.

43. See, for example, Fletcher A. Blanchard and Faye J. Crosby, eds., *Affirmative Action in Perspective* (New York: Springer-Verlag, 1989).

44. Margaret L. Andersen, *Thinking About Women,* 3rd ed. (New York: Macmillan Publishing Company, 1993), p. 194.

45. S. K. Henshaw and J. Van Vort, "Abortion Services in the United States, 1987 and 1988," *Family Planning Perspectives* 22 (1990), pp. 102–108.

46. U.S. Department of Commerce, *The Black Population in the United States: March 1990 and 1989.* Bureau of the Census, Current Population Reports, Series P-20, no. 448 (Washington, DC: Government Printing Office, 1991).

CHAPTER NINE
GETTING RID OF SEX DISCRIMINATION

In 1776, the year the Declaration of Independence was signed, Abigail Adams wrote to John Adams, her husband, the revolutionary, advising him about the new code of laws for the emerging United States:

> In the new code of laws which I suppose will be necessary for you to make, I desire you would remember the ladies and be more generous and favorable to them than your ancestors. Do not put such unlimited power in the hands of husbands. Remember, all men would be tyrants if they could. If particular care and attention is not paid to the ladies, we are determined to foment a rebellion.[1]

John Adams rejected her request, telling his wife to be patient and to realize that other issues were much more important than women's rights. This male view has been common ever since. Women have been told by men, and even by some women, that their rights are not as important as other matters. This has been especially true since the early 1980s, with the emergence of a conservative backlash against women's rights. This backlash was evident, for example, in the statements and actions of presidents Ronald Reagan and George Bush, who, with their associates, were opposed to most women's rights goals. Reagan himself took a public stand against the Equal Rights Amendment (ERA), and the Republican Party platforms expressed open opposition to abortion and affirmative action programs.

From Abigail Adams to today's feminist activists, the challenge has arisen again and again: "If particular care and attention is not paid to the ladies, we are determined to foment a rebellion." In this book we have identified numerous discriminatory barriers facing women, especially in the workplace and at school. We have seen women constantly facing sex discrimination, and we have seen them fighting that discrimination. In this chapter, we examine strategies for change under three general headings: individual pressure for change, change through collective action, and broad societal changes.

One of the biggest misconceptions about sex discrimination is that "you can't fight city hall." Throughout this chapter, boxes entitled "You Don't Have to Take It!" show that women and girls as young as seven years old have done something about sexual harassment and other forms of sex discrimination. *You can do the same!*

INDIVIDUAL PRESSURE TO END DISCRIMINATION

Even today, most men and many women cling to socially acceptable misconceptions that perpetuate discriminatory attitudes and practices. First, women assume that if they work hard and do a good job, their talent and ability will be recognized and rewarded. Second, they assume that gender is irrelevant in the distribution of rewards and that "merit will win out." Third, many assume that someone else will fight the battles for them. Related to this, they assume that, over time, there will be gender equality. Each of these assumptions is wrong, and each maintains the status quo of gender inequality.

Every woman has certain rights under U.S. laws. Knowing these rights, and pressing for them, is a major change strategy for women working as individuals. In the workplace it is illegal for a woman to be fired for filing a sex discrimination complaint against her boss. It is illegal for a male employee doing the same work (even under a different job title) to be paid more than a similarly experienced female employee. It is illegal to force a woman to leave her job in the sixth month of pregnancy. And it is illegal to fire a woman employee who is talking to others about unionizing. In education, it is illegal to exclude women from government-paid work-study opportunities, monetary support through scholarships and fellowships, equal access to institutional facilities and athletic benefits, and entry into all areas of study. In domestic situations, it is illegal to rape a wife (under some circumstances) in all states and to deny credit, mortgage loans, or other financing on the basis of gender or marital status.

The first step to remedy some types of discrimination is for a woman to identify and recognize the sex discrimination. The second step is to know and stand up for one's rights. Placing the burden of gender inequality on women might smack of reinforcing the "blaming the victim" syndrome. However, most men will not aggressively promote women's rights because of their personal and economic interest in maintaining discriminatory practices. Thus, women must take the initiative in fighting sex discrimination. At the individual level, these strategies differ depending on the type of discrimination that women encounter.

YOU DON'T HAVE TO TAKE IT!
(IN ELEMENTARY AND MIDDLE SCHOOL)

A 7-year-old girl had to ride to school in Eden Prairie, Minnesota, on a bus with boys who called her "bitch" and made fun of little girls because they didn't have penises, and with a driver who thought it was funny. Over five months, the girl's mother sent 22 pages of complaints to school officials, who lectured the boys and briefly suspended several troublemakers from riding the bus. Because the mother felt that the school wasn't doing enough to protect her daughter, she filed a complaint with the state Department of Human Rights.[2]

In Petaluma, California, eighth-grader Tawnya Brawdy had to run a gauntlet of boys gathered outside her school who would begin mooing as she approached. According to Tawnya, the harassment "went on before school, during classes, in between classes and during lunch," but her teacher told her she'd just have to put up with it. Boys continued to moo at her all through high school. The U.S. Department of Education found, in a 211-page report, that the schools had failed to protect her. Tawnya's mother sued her district over "emotional distress" and collected $20,000 in an out-of-court settlement. She now heads a group called Parents for Title 9.[3]

Blatant Sex Discrimination

One remedy is active intervention by individuals who do not discriminate. As one of our readers put it:

[There are] social/personal responsibilities of spouses, parents, teachers, legislators, friends, colleagues and others to act in behalf of victims and themselves. A lot of people won't actively discriminate, but they also won't intervene to prevent or stop discrimination (e.g., "You're a big girl. I assume you can take care of yourself." This translates to "It's really your problem, so it's up to you to find a solution.") There is really a lot to be said for the notion that if a person isn't part of the solution, he or she is part of the problem . . . Men use this "nonintervention" reasoning mostly to avoid confronting one or more men (are they afraid, falsely, of looking "unmasculine"?).

Thus, both women *and* men should actively challenge blatant sex discrimination. Individuals in powerful positions can be especially instrumental in sending loud, clear, and public messages supporting gender equality. For example, the mayor of Annapolis, Maryland, once sent a seven-page memorandum to department heads in city government outlining ways to eliminate sexual stereotyping and the use of derogatory and demeaning language and behavior toward women. The memo also included threats of disciplinary action for discriminatory behavior.

Another strategy is prevention. Some women accept jobs and enter educational institutions that they know have a well-established reputation for sexism. The motivations for such actions are mixed—the company might offer a higher salary, the university might be in an interesting location, the applicant thinks that "my experience will be different" or that she will change the existing discriminatory practices. Such high hopes and idealistic expectations are usually dashed. If, during the course of an interview or application process, the applicant discovers the institution's discriminatory policies or practices, she should cite these as reasons for not accepting the offer and send the rejection letter to the influential decision makers in the community, company, or institution.

Preventing gender discrimination on a more personal level is also important. In recent years, many law enforcement agencies, schools, and media organizations have been more willing to raise, publicize, and discuss such neglected issues as rape, sexual harassment, and child abuse. Consequently, some states have set up rape crisis centers, shelters for battered wives, and fingerprinting programs in elementary schools. However, such responses are therapeutic or reactive rather than preventive. That is, they focus on what to do after the offense rather than on teaching women how to avoid or prevent violence, harassment, and discrimination. If more time and effort were spent teaching children and adolescents that physical violence and sexist behavior are *never* okay in interpersonal relations, the cultural acceptance of gender discrimination might begin to change.

Third, if possible, women should initiate action against the male discriminator. A woman can verbally protest an insult. Or write a memo. Or discuss the problem with other workers who might be in a similar situation. All of these are real remedies for women seeking changes in the sex discrimination they face. Taking action can be a source of empowerment as well as a way of reducing future discrimination.

Gathering information on the organization's policies and records can be important in fighting discrimination. An aggrieved woman should collect data to back up her arguments. A company's poor record of past treatment of women or minorities can be important background data substantiating a claim of recent discrimination. Checking to see if other women employees have suffered similar discrimination can be useful, as can checking court cases against the organization.

Organizations themselves sometimes have data on their own internal problems. Companies doing substantial business with the federal government sign contracts requiring them to take affirmative action to correct discrimination against women and others in their workplaces. Usually, the company must prepare an affirmative action plan that spells out its weaknesses regarding the hiring of women, and that lays out goals and timetables for hiring women to correct its deficiencies. This plan is kept in the files of the organization and should be available to employees. It is enforced by the Office of Federal Contract Compliance Programs (OFCCP), the office within the Department of Labor responsible for supervising the implementation of executive orders on desegregating the workforces of federal contractors.

If discussing the program with the boss does not work, an aggrieved woman can pursue internal grievance procedures, file a complaint with the EEOC, or consider a lawsuit. The 1964 Civil Rights Act (Title VII) prohibits discrimination in hiring, firing, wages, promotions, and fringe benefits on the basis of gender. The 1963 Equal Pay Act requires equal pay for substantially equal work. The 1978 Pregnancy Discrimination Act protects pregnant women capable of doing their job from being fired or demoted because of pregnancy. These laws are enforced by the Equal Employment Opportunity Commission (EEOC). The 1991 Civil Rights Act now permits victims of sexual harassment and other sex discrimination to collect substantial compensatory and punitive damages from discriminating employers.

The National Association of Working Women recommends that an individual who is being sexually harassed at work should do at least these things: (1) keep a diary of each incident, with key details; (2) face the issue early on by telling the perpetrator that the sexist words or actions are highly inappropriate; (3) follow up on this confrontation with a written statement on the events; (4) organize against sexism with fellow workers; and (5) know and use the firm's grievance regulations. If following company grievance procedures does not work, then she should go to the EEOC.[4]

In 1980 the EEOC put out a statement conceptualizing sexual harassment as a form of gender discrimination, one that clearly violates the 1964 Civil Rights Act.[5] (EEOC data for 1986 and 1990 show that the number of harassment complaints increased by 25 percent in the intervening period.)[6] Sexual harassment can significantly affect a woman employee's mobility and must be substantially eradicated if women, at all employment levels, are to make further progress. A woman with a harassment or other sex discrimination complaint has six months after a discriminatory act to file a complaint with the EEOC. Unfortunately, the EEOC is seriously underfunded and has generally had a huge backlog; it may take a long time for the agency to make a ruling in a particular case.[7]

If the EEOC cannot help, a woman can sue on her own. Since the late 1980s, there has been a significant increase in the number of lawsuits in this area of sex discrimination, a few with costly settlements for employers. Recent lawsuits by individual women have begun to change the workplace climate in some firms and government agencies. The first major court decision on sexual harassment came in 1986, when the Supreme Court (in *Meritor Bank* v. *Vinson*) ruled that harassment *is* discrimination under the 1964 Civil Rights Act. Subsequently, the EEOC ruled that firms must implement "immediate and appropriate corrective action" in sexual harassment situations.[8]

In 1993 the court made proof of harassment less difficult for women complainants by dropping the previous requirement of a victim having to demonstrate "severe psychological injury." In November 1993, the Supreme Court ruled in *Harris* v. *Forklift Systems, Inc.* that Teresa Harris was not required to show she was "severely psychologically injured" by the sexual harassment of her boss in order to get compensation for sex discrimination.

The court ruling should make it possible for women to successfully pursue sexual harassment cases in the federal courts. In the decision, Justice Sandra Day O'Connor indicated that "no single factor [is] required" in establishing this type of sex discrimination: "Whether an environment is hostile or abusive can be determined only by looking at all the circumstances. These may include the frequency of the discriminatory conduct; its severity; whether it is physically threatening or humiliating, or a mere offensive utterance; and whether it reasonably interferes with an employee's work performance."[9]

Challenges to sex discrimination are more effective when they involve women who are backed up by other women and sympathetic men. Friends, family, coworkers, and supervisors should actively support women challenging sexual harassment and other sex discrimination. Related to this, working women should develop networks with the wives of offenders. Very often, there is a rift between women working outside the home and housewives. Working women and students are sometimes self-righteous about not being "just housewives"; housewives—however intelligent, well educated, and talented—may feel threatened by stereotypical images of young, attractive, and successful women who are out to seduce their hardworking breadwinners. If such misconceptions were reduced on both sides, through seminars, lunches, and workshops, for example, women could attack and reduce gender inequality more effectively in both the home and the workplace.

Because of pressure from individual women, some organizational and institutional changes have occurred, especially in regard to blatant forms of gender discrimination. By choice and out of economic need, women have moved into the workplace in ever greater numbers in recent decades. Many women now enjoy greater economic independence. This outside work can change relationships with men, since women can choose to divorce or marry with less concern for the economic repercussions. The movement of women into the workplace helps women build bonds with other women. Moreover, working women increasingly interact with men in nontraditional settings as lawyers, accountants, doctors, and police officers. This gives women a greater sense of their own personal worth and identity, which, in turn, increases the willingness of some to press against all barriers to achievement, be they blatant or subtle. In addition, men learn how to be equal or even subordinate rather than to dominate from these new women at work.

YOU DON'T HAVE TO TAKE IT! (IN HIGH SCHOOL)

A high school student at Duluth Central High School in Minnesota felt humiliated by the vulgar graffiti in the bathroom stalls. She complained for a year and a half. When school administrators ignored her complaints, she filed charges with the state and prepared to go to trial. She finally reached a settlement that clarified sexual harassment policies and paid her $15,000 for "mental anguish." This was probably the first school in the nation to pay damages to a student who was sexually harassed by her male peers.[10]

Subtle/Covert Gender Discrimination

Implementing remedies to change subtle and covert gender discrimination is more difficult because, as we saw in earlier chapters, most Americans (especially men) are not conscious of these barriers. Because these obstacles can be difficult to measure and document, many people assume that subtle and covert sex discrimination issues are not worth pursuing. Such assumptions are wrong. It is critical to educate women and men about the existence, processes, and harmful effects of subtle and covert sex discrimination.

1. Raise people's consciousness. Talk to each other. Compare experiences. Share information about in-house politics and abuse of women workers and students. In doing so, assume that sex discrimination is environmental rather than "natural" or innate.

2. Reevaluate definitions of stereotypically masculine or feminine behavior in mixed groups. For example, why do we penalize women for crying but accept male outbursts, when both are acceptable for showing such emotions as anger or disappointment?

3. At the end of the day, think about the situations that made you feel angry, defensive, humiliated, or tense. Were such reactions based on your lack of performance or other people treating you as a woman rather than a person? Were you treated fairly? Or were you exploited, manipulated, ignored, or demeaned? If so, was this because you are a woman or because you "screwed up"? In answering such questions, compare your experiences with those of men in comparable situations or predicaments.

Then, do something!

To counteract subtle and covert sex discrimination, women and men can implement a variety of equally subtle and covert strategies.

1. *Help yourself.*   Find out who the respected leaders are and solicit their help and advice on things such as presentations, reports, and procedures. Ask them for tips about how to improve. Do some careful research. Compare your work loads and responsibilities with those of others (especially men's). If you are doing more, point this out—politely, but firmly—to supervisors at every opportunity. Point out your important accomplishments to your supervisor. Compare your salary with that of men with similar achievements. Volunteer to help colleagues, do the job seriously, and communicate that you expect to be acknowledged. Ask your "enemies" (for example, male chauvinists) to evaluate your products, devise cooperative strategies to improve your work, and solicit their help in making your contributions known to others. In terms of committees or similar assignments, be selective: Devote your time only to important committees, volunteer to chair an important committee to avoid serving on two or three meaningless committees, and do your homework. Be active during meetings, but don't be the first to speak to problems. Be brief and well informed in your comments, don't take silly comments seriously, and don't be on the defensive. If you feel you'll be in the minority, especially when the majority of the opposition is male, don't start with

a compromise. Argue for more than you expect; work toward a compromise and make it clear that you are compromising because you're willing to "carry the ball" in the "team effort."

2. *Help other women.*   Whenever possible, nominate women to prestigious or powerful committees, work assignments, or other visible and important responsibilities. If men are suspicious about a "women's bloc," throw them off guard by having the most outspoken, feminist woman nominate a male. Follow that nomination with women's names. If you are in a position to evaluate women, don't be shy about comparing the "double-day" obstacles of married women (especially mothers) with the lack of such responsibilities of single men, husbands, and fathers who have more time to devote to employment. Be sure to encourage other women evaluators to do the same. Evaluate women honestly—encourage their accomplishments but be honest and constructive about weaknesses and limitations. If a woman suggests a worthwhile policy, procedure, or idea, reinforce her immediately, both in writing and in informal communications. Never assume that the proposal is too good, intelligent, or worthwhile to be ignored by decision makers. Never assume that feminists or women working in such female-dominated areas as social work, nursing, and clerical work are too unsympathetic, close-minded, calloused, or too successful to accept constructive criticism or help. The women (and men) who work to improve women's rights may appear publicly to be very tough, independent, and strong. Privately, they are the most likely to feel embattled and isolated because they are often attacked. Give them your support, especially in public and in writing. Such support might motivate fence-hangers to get more involved in gender inequality issues:

> We had a "women's libber" in the department for about six years. She didn't get tenure—I'm not sure why—and left last May. I can't believe I'm saying this, but I miss her. I didn't agree with a lot of things she did—like lobbying for day-care facilities and raising sex harassment issues—but she made me think. . . . Why do I put my wife down at parties even though I really love her? . . . I flirt with students. . . . I tell sexist jokes in class. . . . I have a lousy relationship with most women . . . I'm glad she's gone, but, damn, if I don't miss her. (Male faculty member in an economics department)

3.   *Recruit the help of men.*   Develop alliances with sympathetic men. Solicit their support, communicate openly, and don't put them on the defensive. Work together, coauthor projects and papers, and encourage the involvement of men who do not have professional relationships with women. Become more aware of men who have good intentions, but who behave in sexist ways. Very often, men who are fathers are at least concerned about daughters (if not about wives, mothers, or girl friends) and are more open to discussions about sex inequality.

YOU DON'T HAVE TO TAKE IT! (IN A COLLEGE OR UNIVERSITY)

Frustrated by the institution's ineffective handling of complaints of sexual assault and harassment, students at Brown University listed the names of men they accused of raping women on the walls of women's bathrooms. When university officials ordered the list eradicated, graffiti reappeared in indelible ink and spread to other bathrooms. Brown's president denounced the students' actions, but he also proposed changes in university policies for dealing with sexual assaults on the campus.[11]

Four women students sued Carleton College in Minnesota, charging that the college failed to protect them from two male students who the women said were known by Carleton administrators to be harassing and dangerous. The women contended that the college bungled their cases by advising them not to go to the police when they were harassed and attacked and then they failed to punish the men adequately through its own judicial proceedings. The students said that they were among seven women at Carleton who made complaints to the Carleton dean of students' office between 1984 and 1987, accusing the same two men of sexual assault.[12] Carleton College settled the lawsuit out of court for an undisclosed amount of money.

GROUPS ORGANIZING FOR CHANGE

There are limits to the changes that individual women and men can bring in the area of sexism and gender discrimination. Group efforts are essential as well.

The Feminist Movement: 1848–1960

The women's rights movement in the United States has been alive for nearly 150 years. In 1848, several hundred people, including 40 men, attended the first major women's rights convention in Seneca Falls, New York. Led by Elizabeth Cady Stanton and Lucretia Mott, the convention represented women organizing collectively for major social change. The convention passed one resolution, in a close vote, calling for the "elective franchise," the right to vote for women. This convention launched the women's movement. From the 1850s to the early 1900s, the women's movement, although small in numbers, was active in demonstrations as well as other political and legal activities. In numerous states, women attempted to vote. Occasionally, small groups were successful, even though their votes were "illegal." Women also demonstrated for voting rights at the 1876 Centennial exposition in Philadelphia.

In the years 1910–1912, Washington, California, and several other states yielded to suffragist pressures and established the right of women to vote. Between 1910 and 1917, the number of members of the National American Woman Suffrage Association grew from 75,000 to over 2 million. Demonstrations and other protest activities secured passage by Congress of a full-suffrage constitutional amendment in 1919. After this major victory, the women's movement became relatively dormant, until its resurgence in the 1960s.[13] Women have *organized* to fight for women's rights since at least the 1840s.

Organizing Today

Since the 1960s, there has been an increase in women's organizations, including political action groups, unions, and smaller groups of women working in companies and government agencies. One of the best things women and feminist men can do is to organize against sexism. In the 1991 Senate Judiciary Committee hearings, Anita Hill, a former staff member under Clarence Thomas, a nominee for the Supreme Court, charged Thomas with sexual harassment. Although the Senate Committee managed to duck the implications of the charges, the Hill-Thomas hearings radicalized many women and increased their participation in women's organizations and in politics.

Class-Action Lawsuits

In a number of discrimination cases, women employees have begun to fight back as a group, often in the form of a class-action lawsuit. Recently, four women workers in California, who were employed at the Chevron Information Technology Co., instituted a class-action suit on behalf of all the women who had been sexually harassed at the company—only the fourth class-action suit ever filed for this type of sex discrimination. The women, according to one press report, reported that male managers "grabbed women workers, told filthy jokes and sent pornography, underwear and hostile notes through the interoffice mail."[14] Unfortunately, in February 1994 a California federal judge ruled that the case could not be prosecuted as a class-action suit in regard to the sexual harassment charges (because he thought the harassment was an individual problem, not a Chevron problem) and that each woman would have to pursue her case individually. Nonetheless, this suit received wide media coverage and showed women employees that there can be strength in numbers.

The first successful class-action case dealing with sexual harassment, filed in 1988 and approved as a class action in 1991, involved women complainants at Eveleth Taconite Co., a mining firm. The lawyers for the women said that male employees grabbed the crotches of women employees and scribbled sexist graffiti indicating women's "hot spots." The harassed women workers testified that the management had allowed the harassment to persist and thereby created a difficult work climate for women employees. A federal court decided in mid-1993 that the firm was responsible for the hostile workplace and must pay damages to women workers.[15]

Some of the group cases have brought considerable remedial settlements. In December 1993, the Commonwealth Edison Co., a large midwestern utility, agreed to distribute $3.3 million to several thousand female job applicants as settlement of a legal suit brought by the EEOC on behalf of the women. The court suit argued that some officials in the company had discriminated against women in hiring for meter readers and nuclear-plant operators.[16]

As we have noted previously, in the spring of 1992 State Farm Insurance company agreed to pay $157 million to hundreds of women workers in order to settle a 13-year lawsuit brought by female employees who charged that they had been denied jobs as insurance sales agents. In addition, a female manager of a savings-and-loan branch in Washington, D.C., sued the bank and one of its top executives for gender discrimination. She said he pressured her to have sex, which she acquiesced in out of fear of losing her position. The male executive denied the allegations, and the bank officials said they knew nothing about them. Although a district court ruled against the woman, a federal appeals court reversed the lower court decision, putting companies on notice that they are responsible for sexual harassment by a male supervisor.[17]

Corporate Action

As a result of these court cases, and the Anita Hill-Clarence Thomas hearings in 1991, many corporate executives have become more sensitive to issues of sexual harassment and have implemented grievance procedures to reduce hostile work environments. A number of observers have argued that corporate changes will eventually bring a revolution in this regard: "But the next step in this revolution . . . is how ever-clearer definitions of sexual harassment are being implemented by more and more corporations around the country. . . . companies are searching for better ways to protect themselves, laying down their own laws to stop behavior that isn't just unwanted, but is also illegal."[18] Many companies and public organizations are now providing new regulations, hotlines, and training sessions on sexual harassment. The Corning corporation has used videotapes showing different types of harassment that women employees face; and First Boston investment company requires its workers to sign an agreement indicating they will observe the firm's sexual harassment regulations.[19] Some government employers are also attending to sexual harassment problems. For example, at the University of Florida, the provost, working with other university administrators and faculty and staff members, has instituted monthly sexual harassment sessions and workshops for faculty and staff members (with 200 to 300 present at each): Strong informal pressures are placed on university departments and units to send employees to the sessions.

Still, there are many workplaces where no serious action is being taken. One of the serious offenders is, ironically enough, the law firm. A 1993 survey of about 800 lawyers in large law firms in 14 cities found the following: Three quarters of the firms had official regulations against harassment, up from 38 percent in 1989. Not surprisingly, the male and female lawyers had opposing views on the presence of sexual harassment in their workplaces. While the majority of men felt it did *not* exist, about 70 percent of the women lawyers said it *did* exist on the job. In addition, just over half the female lawyers, but only 6 percent of the male lawyers, personally reported being a victim of sexual harassment in the workplace. Clearly, the legal institutions in the United States need as much attention as other workplaces.[20]

NOW and Other Women's Organizations

The women's equality movement came dramatically onto the national stage in the 1960s. More women were working outside the home, but wages and working conditions remained poor, and male domination remained entrenched. Women had previously joined in various movements for reform, such as movements for black civil rights, but now they pressed their own cause. Protesting women became the target of rage for many in the dominant male group, who ridiculed them as "libbers" and "bra burners." But the counterattacks did not stem the rise of this movement. Various organizations were created, ranging from the National Organization for Women (NOW), to the Women's Equity Action League, to the New York Radical Feminists and the National Black Feminist Organization.

Founded in 1966, NOW has fought for a variety of antidiscrimination remedies at the state and national level. In 1984, NOW set up the National Committee to Support Women Strikers at Yale. It helped raise money to assist strikers with expenses and to pay for a nationwide publicity effort. The strike for equal pay for work was successful. In addition, NOW groups have registered voters during presidential campaigns. In the 1980s and early 1990s, NOW groups charged presidents Ronald Reagan and George Bush with failing to protect women's rights and with reducing the effectiveness of civil rights enforcement programs. They and others protested the ways both Republican presidents had encouraged the EEOC to gut employment rights law enforcement.[21]

Women's organizations such as NOW have used a variety of strategies to bring about changes in society. One common strategy is to change the law. This has been accomplished in civil rights and equal opportunity legislation from the 1960s to the 1990s. New laws are often activated by court cases, some of which have led to improvements in the conditions of women. Normally a conservative force, the law has sometimes been used to expand the rights and opportunities of subordinated Americans. For example, Title IX of the 1972 civil rights law bans sex discrimination in college programs that are federally funded. In the last few years, women athletes have filed suit against discrimination in athletic programs at California State University, the University of Texas, Colorado State, Auburn, Brown, and Colgate. These lawsuits have often been won, thereby suggesting an effective remedy when neither the national athletic associations (for example, the NCAA) nor the federal government have been active enough in eradicating this type of discrimination.[22]

Women athletes have been assisted by women's organizations. Local and national NOW organizations have filed several lawsuits to bring equal treatment to women athletes in college athletic programs. For example, in

October 1993 the California State University system settled a NOW lawsuit by agreeing to implement gender equity in athletics by the year 2000.[23]

Other strategies used by women's movements to protest inequality include electoral strategies, nonviolent civil disobedience, and legal marches and demonstrations.

Women in Unions

Most leaders in the AFL-CIO, an association of nearly 90 unions and more than 13 million unionists, are still white men, although the number of women in top posts has grown slowly in recent years. In part because of this exclusion, women have organized their own unions to fight sex discrimination in the workplace. Such groups as the Women Office Workers (New York), Women Employed (Chicago), Union W.A.G.E. (Oakland), and 9-to-5 (numerous cities) are fighting for better conditions in the workplace. These unions are concerned not just with the usual workplace concerns such as wages and working conditions, but also with women in the workplace. In recent years, the number of women workers in unions has grown substantially, even though union membership in the United States in general has declined. More than half of all workers signed up by unions since 1970 have been women. Women in unions earn substantially more than nonunion women, and they typically have better working conditions and fringe benefits. Union organizing has often brought improved pay and conditions to many women employees. The unionization process is usually started by workers sharing a common grievance; the workers hold meetings and then conduct a legal election to see if the majority of employees support a union. Under U.S. law, management must negotiate in "good faith" with the workers' association about wages, hours, grievance procedures, and working conditions.

One of the most important of the national women's organizations, 9-to-5 (National Association of Working Women), had grown to 15,000 members by 1993 and had members in 250 U.S. cities. The group operates a hotline to help women in white-collar jobs with discrimination.[24] This organization's lobbying efforts also helped to assure that victims of sexual harassment were covered in the 1991 Civil Rights Act.

The American Federation of State, County, and Municipal Employees (AFSCME), a union with a large number of women employees, has been an active advocate of comparable worth. AFSCME, which has a legal section that works on employment issues, has been aggressive in getting comparable worth into bargaining sessions with public employers. In 1983, federal district judge Jack E. Tarner ruled in *AFSCME* v. *State of Washington* that the State of Washington had violated Title VII of the 1964 civil rights act by paying people in predominantly female jobs less than those in similar-skill, predominantly male jobs. Judge Tarner ruled that the discrimination against women "has been and is manifested by direct, overt, and institutionalized discrimination." This case affirmed the principle of equal pay for work of comparable value that had been established in the Supreme Court case *Gunther* v. *County of Washington* (1981). However, in 1984 the Reagan administration's Department of Justice quickly moved into the appeal process against the women and for the State of Washington. This AFSCME case was appealed to the Ninth Circuit Court, which in 1985 decided against the principle of comparable pay for comparable work.[25]

Another major union with a large number of women members is the Service Employees International Union (SEIU). Between 1975 and 1994, this union nearly doubled its members. The union grew from 400,000 in 1975 to more than 1 million in the mid-1990s, one of the biggest increases for any union in the United States. Working aggressively to organize women and minorities in service jobs—including office, health care, janitorial, and public sector workers—SEIU has challenged institutionalized discrimination in a number of companies.[26] Another group, Women Employed, was created in the mid-1970s to fight discrimination in both pay and working conditions. Women Employed has set up career counseling, networking information, and professional development seminars. These programs and workplace discrimination counseling services have been established for the 1,800 members in the area around Chicago. The Women Employed Institute (WEI) is a national leader in research and advocacy to advance women's rights in the workplace.[27]

Many other groups designed to help women with work problems have been formed in recent years. In Oakland, California, the Asian Immigrant Women Advocates organization works on labor and other economic concerns and works to empower its members. In Boston the Women's Economic Development (WED) Project, begun in 1991, works in poorer neighborhoods to provide job training and job access. This group focuses on single welfare-dependent mothers. Latinas are also organizing. Mujer Obrera, a community-based workers' organization of mostly Latino female garment workers, was established in 1981 in El Paso, Texas. Encompassing domestics and restaurant workers, this group has joined in strikes against sewing shops in El Paso, pressing for paid overtime and other major benefits, as well as improvements in working conditions. To meet the needs of its members, Mujer Obrera has developed a broad array of community development projects: a food cooperative, a clinic, and a credit bank that makes small loans to members.[28]

In recent years there has been significant worldwide organization by women workers. Currently headquartered in Geneva, the World Women's Committee of Public Services International (PSI) encompasses approximately 370 national unions and 16 million government workers in more than 100 countries. In the fall of 1993, Catherine O'Reilly Collette, former head of the Women's Rights Department at AFSCME, became the new chair of the international organization. This international group seeks pay equity and an end to sexual harassment for women workers around the globe.[29]

YOU DON'T HAVE TO TAKE IT! (FACULTY IN HIGHER EDUCATION)

A professor at the University of Hawaii who was fired from her English-teaching position in 1982 has settled for $1.27 million. The U.S. District Court found that she had been discriminated against, that her physical and mental health had greatly deteriorated because of her battles with the university, and that some of her health problems were partly due to a stressful work environment.[30]

Shyamala Rajender, a native of India, began teaching in the University of Minnesota's chemistry department in 1969. When the university failed to offer her a tenure-track faculty position in 1971, she filed an internal grievance, claiming she had been refused the appointment because of her sex and national origin. She filed a sex discrimination lawsuit against the university in federal district court two years later.

In 1975, the complaint was expanded by Ms. Rajender's lawyers to a class action suit on behalf of all 1,300 academic, nonstudent, female employees in the University of Minnesota system.

In 1980, the university signed a consent decree agreeing to policy changes. The decree's broad scope is still considered by legal experts to be unmatched in higher education.

In the past 10 years, 329 individual and group sex-discrimination claims have been filed against the system. Of the claims filed so far under the Rajender decree, 10 went to trial, 195 were settled or decided by special master, 110 were dismissed by the court or abandoned by the claimants, and 14 are pending. The university has already paid almost $7 million in legal fees and settlements, including $1.6 million to settle Ms. Rajender's lawsuit—a $100,000 award to Ms. Rajender and $1.5 million in legal fees for her lawyers.[31]

The Superior Court of the District of Columbia ordered Howard University to pay its women's basketball coach, Sanya J. Tyler, $1.1 million in damages. Ms. Tyler sued Howard in 1991, claiming that she had been unfairly passed over for the job of athletics director and that she had been paid less than her male colleagues and treated differently because she is a woman. It was the first judgment in which a court awarded monetary damages to a plaintiff in a sex bias case under Title IX.[32]

A woman who once worked at Alabama State University won a sexual harassment lawsuit against one of the institution's former presidents. The woman charged the former president, Leon Howard, with sexual harassment, invasion of privacy, and assault and battery. The jury upheld the charges, awarding $80,000 in her civil complaint against the former president and an additional $250,000 for a separate claim she had filed against the head of the governing board.[33]

Women in Education

Changing the behavior of male students, teachers, and administrators in educational institutions is another major challenge. Faculty members, staff, and students can take action to improve the climate in educational institutions. They can, individually or in small groups, participate more actively in classroom settings. They can organize women's caucuses and other support groups for female workers and students. They can organize informal seminars to discuss sexism in the classroom and in informal social settings. They can conduct surveys of women students and faculty to ascertain the extent of and change in gender bias and sexual harassment on the campus. Students can, with the help of faculty members and administrators, develop videotapes and other media to teach about discrimination in education. Students can also use the campus newspaper to publicize gender bias issues, and they can demand the inclusion of women's issues in all relevant courses.

Working together with sympathetic female and male faculty members, women students can organize to pressure the high school or college administration to reduce sexism; to issue policy statements making it clear that sexist humor and gender discrimination in and out of the classroom by teachers will not be tolerated; to revise teacher evaluations to include an assessment of the presence of sexist behavior or language; and to implement student grievance procedures against teachers who engage in sexist behavior. Individual teachers can be pressured to change their behavior: to stop using sexist humor, language, and disparaging remarks about women's professional and intellectual abilities; to disregard a person's gender in evaluating her or his work; to encourage rather than question a woman's seriousness in educational pursuits; to make sure that women students are drawn into classroom discussions on an equal basis; to ensure that women receive the time and professional attention that men receive; and to urge women to consider higher-paying, traditionally male careers.[34]

SOCIETAL CHANGES TOWARD EXPANDING WOMEN'S RIGHTS

What can we, as a nation, do about sex discrimination? To answer this question we can examine government actions—including civil rights laws, executive decrees, and court decisions—as well as those of employers in the private sector.

Government and Employment

Consider, for example, government action in regard to employment. In the twentieth century, little government action was taken to deal with employment discrimination until the 1940s and 1950s, when a few state and local governments adopted fair employment laws, usually with weak enforcement powers and relating to men of color and not to women. Until the 1960s, only token action was taken by the federal government to desegregate employment by racial group or gender. Several presidents did take a few steps in the direction of enforcing passive nondiscrimination—for example, Franklin Roosevelt's establishment of a Fair Employment Practices Committee in the early 1940s—but there was no significant antidiscrimination action at the federal level until the 1960s, when civil rights groups accelerated pressure on government. The executive orders issued by President Lyndon Johnson in the 1960s required, at least on paper, government contractors not only to cease discriminating but also to act affirmatively to desegregate their labor forces. These orders were the official beginning of modern affirmative action programs. "Affirmative action" simply refers to *positive* remedial practices going beyond passive nondiscrimination to bring previously excluded women and minorities into historically white male institutions.

In the mid-1960s, enforcement of federal contract compliance in regard to employment desegregation came under the Department of Labor, the agency that supervises employers holding federal government contracts. According to Department of Labor studies, compliance reviews of contractors have had some impact in improving women's employment. The Office of Federal Contract Compliance Programs (OFCCP) has issued regulations that, when built into contracts, require all federal contractors to take affirmative action to eliminate discrimination in recruitment, hiring, and promotion procedures.

Since the late 1960s, federal contractors have been required to submit written affirmative action plans indicating the current representation of women in job categories and providing for affirmative goals and timetables for categories where underutilization of women exists. The OFCC has delegated compliance actions to other agencies, which are supposed to review federal contractors in their area to see if they are taking remedial action. The effectiveness of OFCC-fostered affirmative action has been questioned. Compliance reviews by the U.S. Commission on Civil Rights and other agencies have indicated that *few significant penalties* have been applied to nonconforming contract employers. Grossly deficient antidiscrimination plans have been approved. During the 1980s, the conservative Republican administrations kept the OFCCP from doing an aggressive job, but in the summer of 1991 the OFCCP started a small project to look at the "glass ceiling" faced by women and minority workers in nine companies doing business with the federal government. The study found that there was a glass ceiling—that women and minorities rarely made it into top management. In the first years of the Clinton administration, Department of Labor officials, including Labor Secretary Robert Reich, made strong commitments to eradicate the ceiling.[35]

The 1964 Civil Rights Act, together with its later amendments, prohibits discrimination in employment by larger employers. The EEOC was created to enforce Title VII of that act, primarily to deal with complaints of employment discrimination. The EEOC has the responsibility of investigating legitimate complaints, of seeking conciliation, and, failing that, of going to court to end discrimination. The EEOC's Uniform Guidelines on Employee Selection Procedures, in principle, cover employers with patterns of discrimination against women and in theory should put federal pressure on them to change. Yet, because of the EEOC's management problems and lack of staff, a large backlog of cases has built up, to the point where many complainants have found no practical remedy through EEOC procedures. During fiscal 1993, the number of employment discrimination complaints made to the

EEOC, was about 88,000. This was the largest ever for the EEOC. The cases won that year brought money damages of $161 million, mostly through administrative hearings, rather than through lawsuits. Sex discrimination was the issue in 27 percent of the cases, the second largest category of cases after racial discrimination. In spite of increased resolution of EEOC complaints, however, there was still a large backlog of 73,000 unresolved cases as fiscal 1994 began, much higher than in the previous year. Today, political action needs to be directed at expanding the staff and funding of civil rights enforcement agencies such as the EEOC.[36]

YOU DON'T HAVE TO TAKE IT! (IN BUSINESS AND INDUSTRY)

Five women employed at a brewery in St. Paul, Minnesota, filed suit against Stroh Brewing Co., charging that the company's television ads featuring bikini-clad women created a workplace climate conducive to sexual harassment. The lawsuits claimed that Stroh has produced "sexist, degrading promotion posters and advertisements."

In one ad, known as the "It Does Get Better" ad, scantily-clad women from the "Swedish Bikini Team" parachute with beer into a rocky campsite occupied by men. The lawyer for the plaintiffs said the company's advertising created a climate in which sexual harassment was more easily tolerated. Lawyers for Stroh were willing to settle but rejected one condition: eliminating other sex-oriented advertising.[37]

Tobacco companies have tried for years to attract female smokers with slogans such as, "You've come a long way, baby." A state advertising campaign in Minnesota is telling women they've been exploited for too long. One commercial shows a billboard with a young, leotard-clad woman smoking a cigarette. Two male ad executives stand admiring it, and one exclaims that women "will love it." The woman on the billboard suddenly becomes real and stubs the cigarette out on one executive's head. Another 30-second spot shows a billboard with three smiling women smoking cigarettes and the slogan "Women are making the rush to rich flavor." Panels peel off, changing the message to "Women are making us rich."[38]

Marriott Corporation—one of the nation's 10 largest employers, with 220,000 employees—agreed to adopt specific goals for promoting women to managerial and supervisory jobs in the food and beverage division of its hotel chain for the next 4 years to settle a class action sex discrimination suit. In addition, the hotel chain agreed to put $3 million into a settlement fund to cover back pay claims by as many as 3,000 women who were denied promotions in the past. The suit was filed against Marriott in 1988, claiming that the company's promotion practices discriminated against women because the male-dominated committees systematically excluded women as candidates for jobs above a certain level.[39]

There is no systematic evidence available on the impact of government enforcement activity on the economic mobility of women. The data on actual changes in the workforce reveal a mixed picture. There have been some gains as the result of government enforcement, but the reasons for these gains are many, including women's protests and organization as well as government action.

Much remains to be done. U.S. employment policy must give much more attention to women workers. Meredith Ann Newman has underscored the point:

> Policies that treat all workers as if they were men can no longer be justified in light of the changing demographics of the work force. Reasonably priced quality child care, parental leave, and flexible work schedules affect and potentially benefit both genders. Such increased flexibility in accommodating family responsibilities is crucial to integrating women into upper level management positions. These policies should be advanced in terms of a reflection of society's needs, not as "special favors" for women in the work force.[40]

In addition, federal action should eradicate pay inequities in the workplace.

Legislative Action

New civil rights legislation was difficult to pass between 1981 and 1991 under the Reagan and Bush administrations. In June 1984, the House of Representatives voted overwhelmingly for the 1984 Civil Rights Act, which would have barred gender discrimination in all education programs if the college received federal aid in only one of its programs. The purpose of the act was to overturn the Supreme Court's narrow *Grove City College* ruling. Following the desires of the White House, however, the Senate's conservative leadership killed the bill. In 1984, the Federal Pay Equity and Management Act passed the House in a nearly unanimous vote. But again, the bill was blocked in the Senate by the conservative Republican leadership.

Finally, in 1991 the most important civil rights act since the 1960s was passed, after much opposition from President George Bush and most other conservative politicians. As we noted previously, the 1991 Civil Rights Act permits victims of sex discrimination to collect compensatory damages and makes jury trials available to them. Significantly, it was passed only after much heated discussion between Republicans and Democrats—"and only after the Anita Hill-Clarence Thomas hearings highlighted the problem on television."[41]

Remarkably, as we approach the twenty-first century, equal treatment for women and men is not guaranteed by our basic legal documents. The U.S. Constitution is a document reflecting racial subordination in its legitimizing of slavery and the slave trade, and it was not until the Thirteenth, Fourteenth, and Fifteenth amendments that this legal recognition of racial inequality was removed. It is revealing of the sexist nature of the U.S. legal system that even the liberating Fourteenth Amendment speaks only of the right to vote of "male citizens." This first explicit reference to gender in the Constitution made it clear that no women, black or white, had the right to vote. Women did not get the vote until the Nineteenth Amendment (1920), which stated, "The right of citizens to vote shall not be denied or abridged by the United States or by any state on account of sex. Congress shall have the power to enforce this article by appropriate legislation."

In recent decades, a Constitutional amendment has been proposed to give women equal rights with men. The wording is similar to that which expanded black civil rights in the Fourteenth Amendment: "Equality of rights under the law shall not be denied or abridged by the United States or any state on account of sex. The Congress shall have the power to enforce, by appropriate legislation, the provisions of this article."

As of the mid-1990s, the Equal Rights Amendment (ERA) has not been ratified by the necessary number of states—largely because of strong opposition by male legislators and other conservatives who believe the amendment will break down traditional gender roles for women and men. Attempts to resurrect the ERA have been difficult because of opposition from the male leadership in the White House and in the U.S. Senate. In our view, additional efforts to put the ERA into federal law are critical to women's future progress. Challenges to the sex-biased character of U.S. laws are essential to undermine the patriarchal underpinnings of our economy, our educational system, and our political system. Most women's organizations have pressed for the ERA, which, as many opponents recognize, will undermine the patriarchal character of U.S. workplaces, schools, and legal institutions.

Federal Courts and Employment

As we have seen previously, lawsuits brought by individual women and groups of women have forced some organizational and societal changes. Yet, court cases often have a limited impact because the remedies are case-specific and affect only one individual or, at most, one plant or company. The courts' ability to reshape employment in an entire industry or other sector is restricted. A company or organization is first examined for practices that must be demonstrated to be discriminatory before court remedies can be imposed. Once discrimination has been demonstrated in court, however, the remedies provided by federal courts have usually been specific in attempting "to make whole" the injured parties. While there is no way in which a female victim can be completely compensated for the loss of energy, status, and money resulting from discrimination and the delays in obtaining remedies, some federal courts have made attempts to provide significant monetary compensation for injustice.

Most change coming from the judicial branch has, of course, resulted from legal cases brought by women. Court action benefiting women is relatively recent. Not until 1971 did the U.S. Supreme Court rule against a legislatively-drawn gender discrimination barrier. In recent years, we have seen a slowing of progress in the federal court system. It is still the case that many sections of the U.S. legal code have a gender bias or use sex-based terminology that conflicts with the ideal of equal rights for women. Many state laws are similarly gender-biased.

The Supreme Court has been an inconsistent defender of women's rights. As we noted previously, in 1984 the Court ruled that an entire college is not subject to civil rights laws protecting women, even if one of its programs receives major federal aid. In 1986, however, the Court ruled that sexual harassment is illegal gender discrimination. In 1994, the Court reinstated a NOW lawsuit and decided that the antiracketeering law (called RICO) covered the violent acts of antiabortion activists. Potentially, antiabortion groups such as Operation Rescue could be bankrupted if they lost lawsuits, for the law permits very substantial compensatory damages for victims.[42]

Action by State Governments

In 1979, the National Committee on Pay Equity was created by a coalition of labor unions and women's groups to work for equal pay for women in the United States. As a result of their efforts and other organized pressures, a number of states have implemented the comparable-pay-for-comparable-work principle for government employees. Thus, in 1982 Minnesota adopted pay equity for all local and state government workers. A recent study found that the law has greatly benefited women who are government employees. Contrary to the predictions of critics, there has been no reduction in state employees, and women workers saw their pay increase by more than 10 percent. Five other states (Iowa, New York, Oregon, Washington and Wisconsin) now have similar pay-equity laws, and many other state legislatures have more nearly equalized the wages or salaries for some comparable male and female jobs.[43]

The Need for Political Change

Recent books such as Naomi Wolf's *Fire with Fire: The New Female Power and How It Will Change the 21st Century* argue that the 1990s are different from the "backlash" 1980s, that they are already a decade in which we have experienced a resurgence of women's political power. Wolf rejects "victim" feminism for a "power" feminism that encourages all women to press for greater political influence.[44] Wolf may be too sanguine about current political realities. The political difficulties women face are reflected in the slow pace of change in concrete electoral and other political attainments. In 1992, women were only 6 percent of the House of Representatives and 2 percent of the Senate. While the 1992 elections added some legislators, including a few more women in the Senate, women still make up less than a fifth of all elected officeholders in the United States. Rutgers University's Center for the American Woman and Politics has noted that in 1992 women legislators held a fifth of the seats in state legislatures, up significantly over the previous decade. The Center has found that, as a group, the women are more liberal than male legislators; women politicians are more likely than the men to press for legislation dealing with human resources issues such as health care, education, and child welfare.[45] Assessing these data, one news report noted: "It's no coincidence that, as the ranks of women legislators increased in the 1980s, many states markedly increased their spending on education and other programs for children."[46]

Although women are half the population, no woman has ever served as president, vice-president, or speaker of the House. Very few women have ever served in the U.S. Senate—fewer than two dozen between 1920 and 1994—and only modest numbers have been members of the House of Representatives. Some observers have forecast major changes in the political representation of women in the next decade. Public opinion polls are encouraging in this regard. For example, a recent *U.S. News & World Report* poll found that 61 percent of Americans nationally felt "the country would be governed better" if more women were elected. This figure was up from 28 percent just 8 years earlier.[47]

LOOKING AT OTHER COUNTRIES: A COMPARATIVE VIEW

Some European nations have made greater progress in gender equality than the United States has. It is not easy to create a society with true equality between men and women after centuries of institutionalized gender inequality. But several countries are strongly committed to this goal and have made some progress. For example, in the 1940s and 1950s, legislative action in Sweden made it easier for women to combine work outside the home with family responsibilities. In the 1960s and 1970s, the principle of gender equality became firmly embedded in Swedish law. Although there are not enough of these facilities, Sweden has numerous government-financed daycare centers for the young children of working parents. The daycare services make it easier for women to develop careers outside the home. Moreover, when a child is born or adopted, parents are entitled to nine months of paid parental leave between them. While it is mothers who make the most use of this opportunity, some fathers have also taken advantage of parental leaves. The Swedish health and other social service programs also provide benefits to individuals, not to family breadwinners. Consequently, women generally receive the same health benefits as men.

In the decades of the 1970s, 1980s, and 1990s, progress toward greater gender equality in Sweden has continued. There has been more discussion of human roles, not just of women's roles. The 1979–1980 Act of Equality between Women and Men at Work bars sex-based discrimination in hiring, promotion, training, working conditions, and salary. The law explicitly allows affirmative action on behalf of women who are underrepresented in a job category. Sweden has comparable-pay-for-comparable-work laws. Government officials require private employers to take affirmative action to promote equality. Discrimination in hiring and promotions is banned by law. However, these employment laws have decreased but not eliminated inequalities in working conditions and pay.[48]

The tax laws were also reworked to get rid of gender bias, and the educational system has been reformed so that both boys and girls take home economics and metalworking classes. Swedish law and practice have also encouraged greater participation by women in politics. One third of the

Swedish parliament is now composed of women, several times the proportion to be found in the U.S. Congress. Major political parties often try to put equal numbers of male and female candidates on their slates. Although Swedish feminists have argued that progress has lessened in the last decade and that new efforts must be made, Swedish society has considerably more equality for women than one finds in the United States.

Other countries, even those less wealthy than the United States, have implemented more progressive policies regarding working women. More than 70 countries have statutory provisions that guarantee a woman the right to leave employment for childbirth, guarantee a job when she returns, and provide cash benefits for children. Comprehensive daycare systems have characterized many European countries for years. For example, in France, West Germany, and Italy most preschool children are in free full-day public programs. Many European countries routinely allow parents to leave work to care for sick children.[49] It is interesting that greater progress has been made in meeting most of these family goals in many European countries than in the United States, where "family values" are often celebrated.

LOOKING AHEAD

When looking at solutions for sex discrimination, we sometimes feel overwhelmed. When we press for moderate changes in existing patterns of economic and social discrimination, are we helping to perpetuate a sexist social system that really needs major overhaul? Do women want to be controlled by bosses, male or female, for whom profit is more important than humane treatment of employees? Working women who gain their independence must question the poor working conditions that many male workers face. They must begin to question the basic values that place profit and jobs over families, the workplace hazards that increase corporate profits, and the work tasks so closely supervised that workers' needs for autonomy and privacy are ignored. Some analysts have suggested that pressure must be brought to bear to change radically the U.S. workplace and to emphasize those human values often said (incorrectly) to be distinctively "female," such as compassion, cooperation, kindness, emotion, and a concern for one's community and other people. In fact, these are basic *human* values. Incorporating these changes might require a fundamentally new system of humanized economic democracy rather than the troubled and exploitative "free market" system currently in place.

Can remedies for gender discrimination be implemented on a large scale without major changes in the structure of the existing economic and social system? The destruction of the mechanisms of gender discrimination on a really large scale might well begin to dismantle the built-in patterns of gender inequality that constitute foundation pillars of the society. Major structural changes, such as revising unequal pay systems so they do not adversely affect women, would have an impact on the larger societal system. Pyramiding a large number of institutional changes might alter the very foundation of what is now a fundamentally sexist society. Indeed, some might argue that the basic socioeconomic system would be completely remade in this process. A humanistic, economic democracy could eventually result.

Discriminatory recruitment procedures, unequal pay, sexual harassment, and unfair real estate procedures could be eliminated without affecting the fundamentally capitalistic nature of the society—that is, the ownership of businesses and industries could still be in private hands. Yet, at the same time, *massive* infusions of women into the organizational structures of this society, particularly the highest decision-making levels, would probably alter the shape of this particular U.S. brand of capitalism. It could no longer depend on certain female/minority groups for the cheap labor and other subordinate positions essential to its operations. Seen from this viewpoint, capitalism in some form might survive a thorough purge of gender discrimination, but some of the fundamental structural and cultural supports of the system would likely be changed, with perhaps the entire system being humanized in the process. Greater power and influence for women now in subordinate positions would necessitate a much greater tolerance for diverse ideas, perspectives, and practices that most in the powerful male groups and networks do not now accept.

The action of women themselves is critical for major reforms in this society. There are top-down pressures for change, and there are bottom-up pressures in the form of people banding together in organized protest against oppressive conditions. The likelihood of substantial future change depends on the willingness of women to keep the pressure on. When the entrenched system of institutionalized discrimination gives a bit, that does not mean that discrimination—whether blatant, subtle, or covert—in other areas will disappear. Even hard-won advances can be rolled back, as has been the case since the early 1980s. For that reason, protest against unjust conditions will need to be repeated for the foreseeable future. Eternal protest, as well as eternal vigilance, seems to be the price of liberty.

NOTES

1.   John Bartlett, *Familiar Quotations* (Boston: Little Brown, 1980), p. 392.

2.   Jerry Adler and Debra Rosenberg, "Must Boys Always Be Boys?" *Newsweek*, October 19, 1992, p. 77.

3.   Ibid.

4.   Susan Harte, "Sexual Harassment: How to Deal with Harassment on the Job," *Atlanta Journal and Constitution*, November 10, 1993, p. F2.

5.   Meredith Ann Newman, "Career Advancement: Does Gender Make a Difference?" *American Review of Public Administration*, Vol. 23 (December, 1993), p. 361.

6.   Ibid.

7. Ellen Cassidy and Karen Nussbaum, *9 to 5: The Working Woman's Guide to Office Survival* (New York: Penguin Books, 1983), pp. 136–139.

8. Kara Swisher, "Laying Down the Law on Harassment; Court Rulings Spur Firms to Take Preventive Tack," *Washington Post,* February 6, 1994, p. H1.

9. Mark Curriden, "Sexual Harassment: Southerners May Find It Easier to File and Win Their Lawsuits," *Atlanta Journal and Constitution,* November 10, 1993, Section F, p. 2.

10. Jane Gross, "Cases Challenge 'Boys Will Be Boys' Status Quo," *Baltimore Sun,* March 11, 1992, pp. 1A, 16A.

11. Michele N-K, Collison, "20 Years Later, Women on Formerly All-Male Campuses Fight to Change Their Institutions' 'Old Boy' Images, *The Chronicle of Higher Education,* December 12, 1990, pp. A23–A24; Mark Starr, "The Writing on the Wall." *Newsweek,* November 26, 1990, p. 64.

12. Michele N-K Collison, "The College Knew This Man Was a Rapist," Carleton Student Charges," *The Chronicle of Higher Education,* May 15, 1991, pp. A29–A30.

13. Aileen S. Kraditor, *The Ideas of the Woman Suffrage Movement, 1890–1920* (New York: W. W. Norton, 1981); Eleanor Flexner, *Century of Struggle* (New York: Atheneum, 1973).

14. Reynolds Holding, "Women Turn to Class Action Suits: New Weapon to Fight Sex Harassment," *San Francisco Chronicle,* January 24, 1994, p. A1. See also Reynolds Holding, "Sexual Harassment Class Action Denied: But Women Can Sue as Group for Discrimination," *San Francisco Chronicle,* February 3, 1994, p. A16.

15. Ibid.

16. John N. Maclean, "Women Get Money, Training in Edison Settlement, *Chicago Tribune,* December 30, 1993, Zone N, p. 1.

17. "Companies Are Liable for Sexual Harassment by a Boss, a Court Rules," *Wall Street Journal,* January 29, 1985, p. 9.

18. Swisher, "Laying Down the Law on Harassment," p. H1.

19. Ibid.

20. Thom Weidlich and Charise K. Lawrence, "Sex and the Firms: A Progress Report," *The National Law Journal,* December 20, 1993, p. 1.

21. See Dean Takahaski, "Workplace diversity; Job Rights Enforcement Agency Comes Under Mounting Pressure: Critics of the Reagan-Bush EEOC Hope for Change under Clinton," *Los Angeles Times,* May 17, 1993, Section D2, p. 8.

22. David Barron, "Increasingly, Women Athletes Go to Court—and Win," *Houston Chronicle,* June 27, 1993, p. 12.

23. "CSU System Agrees to Equity in Sports Programs," United Press International, October 21, 1993.

24. Interview with Barbara Otto, Program Director at 9-to-5, April 12, 1993.

25. "*AFSCME* v. *Washington State* Briefs Due Soon," *National NOW Times,* vol. 17, September–October 1984, p. 5.

26. Nanette Byrnes, "Blue Collar Blues," *Financial World,* November 23, 1993, p. 26. The next three paragraphs draw on Joe R. Feagin and Clairece B.

Feagin, *Social Problems: A Critical Power-Conflict Perspective* (Englewood Cliffs: Prentice Hall, 1994), pp. 427–431.

27. *Women Employed News,* Winter 1993, pp. 1–3.

28. Mary Hollens, "Catfish and Community," *Third Force,* May–June 1993, p. 21; Barbara Goldoftas, "Women Helping Women," *Dollars & Sense,* December 1992, pp. 10–11; Micah Fink, "Weaving Workers Together," *Multinational Monitor,* January–February 1992, p. 8.

29. "AFSCME Women's Rights Director Elected to Head Women's Committee of 16-Million-Member Public Services International," PR Newswire, October 25, 1993.

30. Courtney Leatherman, *The Chronicle of Higher Education,* 1992, p. A18, under "Faculty Notes."

31. Debra E. Blum, "10 Years Later, Questions Abound over Minnesota Sex-Bias Settlement," *The Chronicle of Higher Education,* June 13, 1990, pp. a13–a14.

32. Debra E. Blum, "2 More Coaches of Women's Teams Go to Court to Press Claims of Sex Discrimination," *The Chronicle of Higher Education,* September 1, 1993, pp. A47–A48.

33. Courtney Leatherman, "Jury Upholds Claims of Sex Harassment Against Ex-President," *The Chronicle of Higher Education,* February 17, 1993, pp. A13–A14.

34. See Roberta M. Hall and Bernice R. Sandler, *The Classroom Climate: A Chilly One for Women?* (Washington, DC: Association of American Colleges, 1982), pp. 13–18.

35. Bureau of National Affairs, "Diversity Programs Make Business Sense, Glass Ceiling Commission Official Asserts," *Daily Labor Report,* 244, December 22, 1993, p. d24.

36. Bureau of National Affairs, "Charges of Disability Discrimination Boost EEOC Intake by 22% in Fiscal '93," *Daily Labor Report,* 9, January 13, 1994, p. d4.

37. "Female Employees Sue Stroh over Ads," *Baltimore Sun,* November 9, 1991, p. 3A.

38. "Anti-Smoking Ads Warn Women of Exploitation," *Washington Post,* September 8, 1992, p. A5.

39. Frank Swoboda, "Marriott Settles Sex-Bias Suit with Promotion Goals," *Washington Post,* March 6, 1991, p. C9.

40. Newman, "Career Advancement," p. 361.

41. Daniel V. Kinsella, "Expect Changes in Labor and Employment Law," *Modern Casting,* April 1993, p. 44.

42. AP-Special, "Racketeering Law to Cover Abortion Foes," *Toronto Star,* January 25, 1994, p. A13.

43. Carol Kleiman, "Comparable Pay Could Create Jobs," *Orlando Sentinel,* October 13, 1993, p. C5.

44. Naomi Wolf, *Fire with Fire: The New Female Power and How It Will Change the 21st Century* (New York: Random House, 1993).

45. "Women in Politics; a Different Public-Policy Perspective," *Star Tribune,* January 14, 1994, p. 16A.

46. Ibid.

47. Cited in Patricia Aburdene and John Naisbitt, "Going for the Gold in Political Arena," *The Plain Dealer,* December 29, 1992, p. 1C.

48. Birgita Wistrand, *Swedish Women on the Move* (Stockholm: Swedish Institute, 1981), pp. 5–20. See, also, Linda Haas, *Equal Parenthood and Social Policy: A Study of Parental Leave in Sweden* (Albany, New York: State University of New York Press, 1992).

49. Ann Crittenden, "We 'Liberated' Mothers Aren't," *Washington Post,* February 5, 1984, p. D1.

INDEX